Runner's World
HEALTH FOOD BOOK

by the Berkeley Food Co-op

Runner's World Books

Library of Congress Cataloging in Publication Data

Runner's world health food book.
   (Instructional book series; 14)
   Compiled and edited by Helen Black.
   1. Food.   2. Nutrition.   3. Marketing (Home
   economics)   I. Black, Helen.   II. Berkeley
   Co-op.   III. Title: Health food book.
TX353.R86   1982   641.3   82-20434
ISBN 0-89037-244-6
ISBN 0-89037-232-2 (pbk.)

© 1982 by
Runner's World Books

No information in this book may be reprinted in any
form without permission from the publisher.
Runner's World Books
in conjunction with
Anderson World, Inc., Mountain View, CA

HEALTH FOOD BOOK

Contents

FOREWORD..v
INTRODUCTION..vii
PART ONE: HOW TO BE AN ACTIVE,
INFORMED CONSUMER......................................1
PART TWO: BEFORE YOU SHOP
 1. Being Smart About Shopping.......................29
 2. Everybody's Talking About Nutrition..............47
 3. Planning for Eating..............................77
 4. As the Twig Is Bent, So Grows the Tree...........95
PART THREE: ABOUT FOODS AND BUYING
 5. Beverages.......................................107
 6. Beans and Nuts..................................121
 7. Breads and Cereal Foods.........................131
 8. Fruits..147
 9. Meat, Fish and Poultry..........................153
 10. Milk, Dairy Products and Eggs..................169
 11. Vegetables.....................................185
 12. Canned, Frozen or Fabricated...................195
 13. Tips for Creative Cooking......................205
PART FOUR: KEEPING FOOD SAFELY
 14. Food Spoilage..................................213
 15. Food Storage...................................219
 Recommended Reading...............................228

Foreword

The *Runner's World Health Food Book* should be called by another name, like *Runner's World Health Food, Grocery Shopper's Guide and Helpful Food Hints Book.* But then the title wouldn't fit on the cover.

Originally published as *The Berkeley Co-op Food Book* in 1979, the information was collected over a span of twenty-five years from stories in the *Co-op News.* The *Co-op News* is a weekly publication that goes to all members of the Berkeley Co-op. *Runner's World* has retained most of the information contained in the Co-op book.

But you might wonder, just what is a Co-op? It is a business owned and operated by its members. In Berkeley, California, we have formed a cooperative grocery business. Starting with one store in 1937, there are now ten supermarkets and several non-food facilities in the San Francisco Bay Area.

Anyone can join the Co-op but you don't have to be a member to shop at our stores. Each member has one vote. You buy shares in the company every time you shop, but no matter how many shares you own, you still get only one vote. Profits, known as savings, when earned, are distributed to its members. The refund received is directly related to how much you patronize the Co-op.

While members no longer stock shelves, they still control and advise the Co-op through a volunteer board of directors, committees and area center councils. In today's world of growing conglomerates, having a voice in the marketplace is an important reason for Co-op's continued loyalty from its members.

As we have grown, we have provided more services to our members. We have our own Co-op brand label, we offer consumer and nutrition information, a weekly newspaper, USDA choice beef, bulk grains and health foods, international foods, a credit union, a health plan, mutual service insurance and much more.

Lee Awner
Education Department
Berkeley Co-op
September 1982

Introduction

This book is not a cookbook.

It is true that the Berkeley Co-op's staff of home economists has been engrossed in the subject of food and cooking over the years. Our identification with food is such that if some shopper hollers "Hello, food lady" from across the store, we respond at once. We know who's being addressed.

But our fascination with food extends far beyond the mere pleasure of eating. Aided and abetted by the wide-ranging curiosity of Co-op shoppers, we have gathered information on nutrition, food labeling, food costs, food preparation, additives, toxins, safe storage and handling, meal planning, and — very important — legislation and administrative regulations involving food. We are indebted to all the knowledgeable people who helped us, including our suppliers and many persons in government agencies, cooperative extension services and the University of California.

This information has been relayed to our members through Buy Word, a column appearing in the *Co-op News,* the Berkeley Co-op's weekly publication, through information sheets and special exhibits displayed in the stores. It also is relayed through unique point-of-purchase cards posted on the shelves in the stores and, of course, through direct answers to questions asked by shoppers in person or by phone or letter. It seems to us that shoppers have taken from these writings whatever was practical and appropriate for them and used it to better their eating. This book has been drawn from these materials.

Some of the articles selected for the book are updated. Others have been left as originally written, either because it was impractical to update and reprice them, or because the points made were valid without updating. (Besides, one gains a certain melancholy perspective at the spectacle of yesterday's prices.) The date of original publication has been included on articles that have not been updated. Names of authors appear on Buy Word articles but not on other materials.

Most of the writings come from Co-op home economists, past and present. They are Trudy Ascher, Helen Black, Nancy Bratt, Wendy Gardner, Mary Gullberg, Judy Heckman, Marion Hildebrandt, June Kadish, Mary Ruth Nelson, Thelma Phipps, Julia

Robinson, Catherine Sinnott, Joan Taylor, Jean Tuggle, and Betsy Wood. However, some articles were written for us by others, including the late Jim Hardcastle of Capricorn Coffee Company and Adolph Kamil, pharmacist with the Consumers Co-op of Berkeley. We much appreciate their expert and well-written contributions.

Finally, we are most grateful to Ann Norberg for her painstaking work of classifying our materials for us; and to Max Awner, veteran Co-op journalist, for his help in editing and polishing the selected materials, and for making many suggestions that improved the final product.

Helen Black
September 1982

Part One

How to be an Active, Informed Consumer

A SHORT HISTORY OF THE CONSUMER MOVEMENT

A Play* by Betsy Wood
Scene: Morning, University Avenue Co-op Coffee Bar
Characters: George, a Co-op member; Sally, Coffee Bar Manager

George: Morning, Sally.
Sally: Morning, George. What'll it be?
George: (Reading menu) Breakfast Special looks good!
Sally: (Calling over shoulder) O.J., two eggs, bacon, toast, hashbrowns, coffee.
George: Sally, hold the orange juice. I don't like what Anita Bryant is doing.
Sally: (Calling) No O.J.!
George: And skip the eggs. Been told to cut my cholesterol.
Sally: Hold the eggs!
George: Better forget the bacon. They say nitrites cause cancer.
Sally: No bacon on that order!
George: And leave off the hash browns. (Patting his stomach) All that fat and additives, you know.
Sally: (Calling still) Forget that special. (To George) Toast and jelly coming up!
George: No jelly please. I'm told it's 55 percent sugar. And no butter. Saturated fat, you know.
Sally: (Forever cheerful) Dry toast then?
George: Better not toast it. I just read about high temperatures and the damage it does.
Sally: Here's your bread.
George: (Glancing behind counter) I see it's Wonder Bread. Sally, you know about IT&T.
Sally: Sugar and cream?
George: No. Not me! Not good for me.
Sally: Here's your coffee, friend.
George: Don't bother, Sally. I've heard caffeine causes heart problems...
Sally: We've got oatmeal. Ready in a minute. I just add hot water.
George: N'mind. That stuff is over-processed.
Sally: Nice seeing you, George.
George: Thanks, Sally. I'll just sit here and smoke a cigarette.

*Opened to wild audiences at University Avenue in May, bombed in Washington in June, was a rave at the Co-op family camp at Camp Sierra.

(September 18, 1978)

BIG FOUR MONOPOLY

In 1972 the Federal Trade Commission (FTC) issued a complaint that the "Big Four" ready-to-eat cereal manufacturers have illegally monopolized the market. FTC alleged that for thirty years these companies have maintained a highly concentrated, non-competitive market structure by proliferation of brands, trademark promotion, unfair advertising, restrictive retail shelf space programs and acquisition of competitors.

The Big Four	Dollar Volume of Ready-to-Eat Cereals	Market Share
Kellogg's	300 million	45 percent
General Mills	141 million	21 percent
General Foods	92 million	16 percent
Quaker Oats	56 million	9 percent

The complaint said the companies failed to challenge each other's price increases and by their actions obtained excessive profits, blockaded entry into the market, forced consumers to pay higher prices than they would have had to pay in a competitive market.

Does this all surprise you?

We rather doubt it. This is still in the talking stage. It's called pretrial discovery.

In 1979 the "Big Four" cereal companies still had 87 percent of the ready-to-eat cereal market. The charges brought against them by the Federal Trade Commission went to trial in 1976. Since then, Quaker has been dismissed from the case; they claimed that they did not share in the monopoly profits, among other things, and the judge agreed with them. Kellogg began presenting its defense in April 1978; General Mills followed. At this point, the administrative judge hearing this case retired, and an interval elapsed before a new judge, Alvin Berman, was appointed. The trial will begin again in Washington, D.C., October 1979, with General Foods presenting its defense.

According to the Federal Trade Commission, the trial may end before 1980. There are already some thirty-six thousand pages of testimony. When the trial ends, the various parties must submit their proposed "findings of fact" for the judges to consider. This could take an additional year! When a decision is made, the parties then can appeal the decision. More time will elapse.

What will happen if the decision is made against the cereal companies? Certain remedies have been proposed by the FTC, including divestiture of plants by the cereal companies, making some five new cereal companies out of existing plants; licensing of trade marks so that other companies could produce these brand-name cereals; and prohibiting Kellogg or other companies from offering shelf space plans to retailers, in which case the cereal company makes a computerized plan for arranging the various brands of cereal in the shelf space allotted for cereal by the retailer.

A LITTLE BITTY BREAKFAST CEREAL COMPANY

Skinner's Raisin Bran has managed to capture 3 percent of the raisin bran market with very little money spent on advertising and in competition with cereal giants such as Kellogg's and General Foods. The latter has imitated Skinner's Raisin Bran, spent an estimated $8 million yearly on advertising and now has the lion's share of the $140 million raisin bran market. Skinner's product sells for a little less than the competition. U.S. Mills, Inc., which makes Skinner's, is proud of its high quality standards and feels that this is the reason it has been able to keep a toehold in the face of enormous competition. It was first produced in 1926 and apparently has a loyal following among breakfast cereal fanciers.

Most new cereals these days are formulated and advertised to appeal to children. They have contrived names; like Kellogg's latest "Corny Snaps," they have sugar as a principal ingredient, and they are heavily fortified with vitamins and minerals to compensate for their being made from refined cereal flours.

The battle for shelf space in the cereal section of the supermarket is a really tough one. Slow sellers tend to get pushed to the end of the top shelf while the giants, by adding new products to their existing lines, expand the space they require on the shelves. Kellogg offers to revamp the cereal section for the retailer — using its computer program — to allocate space according to sales. Testimony by grocers at the FTC hearings, which seeks to determine if there are oligopolistic practices in the cereal industry, estimated that 80 percent of the nation's supermarkets have used such help from Kellogg at one time or another.

ON BANNING AND EDUCATION

"Co-op is two-faced," one shopper says. "You tell us not to buy light meat tuna to save the porpoises. Then why does Co-op sell the darned stuff?" The more we urge shoppers not to buy something, the more we get this criticism. But another member says, "Ban things from our shelves? Never! I want freedom of choice. Let's handle it all by education."

Both "sides" are equally vociferous. To both I've said, "Banning of major items is a matter for committees to study and for the board to decide. And besides, education often makes a big difference."

Does education work? Yes. Often.

People from Project Jonah, a group working to save porpoises and whales, approached the Co-op on the tuna issue. The Consumer Protection Committee studied it, and the majority recommended that this be handled by education. The board agreed.

Through a few articles, shelf cards and exhibits, we've urged switching from light meat tuna (the big seller), which may kill porpoises when the tuna is caught, to white tuna or bonito. Our ads have featured white tuna (expensive) or bonito (a tuna-like fish, but cheap). Other groups stressed the issue too.

Sales show these changes in two years.

Light meat tuna	**down 34 percent**
White meat tuna	**up 40 percent**
Bonito	**up 300 percent**

By the end of 1976, bonito, still unknown to many shoppers elsewhere, was selling as much as all five kinds of Co-op tuna combined. Hooray! (Meanwhile, light meat tuna fishermen have developed ways to cut the number of porpoise killed).

Yes, other shopping patterns change.

High-sugar breakfast cereal sales are down by about one half (see September 20, 1976, *Co-op News*) after an extensive education and merchandising campaign. Banning the baddies was suggested by individuals but was never brought to a committee.

Ban? Sometimes.

Grapes and iceberg lettuce not picked by United Farm Workers have been "banned" by the Co-op board for years. So have high-hazard pesticides. And aerosols with fluorocarbon propellant were banned after extensive committee research concluded that continued use not only endangered the user but the rest of us as well. Along with the banning went extensive education, and most people found they could get along fine without aerosols.

WHY NOT BUY AS ADVERTISED?

"There's an adventure in every bite."

I am sure you have noticed that commercials for foods on television use mostly slogans and very little useful information. "Honey Combs has a big bite," "Hershey, the great American chocolate bar." Food, especially breakfast and snack food, is advertised as crunchy, munchy, fun and even American. Some ads promise prizes, excitement, friends, action and tingle for your mouth. Many have entertaining presentations with song, color and great imagination. Ad writers must search hard for gimmicks such as cereal that can be formed into words, like Alpha Bits, or that makes sounds when you add milk. Ad campaigns are like election campaigns. Slogans just say, "Vote for Smith," and if they say it often enough, we do. "Good and "fun" become synonymous with sugar.

The high-sugar monster is still on the prowl

Some parents seem to think that sugared cereals are more nutritious than candy and cookies. They don't know that some cereals contain more sugar than does candy. Adding a few vitamins and advertising the food as healthy seems to make parents feel safe about high-sugar cereals. They may even feel safe enough not to bother providing the vegetables, fruits, whole wheat, etc., needed for good nutrition.

You're on your own

At this point there doesn't seem to be much hope that advertisers will change and just push good food, good nutrition and good toys. Manufacturers don't care about you. They care about profits. As long as relatively cheap products such as wheat and sugar can be changed in shape, color, etc. − to make them highly profitable − this will be done. You are on your own to learn to select foods for good food value rather than jazzy advertising. By now we know that brainwashing is possible. Don't let it happen to you.

ADVERTISERS: CURIOUS ABOUT CONSUMERS

If you've got a creepy feeling that someone's watching – you're right! Only it's not Big Brother, it's just another advertising agency surveying us as consumers.

Advertisers have this morbid curiosity about us. After all, they spend a lot of money to influence our buying! It's only natural that they should scrutinize us up and down, probing for our soft, weak underbellies.

Any parent can tell you that love for the kids is expressed (in part) by giving them good, wholesome food. Betty Crocker did a survey and discovered this basic, pure motive of parents everywhere. Then she twisted it, ever so slightly, for her own purpose: a new campaign to sell cookie, cake and frosting mixes. "Desserts are a way to show others you care associated with strong family values and emotions to nourish the spirit," a spokesman says. Don't be surprised at her new slogan for selling desserts: "Bake someone happy."

Advertisers get panicky when consumers become restive. When beef prices skyrocket, or we worry about wasteful use of land, or health problems from eating too much fat, sales of beef drop off. So, it's time for an ad blitz! Time for billboards showing succulent steaks! Time for magazine ads, with glowing accounts of the nutrients in beef!

And advertisers sure worry about us, too. Such as: Are the kids learning to read and write? From *Advertising Age* a few weeks back:

". . . we all have a tremendous stake in whether people can read and write in this country. There is little point to writing a novel, creating an advertising campaign, or designing an attractive cereal box if nobody out there can read the message."

We consumers have a little morbid curiosity of our own. Such as, what does it cost to influence our buying? Checking this out, I found that Wrigley has reformulated its gum, Orbit, and endowed it with a budget for one month of $500,000. Morton's has a new dessert line with a media budget of $6 million for the first year. For a grand total, the expected advertising expense in the United States for 1979 is $49 billion, up from $44 billion in 1978.

TO HECK WITH PESTICIDES, LET'S HARVEST THE PESTS!

Well, we all know everybody's worried about high meat prices and the shortage of protein foods in the world. At the same time, we've got these horrid pesticide excesses. It's about time we put these two problems together and come up with one solution. Such as, why not harvest these crawling or flying friends and use them for food? If other countries can do it, so can we! Personally, I have a lot of faith in the advertising of the U.S. food industry. I just know they could get us to eat these strange foods. After all, look at what they've got us eating already!

But you're probably thinking, nobody knows the nutritive value of these critters. Wrong! I have a United Nations publication that gives this information on insects eaten in other parts of the world. Under the section titled meat, poultry and insects, the following comes to light:

. . . The protein content of flying ants (carebera sp.) varies remarkably with the sex! The male is 10 percent protein and 1 percent fat, while the female is 3 percent protein and 10 percent fat, which nearly doubles the caloric value. True, dieters would have to limit their intake of high-calorie females. On the other hand, we could package the males as a low-calorie snack.

. . . Caterpillars, palm-weevils and other larvae are available raw, dried, fried, and smoked in some countries. The dried form is a whopping 53 percent protein! Why wouldn't these be great with Hamburger Helper?

. . . Lake Fly Cake (Chaoborus edulis) also has a high-protein content — 49 percent. If it's cake, Americans will love it. Actually, it's probably a dry product called cake, but there's no reason we couldn't sweeten it. Then it'll go over big.

. . . Grasshoppers (Acridium, Zonocerus) are available raw, or as a flour. The protein is a more modest percentage, but it's still twice that of wheat flour. As an added benefit, grasshoppers are high in iron. One serving would provide more than the Recommended Dietary Intake for men.

. . . Termites, too, are available raw, dried, smoked, fried. Their protein is about 35 percent, and they are high in fat. So high in fat that my thought is that we should extract the fat and use it for frying.

It's clear that we've been missing a bet! What are we waiting for?

TV – A SUGAR PUSHER

Your three- and five-year-old darlings are constantly asking for "Apple Jacks, Apple Jacks"... and you feel like a monster as you pass by the HoHo's, Twinkies and soda pop to the chorus of "I wanna, I wanna."

Don't give in, parents... the real monster is television. Children watch television approximately seven hours per day. By the age of sixteen, children have spent thirteen thousand hours in school and twenty-two thousand hours watching television. Each year, most children spend about two hundred hours watching advertisements for mostly high-sugar products. So what's a parent to do? Turn off the tube more often, and:

1. Watch television with your kids. Look at how the advertisers appeal. Note the lack of programming with positive health messages.

2. Say no!... but more than no. At a recent workshop sponsored by the Committee on Children's Television (CCT) guidelines for parents were created, including the suggestion that parents explain to young children that the people who make sugary foods make lots of money when children buy the products that they sell. Discuss with your children the clever ways the advertiser sells a product. Also express your concern to your child that he or she will have a healthier body by eating good basic foods than they would eating junk food. Remind them of good-tasting foods other than sweets, such as crispy apples, cold milk or whatever.

3. Praise or complain to the companies that advertise. You'll find the address, required by law, is on the package.

4. Boycott the sugar products.

5. Praise or complain to popular programs where characters are models for children. Perhaps the Six Million Dollar Man or Wonder Woman should eat raw vegetables. Should Cookie Monster become Salad Monster? Find the address and telephone number of the TV station and broadcasting company in the yellow pages of your phone book. Send a copy of your letter to the Federal Communications Commission, 1919 M. Street, N.W., Washington, D.C. 20554.

HOW TO BECOME A SCHOOL LUNCH ACTIVIST

You're still working on that uphill battle to use basic foods. But your efforts are being wiped out by your child's school lunch experience.

There are vending machines enticing your child to divert school lunch money to buy soft drinks, potato chips and candy. The lunchroom atmosphere is chaotic, and children's bag lunches with candy and cakes are swapped between youngsters.

The lunch menus seem to reflect the high salt, high fat, high sugar diets that the U.S. Senate Committee on Nutrition & Human Needs warns may contribute to obesity, high blood pressure, heart problems, and certain kinds of cancer. For example, there are frequent appearances of salty, high-fat pizzas, hot dogs, gravies, ham and sausage on luncheon menus. There is white bread, sweet desserts, and your child selects the sweet chocolate milk or whole milk. (Assuming your child was accustomed to nonfat milk at home.)

Start Where the Action Is

April is a month when budgets and menus for the next school year are being planned. Although school lunch programs are federally and state regulated, they are run on the local level and are sensitive to local pressure. Anytime is right to get the action started.

1) Send for: *School Food Action Packet,* Center for Science in the Public Interest, P.O. Box 7226, Washington, D.C. 20044. Cost is $1.50.

This book outlines problem areas to look at and suggests how to go about getting solutions.

2) Arrange a visit to your child's school.

Ask about vending machines, school lunch menus, additives in foods, frequency that very sweet or salty foods are served, etc.

3) Talk up your ideas. Call a meeting, organize a committee, do some research. Set some goals and priorities. Negotiate with staff. Involve older children in the process.

After doing research and sharing your concerns with parents and staff, you may discover that requiring vending machines to carry more nutritious foods is a priority. Or you may find that attending the board of education budget meetings is the way to start to make certain the business aspects of serving a school lunch do not overrun the nutritional welfare of your children. Or you might write letters to the board of education or the food processors involved. Getting the message to them is very important.

LOOK, JOHN! LOOK, MARY! SEE THE UPC

See the UPC on food labels! See the stripes, broad and narrow! See the numbers underneath! See the UPC on more and more foods! What's it all about? What is UPC?

UPC means Universal Product Code, that's what. The stripes identify the manufacturer, brand, size, etc., of an item. With UPC on food labels a store can use a scanning device to read the code and match it up with the price, fed into a computer. With UPC and the necessary equipment, stores can eliminate "ringing up" of groceries in the old familiar way. And stores can save the expense of putting prices on each item sold. And that's progress, we're told.

Already I'm Getting Nervous

Already it's very hard to compare prices of foods. Without a price on the item, even if it's well marked on the shelf, it'll be even harder. What if I want to compare the price of canned kidney beans, stocked in one part of the store, with dried beans stocked in another section? What if I want to compare nonfat dry milk with fresh milk? It's going to mean more running back and forth to check the shelf price. And I've got to remember the shelf prices, at the checkstand, to be sure I'm being charged the right price.

Supermarkets have been known to be a little sloppy about shelf prices. With UPC and automatic pricing, the shelf system will have to get a lot better. Most frightening is the ease with which prices can be changed in a computer. How can shelf pricing keep up?

Electronic checkstands, when scanners are used, will be faster and that's all to the good. But this speed will also make it harder for shoppers to see what prices are being charged. Even though the new cash register tape will better identify the item and price charged for it, by that time it'll be an extra hassle to change your mind or correct mistakes. If a mistake is suspected, someone will have to go back to check the shelf price to be sure.

We've seen some effective consumer surveillance on prices charged. Shoppers have looked at the price in the ad, on the can, on the shelf, and finally at the price rung up at the checkstand. The sharp-eyed shopper now picks up discrepancies. Some people wonder if a government agency, the Bureau of Weights and Measures, for example, could equal such surveillance on the accuracy of scanned prices. If so, we'll pay a pretty penny for it in necessary taxes.

Already Co-op faces extra expense when the UPC will not fit on an otherwise satisfactory label. A new label for an item can cost several thousand dollars. The UPC may take up space we'd like to use for consumer information. Sadly, the extra expenses of changing labels are roughest on small companies. Some of them, as such new expenses become necessary to compete, will go out of business.

Scanning will save an estimated 2 percent gross sales, or more; the savings from elimination of item pricing is estimated to be from 0.3-0.6 percent of gross sales. It will still be cost effective to item price with scanning. We should point out that in the supermarket industry such savings will go to shareholders in the form of increased profits. In the Co-op, on the other hand, any savings will be returned to the members.

MODERN MYTHOLOGY
or where did all the money go?

You're broke. You sure would like to hobnob with money, but somehow it's always out. It has flown the coop by the time you get through the checkstand. Frustrated and angry, you think things should be better by now. Maybe you're suffering from a chronic case of Modern Mythology brought on in part by these modern myths:

Everything is getting better. Well maybe some things are. But for the average working person real earnings haven't changed since 1967.

Surely there are fewer poor people as time goes on. Dead wrong. During 1975 there were two and one-half million new people "at poverty level"[*] for a grand total of twenty-six million or 11 percent of our population.

The rich pay 75 percent of their income in taxes. Wrong again. The richest 10 percent of our people pay roughly 20 percent of their income in taxes, while the poorest 10 percent still pay about 11 percent in taxes. 60 percent of the people pay a steady 16-17 percent.

The Department of Agriculture says people spend under 20 percent of their income for food. Maybe true for rich people. But if you're in the lowest fifth, incomewise, it would take 53 percent of your income to buy the "Low Cost Plan" diet worked out by the Agriculture Department.

Food stamps go mostly to students and strikers. Not so. Two recent studies show that only 1.3 percent of food stamp participants are students and less than one-tenth of 1 percent are strikers. Less than 1 percent of the food stamp households have incomes over 1½ times the poverty level.

Well, modern myths or not, you're still broke and need help just to buy food. You might investigate these programs: Food stamps — Call your local welfare office for information; WIC — (Women, Infants and Children) provides food vouchers for pregnant and nursing women, and children up to five years. Check with your local health department.

*The "Poverty level" was defined in 1975 as $5050 yearly income for a family of four; in 1979, that level is defined at $6700. (Note: Part of the material for this article came from *The Christian Science Monitor,* September 28, 1976.)

HOW TO GET BY ON FOOD STAMPS

To get by on food stamps, you need to follow all these DO's and DON'Ts.

DON'T have teenagers, because they eat too much. Food stamp allotments are based on families with school-age children. It takes 30 percent more money to feed a teenager than the "average child."

Especially, DON'T have teenage boys, because they take 45 percent more money than the average child.

DON'T have a big family, because after eight people each additional person is only allowed $22 per month for food.

DON'T be old or have diabetes or allergies. Special diets take *money*, which you don't have.

How to Be an Active, Informed Consumer 13

DO have all day to spend. (This means you can't be a full-time worker, getting the minimum wage, trying to stay off welfare and support your kids). You need time: to take the bus, to stand in line at the welfare office to get certified, to wait to pounce on the mailman on the first and fifteenth, to wait in line to cash your check, to wait if the cashier runs out of money, to wait in line to buy your stamps, to get to the office before it closes at 5:15, and of course to wait at the checkstand on the busiest days of the month. And you need time to cook everything from scratch and grow your own vegetables.

DO forget what you've learned about cheap food. Right now, for calories alone, cake mix is cheaper than bread or beans or rice or potatoes.

DON'T live in a time of inflation, because food stamp allotments are always six to twelve months behind actual costs.

DON'T be poor, because poor people's food has gone up a lot more than rich people's food.

DON'T be Oriental or Chicano or anything else with a cultural eating pattern. If you grow up without a cultural eating pattern, maybe you won't be accustomed to rice or beans. (Rice costs double what it did a year ago and beans cost five times as much.)

DON'T be too interested in nutrition, because you might think you should have lots of fresh fruits and vegetables or whole wheat bread — and you can't buy these often. (The U.S. Department of Agriculture says that the Economy Plan on which food stamp allotments are based is "designed for temporary use" and "does not provide as nutritious a diet as other plans." It suggests "less milk, meat, poultry, fish, eggs, fruits, and vegetables than other plans.")

DO have a rich aunt so you can eat there often.

DO have lots of extra cash around to pay the cash required to get stamps and to supplement your stamp food with goodies like meat and fresh milk.

DO be thankful that on July 1st your allotment went up. If you are in a family of four, you now get stamps valued at $1.25 per day per person, maximum.

But, you say, you've been making it without my advice? Let me know how you do it.

Note: This is a historical piece. In 1974, the price of beans and rice shot up out of sight. Food stamps are distributed on a completely different basis now and the allotment is now up to $1.67 per day, as of July 1979.

IT'S REALLY NOT ALL THAT SIMPLE*

The total chemical environment and the vast variety of foods available to humankind make any attempt to pinpoint a cause-and-effect in cases of food-related illnesses very difficult. The exception is cases of poisoning due to microorganisms or accidental contamination of the food by grower, processor or consumer.

Foods are probably the most complex part of our total environment, since they contain toxic substances as part of their normal composition and, furthermore, chemicals such as pesticides and food additives may be applied to them during growth, storage or processing. Many chemicals naturally present in foods are the same ones used in efforts to produce, process, distribute and cook them. Most food additives also occur naturally in foods — vitamins, protein components, organic salts of many minerals, spices, flavorings and natural coloring materials.

Only a relatively few additives have been completely made by man. Toxic metals (lead, mercury, cadmium, arsenic, zinc) that may contaminate foods by environmental pollution or processing vessels also are normally present in foods because they occur in soil and water and thus get "built into" the growing plant. Other chemical compounds are generated by the heating, drying, freezing and pickling of foods.

We are able to control quite rigidly what we put into foods during processing, but the natural composition of foods is mostly beyond the pale of regulatory control. Take the potato—one hundred fifty distinct chemical substances have been found, including solanine, alkaloids, oxalic acid, arsenic, tannins, nitrate, and over one hundred more, all with no recognized nutritional value. Orange oil has at least forty-two chemical entities, and all vegetables, fruits and other natural foods are similarly complex.

How do we survive the impact of myriads of potentially toxic substances in natural foods? First, the concentrations are so low that, except when grossly exaggerated quantities are eaten over an extended period of time, the levels that cause toxicity are never reached. If cabbage constitutes a large part of the diet for a long time, its goitrogenic substances may produce goiters. It is the diversity of foods in our diets that protects us from these hazards.

Secondly, our bodies can handle small amounts of many different chemical substances even though larger amounts of any one of them perhaps could not be tolerated.

Lastly, there are natural antagonisms among these trace elements that reduce their toxicity. For example, a toxic level of cadmium in the diet is reduced by an accompanying high level of zinc. High manganese content interferes with iron absorption but can be offset by additional iron in the diet. Copper antagonizes molybdenum, selenium cancels out mercury, cobalt antagonizes iron.

This principle of "safety in numbers" in a wide variety of foods eaten has been recognized as applying to food additives and pesticides by the joint FAO/WHO Expert Committee on Food Additives. An increase in the number of additives on a permissible list doesn't necessarily mean that the amount used has increased but rather that these are alternate choices that reduce the chances of cumulative levels of any one. Pesticides also have a lower hazard when many different ones are alternately used for a single purpose.

There are other ways that we are protected. Certain processing methods render the foods safer. Heating removes the cyanogenetic glycosides and some of the goitrogens. Refrigeration, canning, freezing, drying and even packaging suppress contamination by harmful microorganisms and chemical changes in the foods that could produce toxins. The worldwide food distribution system dilutes potential hazards caused by local imbalances or environmental factors.

A short summary of some further examples of toxic materials in foods will underline the safety factor provided by a wide variety of food choices. Favism, a form of hemolytic anemia, is caused by a toxin in the fava bean. Buckwheat contains a factor that produces fagopyrism, a photosensitization to sunlight resulting in inflamed eyes, nose and ears in cattle. Similar photosensitizing agents occur in parsnips, carrots, parsley, dill and limes.

Lycopene, which is related to carotene — the vegetable form of vitamin A — can cause illness when it accumulates in the livers of persons who chronically consume large amounts of tomato products.

Nitrates may reach harmful levels in vegetables and forage plants grown in soils high in nitrates. A severe anemia, similar to that caused by carbon monoxide, was produced in children who ate leftover spinach that was not refrigerated. Bacteria growing in the spinach changed the nitrates to nitrites, the chemical form that destroys the hemoglobin in the red blood cells.

Honey poisoning has occurred in both Europe and the United States. Honey becomes poisonuous when bees collect nectar from mountain laurel, rhododendron, azalea and oleander, which contain potent heart stimulants.

Many plants used as food by both people and animals contain glycosides that produce hydrocyanic acid, an extremely toxic chemical, in the stomach. Some of the foods that contain these glycosides are bitter almonds; seeds of peach, plum, apricot, cherry and pear; lima beans and tapioca. Some one hundred eighty plant species are known to contain them and many of these are used for cattle feed.

So the public health agencies are charged with protecting us from many hazardous foods and monitoring the sanitation of all foods offered for sale. We protect ourselves by eating a wide variety of foods and by handling the foods we intend to eat in safe and sanitary ways. And lastly, we should be wary of collecting and eating wild plants, berries, nuts and fruits unless we are quite sure they are safe to eat.

*Summarized from "Natural Food Toxicants — A Perspective" by Julius M. Coon, Ph.D., *Nutrition Reviews*, Vol. 32, No. 11, November 1974.

Food Plants. . . Sometimes are Unfriendly

Of course most plants seem friendly enough. In appearance they have a certain non-aggressiveness, a disarming passivity. But do not be too trusting. Plants, including food plants, do not grow themselves purely for our pleasure. Rather they grow for the survival of their species! Perhaps they increase their chances of survival by being indigestible, or by causing disagreeable bloating, or even by being truly toxic. The food person in each household should know of these crafty ways of plants.

ON BEING CHOOSY ABOUT FOOD ADDITIVES

For those who wish to be selective in their anxiety about food additives, help is at hand. Why worry collectively, if you can single out those chemicals that are most worrisome? *Eater's Digest*, by Michael Jacobson, is an easy reference to the food additives in greatest use. Published first in 1972 by Anchor, it was updated in 1976 and costs $2.95.

The first chapter discusses the possible dangers of additives, gives some basic classification of additives, plus fascinating bits about the functioning of the Food and Drug Administration. The second chapter is the most interesting and useful to me. Food additives are listed in alphabetical order. Jacobson gives a brief rundown on the ways each additive is used in food processing, describes the knowledge, or lack of knowledge, of its safety or danger as used in food, and winds it all up with references. The last chapter looks at standards for foods, including information on optional ingredients and labeling requirements or lack of requirements for additives. There are four appendices, including a list of banned additives, a partial list of Generally Recognized As Safe (GRAS) substances, with their functions, the chemical formulas of some additives, and a glossary.

Jacobson was graduated from the University of Chicago with a bachelor's degree in chemistry and holds a doctorate in microbiology from Massachusetts Institute of Technology in 1969. He has worked as a consultant to the Center for the Study of Responsive Law and is one of the founders of the Center for Science in the Public Interest. The Salk Institute of San Diego provided him with financial support while he wrote this book. He is also a co-author of the pamphlet, *The Chemical Additives in Booze*, as well as "Chemical Cuisine," a wall chart on food additives.

CHEMICAL CUISINE

Nutrition Action, a project of the Center for Science in the Public Interest, 1755 S. St., N.W., Washington, D.C. 20009, has prepared a wall chart titled Chemical Cuisine. It lists what the center's experts consider to be the degree of hazard for a large number of food additives. Here are a few examples from the much longer lists in the chart:

Safe — ascorbic acid, carotene, calcium propionate, carregeenan, casein, citric acid, EDTA, glycerin, vegetable gums, hydrolyzed vegetable protein, lactic acid, lactose, mono- and diglycerides, polysorbate, sodium benzoate, sorbitol. Many of these are naturally occurring components of foods.

Caution — may be unsafe or is used in food we eat too much of, such as soft drinks and beer, fats and fat-containing foods, cereals and desserts: BHA, MSG, phosphoric acid, phosphates, propyl gallate, sulfur dioxide, sodium bisulfite.

Avoid — either unsafe or inadequately tested: artificial colors, BHT, brominated vegetable oil, caffeine, quinine, saccharin, sodium nitrite and nitrate. In this group sugar and salt are listed, not because they pose any hazard if one does not overuse, but because many of us do consume too much for good health.

This listing seems to the Co-op home economists to be based on fairly good evidence. We thought we should share it with you since many of you have asked for such information.

THOSE RAT FACTS ABOUT SACCHARIN

Are you familiar with the Bronx Cheer? Lately it's been widely used to ridicule the rat studies that showed that saccharin could cause rat cancer. Some people are hooting over reports that the fateful doses given the rats was about equivalent to the saccharin in eight hundred cans of diet soda. Not even a highly motivated teenager drinks that much soda in one day.

But this kind of rat test is not being questioned by sober scientific types. It is a bonafide method of identifying the weak cancer-causing chemicals whose effects show up twenty to forty years later in humans. In contrast, highly potent chemicals do not usually require the same type of tests before their harm is recognized.

The problem in identifying weak cancer-causing chemicals is that only one out of twenty thousand Americans may be susceptible, yet that means that ten thousand people could develop the disease because of the chemical. There is not enough money nor trained people to study twenty thousand rats to see if only one will develop cancer. Instead, fewer animals are used with correspondingly higher doses. Such dosage indentifies the tumor-producing capacity with meaningful, consistent and reproducible results. This system has been studied using chemicals known to produce cancer in humans and has been found to be reliable. It is now well known that if a large dose of a chemical causes cancer in animals, a low dose will probably cause cancer in some humans.

There is a misconception that large doses of most anything will cause cancer. However, while extremely high levels of most substances can be harmful or even fatal, only a few cause cancer. For example, of one hundred twenty pesticides and industrial chemicals chosen for study because of evidence of toxic effects in humans, only eleven were shown to cause cancer in mice.

NITRITES AND NITROSAMINES

Last report on nitrosamines was a Buy Word in the Co-op News of April 20, 1977. How about an update?

Nitrosamines are known carcinogens formed when nitrite combines with amines from protein, either when the nitrite-containing cured meat, poultry or fish is cooked or in the mouth or stomach when both components are present.

The U.S. Department of Agriculture on May 16, 1978, lowered the level of nitrite that can be added to bacon. There is increasing concern about nitrites since the recent MIT study showed that nitrites can induce cancer in laboratory animals.

The reason for the retention of preservatives in cured meat products is that, in the past, nitrite has functioned to prevent botulism. Industry, FDA and USDA are now forced to develop new methods for controlling these competing health problems. The responsibility for regulating nitrites in our food is shared by two agencies and involves three different laws.

The MIT nitrite study has now been reviewed by FDA scientists who concluded that doses of nitrite fed to rats ranging from 250 to 2000 ppm did increase the cancer risk from 7.9 percent in those fed no nitrite to 12.5 percent in the combined test groups. FDA and USDA have formed an Interagency Working Group for Nitrite Research to review all research in nitrite and nitrosamines, identify gaps in our knowledge and recommend research to fill these gaps.

The above information is from the Joint Statement of Carol Tucker Foreman, Assistant Secretary for Food and Consumer Services and Donald Kennedy, Commissioner of Food and Drugs on behalf of the USDA and the Public Health Service, Department of HEW before the Subcommittee on Agricultural Research and General Legislation, Committee on Agriculture, U.S. Senate.

NITRITES IN FOOD

Are nitrites only in cured meat products? No way! While the figures available for nitrites from foods other than cured meats are estimates, the indication is that only about 2 percent of the total dietary nitrites we are exposed to come from cured meats. The remaining 98 percent comes from other foods, drinking water and saliva. Even smog makes a contribution on days when it is heavy.

Saliva accounts for about three-fourths of the daily nitrite ingestion. An appreciable part of this is believed to come from the digestion of food and the action of bacteria upon it in the small intestine. The remainder comes from nitrates in the saliva reduced to nitrites by the bacteria in the mouth. The human body is exposed to an average of 33 milligrams per day of nitrite, of which only 0.7 milligrams comes from cured meats.

Drinking water in the United States very seldom exceeds the standard set by the U.S. Department of Public Health of 10 milligrams per liter (about one quart) of water. Water from private wells, however, may be higher in nitrate, especially water from shallow wells where the soil is impermeable. This nitrate can come from sewage pollution of the water, or from runoff from agricultural land.

Adults tolerate considerable dietary nitrate/nitrite but infants are more sensitive. Nitrite reacts with the hemoglobin in the red blood cells, transforming it into methemoglobin, which cannot be used to transport oxygen. The body rapidly replaces the defective methemoglobin except in the infant who has such a small amount of blood that a large amount of hemoglobin could be tied up at one time, causing an oxygen deficit. This hazard to infants has only been found where well water high in nitrate was used to prepare their formulas.

(This information is from recently published material from both the National Research Council-National Academy of Sciences and the American Meat Institute. Both base their tentative conclusions on a rather limited amount of published scientific research from MIT and Iowa State University, among others.)

WHAT IS GRAS?

GRAS (Generally Recognized As Safe) is a catchall. Into it were dumped all the food additives the Food and Drug Administration thought didn't need to be tested for safety at the time the

Food Additive Amendment went into effect in 1958. Since 1972 a team of outside scientific experts has been taking a second look at these additives to make sure they are safe by today's standards. So far it has examined about half the four hundred GRAS items and found only a few it considered questionable. Some of these follow.

Caffeine not only occurs naturally in coffee, tea and cocoa, but is added to cola-type beverages. The experts could not agree on the hazard but recommended additional studies in animals, human adults and children to check for birth defects and effect on behavior.

MSG has been alleged to be a possible hazard to infants less than twelve months. The committee felt there was no hazards to adults at the present level of use, although a few suffer from "Chinese restaurant syndrome." Baby-food manufacturers no longer add it to their products.

Protein hydrolysates are okay if derived from casein (a milk protein), but further studies are recommended for those from other sources. They should not be added to infant formulas or baby foods.

Licorice, licorice extracts, and ammoniated glycyrrhizin can cause temporary high blood pressure if used heavily. There is no hazard with normal use.

Regular sugar or corn sugar products are involved in tooth decay but pose no other known hazard. Recommendation is for further studies on the effects of increased consumption.

Nutmeg, mace, and their essential oils are recommended for further studies although there is no evidence of hazard at present.

FDA is committed to review all food additives and currently is reviewing GRAS and non-GRAS flavors and colors. Here are some of the actions FDA has taken:

Placed mannitol on an interim status until more study is done on thymus gland growth in female rats.

Sorbitol was affirmed as GRAS, also dill and garlic.

Proposed that BHT be placed on interim status while checking effects on rat livers. BHA is also on interim status, though there is less urgency than for BHT.

The following are proposed for affirmation as GRAS: beeswax, clove oil, licorice, mustard as a flavor; gelatin as a thickener; iodine and sorbose (a source of vitamin C) as dietary supplements.

(This information was abstracted from "The GRAS list Revisited," which appeared in the May 1978 issue of the magazine *FDA Consumer*.)

HOW NATURAL ARE THOSE 'NATURAL' VITAMINS?

The idea that "natural" vitamins provide special benefits for our bodies has been raging around the Co-op. This has occurred despite repeated assertions by our home economists and pharmacists that vitamins have the same properties whether they are called "natural" or "synthetic." We know of no advantages to justify the higher prices that "natural" labels often command.

Co-op does stock "natural" vitamins for the many shoppers who prefer the products so labeled. In addition to our natural food stores, the pharmacies have been offering an expanded selection, and now our regular food stores have them, too. Spurred by our growing sales, we have been trying to find out more about these products. A few weeks ago I visited two manufacturers of "natural" vitamins in Southern California. These companies make capsules, tablets, and other dosage forms sold under some of the most famous brand names found in "health food" stores, as well as our Co-op stores.

During the visits it became clear that many vitamin products labeled "natural" or "organic" are not really what I had imagined those terms to mean. For example, their "Rose Hips Vitamin C Tablets" are made from natural rose hips combined with chemical ascorbic acid, the same vitamin C used in standard pharmaceutical tablets. Natural rose hips contain only about 2 percent vitamin C, and we were told that if no vitamin C were added, the tablet "would have to be as big as a golf ball." A huge stock barrel containing raw material for tablet manufacture was labeled "Rose Hips – Adjusted to contain 50 percent Ascorbic Acid." Nevertheless, the labels on the bottles read by the consumer were titled simply "Rose Hips Vitamin C." Would you have guessed that the amount of vitamin C coming from rose hips was but a tiny fraction of the amount added as a chemical?

Similarly, the B vitamins turned out to be mostly synthetic chemicals added to yeast and other natural bases.

Vitamin E products are indeed derived from natural sources – mainly vegetable oils such as wheat germ, soy bean, and corn. These are sold as cheaply as the synthetic variety. But in order to concentrate the vitamin in a capsule small enough to swallow, various chemical solvents must be used for extraction and separation. The vegetable material is grown with use of the usual insecticides and chemical fertilizers. Even the gelatin capsule must contain a preservative so that it won't turn rancid.

Again, the labels on the finished products say "natural" and "organic" without qualification. Here the terms are used quite differently from the way I had thought of them before. Apparently, these words can be used freely, because there are no legal definitions of "natural" or "organic." In fact, since the vitamins themselves are identical, no one can tell them apart, either in a test tube or in an animal. A legal distinction could hardly be enforced when no way can be devised to test the difference.

FDA WILL REGULATE OTC VITAMIN AND MINERAL DRUGS

The Food and Drug Administration (FDA), for the first time in its history, is engaged in a massive review of the safety and effectiveness of all over-the-counter (OTC) drugs. This project is now in its eighth year and only about 40 percent completed. Seventeen "expert panels" are charged with recommending changes in product formulations and their labeling. Improvements in areas such as OTC laxatives, cough and cold remedies, dental and sleep aids, etc., are expected to save the consumer money as well as improve the products' usefulness. It is certain that consumer education by FDA, pharmacists, physicians, and the drug industry itself is a key requirement to the success of this undertaking.

The most recent panel to submit its recommendations[1] to FDA is the one dealing with therapeutic vitamin-mineral formulas[2] that make claims on their labels for treating certain conditions. Three-fourths of all vitamin-mineral products make no such label claims and are classified as food supplements. They fall under the regulations applying to foods. It is expected that no changes will be made in these products. According to the panel recommendations, products classified as OTC drugs involve some hazard to consumers and should therefore be regulated as to the amount and types

1) Federal Register, March 16, 1979 and *FDA Consumer*, April 1979.

2) This particular "expert panel" was the Advisory Review Panel on Over-The-Counter Vitamin, Mineral and Hematinic Drugs. Like all the seventeen expert panels, it was chosen from nominations that came from consumer and other organized groups all over the country. The final panel had representatives from minorities, from health and other food groups, from the medical, pharmaceutical and nutritional professions, and one person who represented the general public.

of ingredients permitted as well as to dosage and contraindications. Here are some examples of the panel's comments:

1) Calcium, iron and zinc are effective as single-mineral pills. Magnesium, phosphorus and potassium are not because deficiencies are rare. Copper, iodine, fluoride and manganese are dangerous in high doses.

2) Over a hundred miscellaneous ingredients that make no contribution to the effectiveness of the formula are considered inappropriate. Among them are apricots, brewer's yeast, buckwheat, comfrey root, hesperidin, kelp, lecithin, rose hips and wheat germ.

3) Combinations of the fat-soluble vitamins (A, D, E and K) should not be permitted, since such combinations are neither safe nor rational.

4) Elderly persons do not need so-called "geriatric" formulas, since their requirements are the same as other persons. Women do not need those labeled "for women taking oral contraceptives," because there is no evidence that these persons need additional folic acid.

5) Vitamins A, D and C are toxic in large amounts over various periods of time. Labels should warn of this toxicity.

THE COST OF FOOD LABELS

Who pays? We have received a number of protests from members because we have pointed out that label changes cost money. The food business is one of such low profit margins that increasing the cost of doing business is a serious matter, not to be jumped into lightly. Ultimately, the consumers will have to pay for label changes as a part of the price they spend for food.

What do consumers want on labels? The recent FDA, USDA and FTC hearings held across the country revealed that consumers want:

1. All ingredients listed on food labels.
2. Total sodium and total sugars on labels.
3. Percentage of major ingredients on labels.
4. Open dating on food products.
5. Nutritional information that is understandable.
6. Better government regulation of fortified foods.
7. Education on how to use all this information.

What's the cost of getting this information on labels? There's a labor cost to gather the information and to redesign the label so it is both legible and legal. There are analytical laboratory costs to get the needed information. FDA insists it must be accurate. Changing printing plates for the new labels and losing money when present label inventory is discarded add up to additional costs.

Just suppose FDA makes nutritional labeling mandatory! Or suppose FDA decides to require some type of declaration of the sodium and various sugars in the products? Universal Cooperatives, which is ultimately responsible for all Co-op labels, estimates that such major changes for our six hundred Co-op label products would cost:
$53,000 to rearrange the labels (new designs, printing, inventory loss, etc.)
$28,000 staff time
$105,000, at least, for analytical laboratory tests
This breaks down to an average of $320 per product which, even if spread over ten years, is still a yearly cost of $32 per product.

It's not that we are dragging our feet on this matter. We are as keen for informative labels as anyone in the business. We just think you consumers should know approximate costs and that all of us make sure that when we do change labels we have researched all the problems first.

SPEAK UP IF YOU DON'T LIKE IT

A while ago, I talked to a group of fifty women — all employed as consumer advisors by major food processing companies. These women handle consumer complaints about their companies' products and services. I described how we handle consumer education and quality control problems at the Co-op. They were flabbergasted to learn how we do things and how many shoppers bring products back when something is wrong with them. They said they get very little feedback from consumers and very few complaints about the products their companies make. So I said I would tell you how to complain about national brand products . . . those sold under names such as Del Monte, Best Foods, General Foods, General Mills, Purina et al.

Write a letter! The address is on the label. The company's name the city and state, and the zip code are all you need. Type your letter if possible and keep a copy. Address the letter to "Department of Consumer Complaints" or "Department of Public Relations." Be polite. Be brief. Be objective. Be confident.

Describe the problem including the exact name and size and any code number and/or dates on the package.

Keep the evidence if it is not perishable. Do not send it with your letter. Keep the cash register slip with the purchase date and the price paid for the product.

Three things may happen:

1. Your letter may be ignored.

2. You may receive a form letter with an apology from the company's public relations department.

3. Or, you may hit the jackpot and receive a letter and one or more free samples of the product.

Part Two
Before You Shop

1

Being Smart About Shopping

HOW TO PICK A GOOD SUPERMARKET

Suppose you move to a new town or a different area in a metropolitan district and you're lost without your dear old Co-op; what to do? Case the joints in the new place, take notes as you go, record prices of frequently purchased items, then sit down and rate the various stores you visited. Try your first and second choices to see how they stack up under actual shopping conditions before you decide.

Here are some things (besides prices) to observe as you cruise the unfamiliar markets. These are not listed in order of importance — only you can know if a particular practice is important to you.

1. Pricing. Are most items singly priced or are they, for example, three for 57¢? Do the shelf tags carry unit prices (price per pint, pound or count)? Are the items individually price marked even if the cash registers use a scanning device for ringing up the sale?

2. Frozen foods. Are the foods solidly frozen? Is the temperature of the box near zero degrees? Are frozen foods piled near the front of the freezer where temperatures may not be low enough for long storage? Are stacks of products left in the aisle thawing while the clerk is checking out customers or is out to lunch?

3. Dairy and egg boxes. Are the eggs refrigerated? Is the temperature of these boxes $42°$ F or lower? Are they clean? Do the meat labels give the species, primal cut and retail name (like "Beef Chuck Steak")?

4. Produce. Is it wilted, poorly trimmed, dirty, or untidily thrown into the case? Is there adequate variety for your needs? Are there too many impulse items such as salad dressing, croutons, salad seasonings, salad bowls, etc.?

5. Grocery. Are there too many "out of stocks" on the shelves? Are marked-down items in such poor condition (dented on seams, swollen or badly rusted) that they should not be sold?

6. General appearance of the store. Is the store cluttered with advertising posters, banners and other gimmicks? Is there a directory to help you find things? Are the front end aisle displays filled with junk foods and impulse items?

7. Checkstand area. Is the service good? Are checkers friendly and efficient? Are the checkstands cluttered with impulse items? Do you leave with a feeling that you would like to return because the store management really cares about pleasing you?

THE WORST BARGAINS IN THE SUPERMARKET

Until those guys up front figure out how to be the winning supermarket with the lowest prices, the highest quality and still stay in business, I'll just keep saying the same old thing. Which is, the best way to save money is by making careful choices when you shop — no matter where you shop. Here are a few of the worst choices you can make, in terms of what you get for your money.

• Bacon, hotdogs and spareribs, because you get less meat, more fat or bone than in most other cuts.

• Honeydews, cantaloupes and strawberries in early spring because it's too early in the season and the price is high. Such fruits come a long way at this time of year, and melons especially are apt to be small and not very good.

• 3¼ oz. size "Chicken of the Sea" tuna because the price per can may be low but the price per pound is the highest of any size can of tuna.

• Hamburger Helper because you're paying a lot for a pinch of herbs, some dried tomato sauce, about 1½ cups of macaroni! And you still have to buy the meat! That's a high price for convenience.

• Del Monte individual pudding cups because that's a lot of packaging for a little bit to eat, and what you eat is a product of many additives, artificial color and flavor.

• Birds Eye frozen vegetables in sauces because with all that sauce there's less vegetable. That means less of the nutrients that are hard to get, and more nutrients (fat and calories!) that are too easy to get! Plus, a high price for convenience.

Before You Shop   31

• Don't forget! Almost any food you prepare at home will be more nutritious than a highly processed convenience food.

SECRETS OF A SMART SHOPPER

Prices going up, up, up and away? What to do? Here are some ideas from your home economists. Give them a try.

Before you go to the store:

• Establish a rough limit on what a certain type of food should cost for your family of four. For example, not more than $2.50 (or whatever you decide) for the main dish for dinner; 45¢ - 60¢ for breakfast fruit, or vegetables for dinner or dessert, etc.

• Certain foods are good buys year around. Use them frequently. For example, your list might include frozen orange juice, canned tomatoes, regular or low-fat milk and/or nonfat dry milk, or several bulk grains. Each family will have its own favorites.

• Keep a shopping list in your kitchen. As you finish an item that you use regularly, put it on the list. As you think of ideas for upcoming meals, put the needed items on the list.

• Plan to do a major shopping once a week. Plan your menus ahead for one week, if possible. Check supplies on hand and complete your shopping list accordingly. The less often you go to the store, the fewer opportunities you will have for impulse buying, although you may want to pick up fresh food at least twice a week.

• When planning menus, consider the cost of convenience foods. If you buy "built-in maid service," you usually pay for it. There are exceptions (frozen orange juice, frozen peas) but they are rare. While a convenience food can be a blessing on occasion, regular use can cause the budget to skyrocket. For instance, macaroni and cheese "made from scratch" is much less expensive, almost as easy to prepare, and usually more nutritious than the packaged or frozen products.

• Plan to buy "store" brands of canned and frozen foods, paper products, health and beauty aids, etc. Usually the quality is comparable to nationally advertised brands while the cost is less. A case in point is laundry bleach. Co-op bleach and Clorox are identical in composition but Co-op costs less.

• Check ads for seasonal low prices on meat, poultry, fish, fresh produce and grocery items. Alter your menu when you find a good buy. Buy only amounts you can use before storage time lapses. Compare prices of fresh, frozen and canned versions of the same item. Also compare prices of bulk products with the packaged versions. Sometimes there is considerable price difference, while the nutritive value may be the same. Flavor, of course, may differ considerably.

• Save shopping time by organizing your shopping list according to categories as stocked in the store so that you do not retrace your steps. Plan to buy frozen and refrigerated items last so that they will not warm up too much.

• If you shop for specials at several stores, be aware of impulse purchases, extra transportation, and shopping time, which may negate savings.

• Eat before you shop! Research has shown that a hungry shopper is more likely to indulge in impulse buying.

• Leave the kids home if you can't say "no" and mean it.

• Buying larger sizes? Use unit pricing information to see if it's worth doing. Small sizes on sale may be a better bargain. Beware of optical illusions in packaging. Sometimes a larger bottle, for example a salad oil bottle, contains fewer ounces than one that looks smaller.

• Avoid or choose with care items displayed on center or end aisles or at the front of the store. In some stores these may be "impulse purchases" and poor values. Sometimes they are "in and outs" – products not regularly stocked, which may or may not be poor buys.

• Don't buy a product just because a demonstrator offers you a sample. Consider if this is really something you want at a price you can afford.

• Ask the checker to call the prices as he/she rings up your order. No one can remember all prices accurately. Special prices may not be marked on the package, clerks may ring up the regular price.

After you shop:

• Don't stop on the way home to do errands. Many foods deteriorate rapidly if unrefrigerated for an hour or more.

• Check your purchases against the cash register tag to see that you paid only for what you received and that the prices charged were correct. If you find inaccuracies or discrepancies, report them to the manager the next time you shop.

• Keep track of your food costs. Separate costs of non-foods and pet foods from "people foods."

Before You Shop 33

• Check if you are wasting food by preparing too much or serving foods your family doesn't like. Either prepare quantities that will just feed your family for one meal without leftovers, or plan to have enough leftovers for another meal.

MAKE A SHOPPING LIST

Tired of extra shopping trips and wasting money on impulse items? Instead: (1) Plan your menus a week ahead; (2) Use up perishable items on hand; (3) Look at the recipes used for your menus and note what ingredients you need to buy; (4) Make a shopping list.

Co-op member Tamar Wise suggests that you shop by grocery categories. Add any product you buy regularly to the list below and eliminate items you do not buy. Arrange the rest in the order found in your store. Plan your shopping route to buy cold and frozen items last.

Make a permanent list and Xerox it or enter it in a notebook. Use the list as a reminder or place it next to the paper on which you write your shopping list. If you use a full-size paper, you may have space for brand, size, price, or other comments.

GROCERIES (Staples)

Tip: Compare *price per pound or quart, etc.* (unit prices) before choosing.
- soft drinks, beer
- coffee, tea, cocoa
- dry, evaporated milk
- cereal
- salad dressings, mayonnaise
- catsup, pickles
- tomato sauce, other
- rice, noodles, beans
- Mexican food
- Oriental food

- gourmet food
- crackers, cookies
- bread, muffins
- peanut butter
- jams, honey, syrup
- baking supplies
- spices
- oil
- pudding mixes, gelatin
- canned meat, fish
- soups and prepared foods
- canned vegetables
- canned fruit
- fruit juices

NON-FOODS

- paper products
- shampoo, toothpaste
- pet food
- drug items

- soap and detergents
- cleaning supplies
- housewares

PRODUCE

Tip: Stroll around to look at all the oranges, apples or potatoes before choosing. Sometimes they're not stocked together; you may miss the best buy.

bulk foods
dried fruits
salad makings
fruits, citrus
potatoes, carrots
vegetables

MEAT DEPARTMENT

Tip: Look at the bone and fat as well as price per pound. Compare price *per serving*.

meat
poultry
fish

DELI

Tip: Luncheon meats can be very expensive per pound. Cheeses can be a good buy. One pound of cheese has as much protein as 1 1/3 pounds of ground beef.

cheese
luncheon meats
tortillas
pickles

DAIRY FOODS

milk, yogurt, cottage cheese
margarine, butter
eggs

FROZEN FOOD

ice cream
vegetables, juices

CONFESSIONS OF A WEEKLY SHOPPER

I had fallen into deplorable ways. Every night or so, after work, I was shopping for food. It was awful! Trying to organize my thoughts, hurrying to decide what to buy, waiting in line feeling cranky and mean! Finally I gave up and went back to the One Big Weekly Shopping Trip. It has worked just dandy, now that I'm used to it. Here's what's good about it.

I should be at the store at ten minutes to six to face the most important decision of the day. . . dinner? No, thanks! No longer do I attempt this decision during my precarious late-afternoon mental state. Instead, I do it on my Weekly Shopping Trip. Having decided in advance what's for dinner, I fix it more or less automatically. Thus my brain is free to relax and socialize so that dinner can be the glorious end to a hard day, rather than the final trauma!

Food shopping isn't getting any easier, but it's always been hard work. Now, I allocate prime time for shopping. Nobody does a good job when in a rush, tired out, worried about something else, or hungry. Instead I try to choose a time when I can give the job the attention and judgment it deserves. It takes at least an hour in the store, plus another half hour at home to put the food away. Getting to the store when it first opens, or shopping in the early evening when other people are still eating, may be worth the effort because the stores are relatively uncrowded. However, all items may not be available.

Food costs take up a lot of your income: maybe one-fourth or more. Should you work ten hours to pay for food grabbed in a few thoughtless, frenzied minutes? No! I say. Shopping once a week has some money "smarts." First, I find I have a better idea what I'm really spending for food. (I can easily subtract the total amount for non-food when I get home. It's one lump sum, instead of a few bucks here and a few bucks there, which somehow I never get around to totaling up.) Second, I know about how much of various foods we use per week, how often I need staples, so I take better advantage of specials. Of course, those who have the time and gas can maybe make a killing driving from one store to another, skimming off only the specials.

Admittedly, storage is a challenge. Shopping once a week means for me that we have fresh fish or liver or ground beef or some such perishable food the night that I shop. If this seems too limiting, it's still worth it! It also means using fresh vegetables like asparagus as soon as possible, while buying carrots, winter squash, oranges and grapefruits and other produce that will stand a week's storage. For big milk users, it may mean falling back on fresh concentrated milk or nonfat dry milk after a few days.

When I am very well organized, which isn't always, I may start tomorrow night's dinner while fixing tonight's. Just a small start can be a big help, such as getting out a recipe, or digging out an inconveniently stored casserole. I may even cut up a chicken, mix up a marinade or salad dressing, or trim the fresh string beans for tomorrow night. Whatever little thing it is, I'm grateful that it's already done, when tomorrow night rolls around.

SUPERMARKET PIE-IN-THE-SKY

Where, oh where, is that supermarket in the sky with the very cheapest prices?

Is it Safeway, which recently has increased sales by 11 percent while profits plunged 28 percent? If so, it will not stay cheap long.

Some of us cynical old Co-op hands are doubtful that shopping the cheapest supermarket . . . if there really is one . . . is the best way to save money on food. We've seen price wars before. And we've looked at price comparison between competitive supermarket chains over the years, where long lists of typical foods of equal quality are priced on the same day. We've seen the differences of 5 to 10 percent at most. That's peanuts compared to the savings that can be made by skillful "trading down," meaning choosing a cheaper version of a product usually bought. Trading down may mean buying a different menu item at lower price, or a less convenient, or less fancy, or lower quality item. According to Sylvia Porter, trading down can save 27 to 30 percent on grocery bills.

Trading down takes some effort. It takes a sharp eye for unit prices; willingness to change a planned menu when prices are higher than expected, as well as a good backup of recipes to substitute; and practice. But it's sure great for survival, especially during sudden food price rises, or sudden loss of income, or sudden increase of mouths to feed, or inflation squeeze. For example:

Look for cheaper packaging. Lasagne in a box costs more than lasagne in a plastic bag. The 27 percent saved by buying Co-op's lasagne instead of Golden Grain's in a box is partly due to packaging cost.

Or change your menu. Now try changing from lasagne to spaghetti, both Co-op brands. You'll save 34 percent on that trade-down. But a switch from pastas to rice will result in additional savings. Rice is cheaper and of similar nutritional value. Buy Co-op rice instead of Co-op spaghetti and save 8 percent on that trade-down. If you make a grand sweep and trade-down all the way from Golden Grain lasagne to Co-op rice you save a whopping 55 percent!

Try a more nutritious meat. For example, beef heart has more iron and B vitamins than ground beef. Sometimes it is also cheaper, $1.25 per pound compared to $1.59.

Is this high quality necessary? Maybe jack cheese at $1.89 per pound does as well as sharp cheddar at $2.35 or more. Savings are 19 percent.

Watch that convenience! It's usually high priced. Hamburger Helpers range from $1.70 - $2.09 per pound, more than you may wish to pay for meat.

Before You Shop 37

USING THE UNITS

Every so often we like to remind you about that great shopper's friend — the unit price. It's a little sticker on the edge of the shelf that makes it all possible. No need to worry about the size of the container — you can compare the eight-ounce can for 49¢ with the six-ounce can for 35¢. Complicated figuring or gadgets aren't necessary because all the work has been done by our computer. All shoppers have to do is know about it and use it.

How it works:

The Units symbol on the tag	Unit	Example of item listed on that unit
OZ	Ounce	Instant coffee
PT	Pint	Salad dressing
LB	Pound	Breakfast cereal
QT	Quart	Infant formula
E	Each	Cigars
100	100 Count	Paper plates
10	10 Count	Lawn leaf bags
100SF	100 Square Feet	Aluminum foil
1000	1000 Count	Toothpicks
MXD QT	Mixed Quart	Canned soup
MXD PT	Mixed Pint	Frozen juices

It's the unit price that gives the important information. Unless we've made a mistake, the units are always the same within any one group of foods. All you need to do is compare the unit price and you know immediately which is the better buy in terms of cost. (Of course, you may not always want to buy the least expensive item, but unit pricing can help you decide whether the extra cost is worth it to you.) The unit price even helps you compare all those odd numbers and sizes of facial tissues, toilet paper and paper towels by giving the cost per one hundred square feet.

There are still many items that aren't on unit pricing. These may be things like spices that are so tightly shelved that there just isn't room for the tag. Or they might be "outside vendor" items, such as crackers, or health and beauty aids where the "units" are not all the same.

We hope you use unit pricing. When trying to stretch dollars it can be one of the best friends you've got.

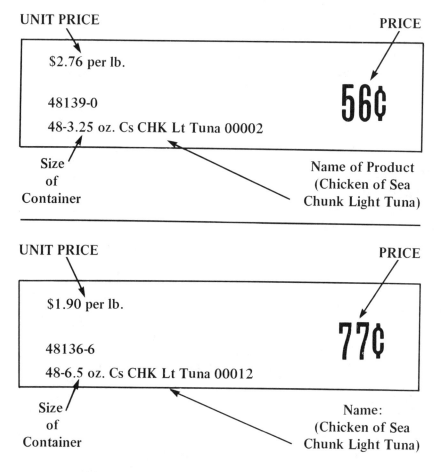

WHAT YOU CAN FIND ON A LABEL

by Joan Taylor

More and more people are becoming concerned about what they are eating and what is added to their food, such as sugar, fat, salt and chemicals. Labels can help you. If more than one ingredient is used there must be a list of ingredients. The ingredients will be listed in order of decreasing *weight*. The largest amount is listed first.

Sugar. You may find sugar in products listed in different forms of sugar. They are still sugar.

sucrose	fructose	corn syrup
dextrose	molasses	honey
lactose		invert sugar

Nutrient Label. If nutritional information is on the label you will find the serving size, servings per container, and nutrients found in the product.

Weight. Don't forget to look at the weight of containers. Sometimes packaging can fool the eye when you want to compare size.

For information and complaints. There is a company name and address that consumers can write to for information or to make product complaints.

NUTRITION LABELING

Take a good look at food labels when you shop. You will find that the labels of some foods now show the amounts of certain nutrients per serving. The new nutrients labeling regulations, adopted by the Food and Drug Administration in March of 1973, have made it possible for manufacturers to label the nutrient content of their products. These regulations require that the nutrients be labeled as a percentage of the U.S. Recommended Daily Allowances (U.S. RDA). The U.S. RDA, a liberal daily nutrient allowance, replaces the now outdated Minimum Daily Requirements (MDR), which we may particularly remember from the labels of ready-to-eat cereals and special dietary foods.

What is a Nutrient?

A nutrient is a substance that is required for nourishment of the body. There are over forty nutrients that are known to be essential for humans. Protein, fat, carbohydrate, calories and the numerous vitamins and minerals are among the nutrients shown on the Nutrition Information Panel of the label. You can now learn what goodies are present in various foods so labeled. You may also discover that some snack "foods" really contain so few nutrients that they may not be worth the calories they add to the daily diet!

Labeling is voluntary except for foods that are enriched or fortified with added nutrients such as dry cereals, bread, flour, rice, macaroni, noodles, milk and margarine. Additionally, if a manufacturer makes a claim mentioning calories, protein, vitamins, minerals or any other nutrient, then that food must have nutrition labeling.

What's Required?

The following information is required on all nutrition labels and in the order as listed:

Nutrition Information Per Serving
Serving Size
Servings Per Container
Calories
Protein
Carbohydrate
Fat

Percentage of U.S. Recommended
Daily Allowances (U.S.RDA)

Protein	Riboflavin
Vitamin A	Niacin
Vitamin C	Calcium
Thiamine	Iron

The serving size is established by the manufacturer. Take care when figuring daily nutrient intake based on the serving size; it may be more than is normally eaten at a time. The servings per container vary with the size of the container and the type of food.

Calories per serving will help us make food choices depending upon whether we need more or fewer calories. For example, two foods might provide similar amounts of vitamin A per serving, but the caloric content could vary greatly.

The protein, carbohydrate and fat per serving is stated to the nearest gram. (Think of a level teaspoon of sugar as weighing about five grams.) This information will be useful to those on special diets.

Nutrition information as a Percentage of the U.S. Recommended Daily Allowances (U.S. RDA) is mandatory for only eight of the forty-plus nutrients needed by humans. The U.S. RDA is a liberal allowance set about 40 percent above the amounts needed to prevent symptoms of deficiency in most of the population. However, if you select naturally occurring foods that supply adequate amounts of these eight nutrients, it is very likely you will get enough of all of the other needed nutrients.

A Few Hints on How to Use the Label Information:

1. Learn the names of the eight nutrients for which a percent U.S. RDA must appear on the label. (Check closely. Some products will not have the standard list of eight, but will refer to the

Before You Shop 41

missing ones in a footnote.) You will discover that only certain foods contribute sizeable amounts of these nutrients. One needs to eat a variety of foods to meet these allowances.

2. When planning meals, always compare the nutrient and caloric content of foods that may be substituted for a similar type food in the meal, such as vegetables for other vegetables, milk products for milk, and so on.

Additionally, plan meals in terms of the four basic food groups: 1) milk and milk products; 2) meats, poultry, fish, eggs, cheese and dry beans or peas; 3) vegetables and fruits; and 4) bread and cereals. Each group makes a different contribution to the diet and each should be included in every meal.

3. Warning! Don't buy foods solely on their high vitamin and mineral content. Many fabricated foods, such as the highly processed cereals, may contain 100 percent of the eight nutrients. However, these foods probably are lacking in many nutrients that are present only in naturally occurring foods. The constant use of highly processed foods could result in a deficiency of some nutrients not included in the mandatory U.S. RDA.

4. Don't fret if every member of your household is not getting 100 percent of the eight mandatory nutrients. Almost without exception, the levels for each of these nutrients represent the highest values for all the various age sex groups and probably not everyone needs those amounts.

5. Do not expect your family to eat foods just because they are "good for you." Nutrients are wasted if foods are not eaten. Therefore, choose wisely the foods you *know* your family likes to eat.

THE WAY THINGS ARE

Some companies have chosen to put nutritional information on their labels, including Co-op, Del Monte, Green Giant and Campbell's Soup. One by one the products with these labels are appearing on our shelves. Even with those few available so far, marvelous truths are revealed!

The Awful Truth About Pears and Peaches

A glance at the labels of Co-op Canned Pears and Del Monte Canned Peaches tells it: Peaches have significant amounts of vitamins A and C, while pears are low in both.* And neither has much else of importance. This is no criticism of Co-op! Far from it! It is a matter of the way things are, with peaches and pears.

---

*Remember, figures given are percentages of the U.S. Recommended Dietary Allowances (U.S. RDA) adapted for label use by the FDA. When those figures are lower than 10 percent, consider the amount of that nutrient to be on the low side, usually.

Amazing Difference in Bean Types

Del Monte nutrition labels show that one cup of Italian Green Beans provides 15 percent of the U.S. RDA for vitamin A, 40 percent of the vitamin C, and even 10 percent of the riboflavin. As for Blue Lake Green Beans, vitamin A is 26 percent and vitamin C is 15 percent of the U.S. RDA.

Knotty Knowledge of Mixed Foods

Here's a tough one. Even if you know about peas, beans, corn and rice, how can you figure out the nutritional value of mixtures of the same, or of creamed vegetables? Well, Green Giant figures it out for you. Their nutritional label information will provide you with fascinating tidbits. Particularly, it is interesting to see the way caloric value, protein and fat vary in the different combinations.

Much, Much More? Maybe

Shoppers should register their approval by writing companies to request this labeling, or by buying products that have this labeling already. When the time comes to order a new batch of labels, food companies will decide whether the expense is worth it to them. For your sake and mine, the decision should be in favor of this real buyer's boon, nutrition information on the label.

HOW TO TAKE YOUR KIDS SHOPPING FOR BREAKFAST CEREALS

When vacation is upon us it means taking the kids along when you shop. You crotchety old Co-op Home Economist suggests that it is never too soon to start teaching kids to read labels! They can practice on something exciting, like breakfast cereals.

First and second graders can read the net weight. Don't tell them to pick out the big box — let them hunt for the eighteen-ounce or whatever size you need. Maybe they'll find out how many ounces in a pound, too.

Third and fourth graders can look for sugar. It'll take them a little time to find "ingredients" in that small print. But it's worth it. Tell them to skip any cereal that lists sugar as the first ingredient. Tell them the first ingredient is the most, the last ingredient listed is the least. Then let them hunt the cereals with the least sugar.

Fifth graders can check added vitamins. Fifth graders are old enough to face such hot controversies! Are vitamins A and D added? How much? Many authorities think that these vitamins, known to be toxic in large amounts, should not be added to breakfast cereals.

Sixth graders can figure the best buy. With paper and pencil, some sixth graders have fun figuring out price-per-pound of different sizes and brands. Others call that cruel and unusual! So let them check the unit price shelf labels instead.

LET'S HEAR IT FOR OPEN DATING

Let us all observe one minute of praise for open dating! Here we are taking for granted this great boon to food buyers, when just yesterday, it seems, we bought milk, eggs, luncheon meats, etc., without the faintest idea when the food was packed or how long it should keep.

This is not to say the battle is won! Not on your tintype! For one reason, still with us is the scarcely legible date. What good is a date you can't read? Second, there's still confusion among food packers as to when to use pull dates rather than pack dates, or whether to use an expiration date. A date needs those few words of explanation that clearly indicate whether it's pull, pack or expiration. Third, sad to say, there are still plenty of mavericks, such as the canning companies, holding on for dear life to their secret codes. And last, even well-dated products seldom describe the temperature and storage conditions under which the product will stay safe. So we aren't exactly hurtling toward Grade A perfection! But making progress, anyway.

Just so you could see how they're going, I thought I'd pass out a few "grades" on food dates.

Kellogg's and Skinner's breakfast cereals rate A. Hurray for these clearly visible dates! And they tell us what it is, right on top, "Better if used before 6 Dec. '80." Post cereals get only B; they've got a date, but no explanation. General Mills, Quaker, Ralston Purina and Nabisco all get F for using indecipherable codes, such as G310Z.

I wish I could give Oroweat an A, because Oroweat is a bread company using a date rather than a color-coded twist. Alas, the pull date is obliterated in the packaging, and there are no words of explanation. So mark Oroweat down to B.

Calumet gets A. What a delight to have an expiration date on baking powder! Right on the top are the words, "Use before date on bottom."

Co-op flour has climbed to B. For a while we had a sticky situation where the supplier of one kind of flour was using a pack date, while another was using a pull date. Now they're both using a pull date but with, alas, no explanation. I'm sorry to say that Gold Medal (General Mills) gets an F on flour, too, as well as on breakfast cereal; they're using a code.

Campbell's soups, bless'em! Most canners have made no move toward open-dating their products. Campbell's has taken the plunge, with a legible date embossed on the end of the can. Alas, there's nothing to tell us it's a pull date, not a pack date.

Too bad, Co-op margarine gets C, because sometimes it has a date, sometimes, a code. Not really puzzling! We have two suppliers of Co-op margarine. One provides this service, the other doesn't, yet. Nice to see that Parkay and Saffola both have dates, with the words clearly visible, "Best when purchased before. . . "

Thank you, Asumaya Tofu! Here's a date we've really needed. Tofu has climbed up from no information at all, to a date that we've been told over the phone is a pull date. When they get those few extra words on the label, we'll give'em an A.

Pull Date:

The date after which a product should not be sold. If properly stored, the product is good for a certain period after the date.

Pack Date:

The date when the product was packaged.

Expiration Date:

Date after which the product may not be good.

HOW MUCH ARE YOU WILLING TO PAY FOR THE WORD "HEALTH" ON YOUR TOMATO SAUCE?

Consider two 15 oz. cans of tomato sauce, available side by side at the Co-op Natural Food Store:

HEALTH VALLEY

85 c

The label says:

"No citric acid"
"No sugars"
"No preservatives"
"No artificial colors or flavors"

Health Valley Ingredients:

Tomatoes, (water, tomato paste), sea salt, natural spices and herbs, tamari soy sauce (water, soy beans, wheat, sea salt).

CO-OP

29 ¢

But Co-op:

Contains no citric acid
Has no sugar
Also has no preservatives (canned foods are preserved by the heat of the canning process). Likewise has no artificial color or flavor. (These additives are almost never in canned food. One exception: maraschino cherries).

Co-op Ingredients:

Tomatoes, salt, dehydrated onion, dehydrated garlic, spices, natural flavors.

Co-op is fairly typical of other "commercial" tomato sauces. We have a second "natural" brand, Gerardi, also costing 85 ¢, containing "tomatoes, salt, pepper, spices."

WHAT'S NATURAL

What's natural? A simple definition is "existing in or produced by nature." I like that. It's uncomplicated.

So, what's it mean when we talk about natural foods? Once the processors change the vegetable, grain and meat shapes by puffing, compressing, grinding, reforming or extending, we've left natural and are into processed.

Some Labels Take Liberties

Have you read the ingredient label on Daisy Fresh Natural Mango Flavored Juice Drink? It says "water, juice, citric acid, potassium alginate (stabilizer), natural flavors and artificial colors." What's so natural about that?

Quaker's 100% Natural Cereal with Apples and Cinnamon is "naturally sweetened with brown sugar and honey." At least it's not "unnaturally" sweetened. That's a plus.

Don't be misled by the word "natural" on a label. Read the ingredient list. Stick to basics as often as possible.

LABELS
THAT SAY

"No preservatives," "No cholesterol," "No artificial color or flavor" may imply falsely that other similar products do contain these things.

Oil labels that do not list preservatives do not contain them.

The Food and Drug Administration requires that preservatives be listed on all labels.

No vegetable oil contains preformed cholesterol. It is found only in animal fats.

2

Everybody's Talking About Nutrition

BUT WHAT ARE THEY DOING ABOUT IT?

Woman's Day magazine conducted a survey ("Family Food Study" by Yankelovich, Skelly and White) recently, which turned up some interesting findings from the one thousand one hundred eighty-eight persons surveyed. Sixty percent of those questioned would settle for fewer children's TV programs in exchange for a ban on advertising directed at children under twelve. Fifty percent wanted pesticides banned even though it might mean fruits and vegetables would cost more. Further, 71 percent worry about pesticides, 62 percent are concerned about food additives, and 68 percent think natural foods are healthier than processed ones.

People think physical fitness and nutrition go hand in hand, according to survey findings. However, almost half those surveyed felt that the whole day's food should be balanced but it's not necessary to eat three meals a day nor are there special foods for breakfast, lunch or dinner. These people seem more relaxed, less rigid in their lifestyles.

Interest in nutrition is high, with 77 percent admitting to recently activated interest in this subject. Fifty-one percent want more information on how to choose better foods, 40 percent want to avoid harmful ingredients. One out of five was on a diet and 44 percent of the families had one or more members overweight.

But has all this interest changed eating habits? Three out of four said they eat what they like. Seventeen percent of them don't worry about this behavior, while 59 percent try for a balanced diet but not too hard. Only 14 percent feel strongly about "eating what's good for you" and 10 percent are watching their calories. Major barriers to good nutrition were felt to be snacking (45 percent), no time to cook (51 percent of the employed women) and television advertising to children (36 percent of the parents).

WHO'S IN CHARGE? NOBODY

Everybody knows the right thing to do is to eat right! There is no disagreement on this point. The problem is, who's in charge of eating right?

Not Me, Said the Eater

I eat what I like! I eat the doughnut, because it's sweeter than plain bread. I load up on soft drinks, because they go down easy. It's not my fault that all these things are so handy when I'm hungry, at vending machines in schools, at coffee shops, at doughnut shops, at end-aisles in supermarkets . . . it's not my fault that I eat the way I do!

Not Me, Said the Cook

I fix what they like to eat! If it's not too much trouble, that is. It's not my fault that they're finicky eaters!

Not Me, Said the Shopper

I buy what I know they'll eat. Besides, I can buy only what's in the store. It's not my fault that there are so many too-sweet, too-fattening, easy-to-fix products in the stores!

Not Me, Said the Supermarket

I sell what I know people will buy. And I put it where they can't miss it when they shop! It's not my fault that I have to sell what's on the market, what's been advertised, what people ask for.

Not Me, Said the Manufacturer

I only make what people want. And I have to scream, to rave, to advertise! Otherwise, people wouldn't know they want our sweet, spicy, over-seasoned, easy-to-eat products!

So Nobody's in Charge!

Instead, maybe it's everybody's responsibility. The manufacturer could choose to scream about some more nutritious products.

The supermarket could choose to put them where people couldn't miss them. The shopper could choose to find them. The cook could choose to learn to cook them. And the eaters? They could solve the whole problem — they could choose to eat right!

The Great American Diet and How to Change it

This time, it's a committee of the U.S. Senate recommending that we change our diets.*

This is not the first semi-authoritative body of recent years to issue stiff warnings about the excesses of the American diet. Others have offered similar advice. One reason for concern is that death rates from heart disease, diabetes and certain kinds of cancer in various countries, when compared to food eaten, seem to indicate a possible relationship with excess calories and high dietary fat, sugar or salt.

The Senate committee's seven goals have the support of some very eminent authorities. Most nutritionists will agree with most of the goals but will restaurant operators and food processors cut down salty, sugary and fatty foods? Others may wonder why limits on alcohol were not suggested. But can we wait until everybody agrees before taking steps to attain these goals?

My opinion is that at least these goals represent the direction in which we need to go.

The Senate committee's seven goals:

1. Avoid overweight. Do this by avoiding excess calories and by increasing energy expenditure. Reducing food intake to less than 1200-1400 calories is not recommended for average-sized people because that amount of food will not provide adequate vitamins and minerals.

2. Eat less fat. Presently, we're getting about 40 percent of calories from fat; the goal is to reduce it to 30 percent. To meet this goal a person who needs about two thousand calories per day can cut out about two tablespoons of butter or margarine or other fat.

3. Eat less saturated fats. They recommend that 10 percent of our calories come from saturated fat, plus 10 percent each from polyunsaturated and monounsaturated fat. This means choosing some oils and margarines to replace butter, lard and hydrogenated fats; choosing poultry and fish to replace some beef, pork and lamb; choosing lowfat or nonfat milk in place of some whole milk.

4. Eat more starchy foods. Eat more complex carbohydrates,

---

*U.S. Senate Select Committee on Nutrition and Human Needs, December 1977.

such as are in bread and potatoes, and more natural sugars as in vegetables and fruits. The goal is to increase this section from a mere 28 percent up to 48 percent of calories.

5. Eat less sugar. Reduce refined sugar intake from the current 18 percent of calories to 10. On a two thousand-calorie diet, this would be equal to about four tablespoons sugar per day. Note: one twelve-ounce can of soda has about three tablespoons sugar!

6. Eat less cholesterol. From an average intake of 600 milligrams of cholesterol, the recommendation is for three hundred milligrams per day. By reducing total fat and saturated fat, cholesterol tends to be reduced, too. Though eggs are very high in cholesterol, an egg every other day can be included at this level.

7. Eat less salt. Americans eat from six to eighteen grams of salt a day; the goal is to reduce this level to five grams (two thousand milligrams sodium). This would mean not adding salt at the table, and avoiding highly salted foods like potato chips, soy sauce, etc.

Fight the Fat

How to Eat Less Fat

Lately, we're being advised to eat for health and longevity. The most staggering advice is that we reduce calories that come from fat in food to 30 percent of the total calories eaten each day.

This recommendation, from the Senate Select Committee on Nutrition and Human Needs, assumes we all know that calories also come from protein, carbohydrates and alcohol in the diet as well as fat. It comes at a time when Americans are reported to be weighing more for their age than a few years ago: the average weight for height of adults has increased by four pounds since 1962. This seems like a worrisome trend toward more obesity, but the advice is not aimed only at people who are overweight. Instead, it is said that even normal weight people would derive health benefits by cutting down fat calories and making up the deficit with starchy foods such as potatoes, bread or rice.

Great! But how on earth do you translate the 30 percent-calories-from-fat diet into real food? Where does the bacon and eggs breakfast, the hamburger-milkshake lunch, the beef stroganoff dinner fit into such a diet? I set about figuring this out and as a result of my diligent calculations I can now report which typical combinations of foods are on the unhappy side of 30 percent fat calories, and vice versa.

Before You Shop 51

The Cereal-Milk Breakfast Makes it; Bacon and Eggs Don't

Shredded wheat, whole milk and orange juice are an 18 percent fat calorie breakfast. With low fat milk, the same breakfast is only 15 percent fat calories and with nonfat milk, it's down to 7 percent. On the other hand, pour half and half on your cereal and the fat calories shoot up to 44 percent. The bacon and eggs breakfast, even with a poached egg (no added fat) and a skimpy one-half teaspoon of butter or margarine on toast does not make it either. It is, alas, 55 percent fat calories.

What's for Lunch?

The peanut butter sandwich, whole milk and apple lunch scandalized me with fat calories reaching 48 percent. A cheese sandwich in place of peanut butter is even worse, at 56 percent fat calories. However, switching to nonfat milk dropped fat calories down to 34 percent and 38 percent, respectively. The hamburger, milkshake and French fries luncheon came out at 43 percent fat calories.

Dinner — the Biggest Challenge

For dinner, I calculated a recipe from the *Co-op Low Cost Cookbook*. Hamburger Stroganoff. Assuming that one-fourth of the recipe was eaten with one cup cooked rice, the fat calories are, sob, 44 percent. This is based on using lean ground beef, 15 percent fat. (With higher fat ground beef, some but not all of the extra fat would cook out and probably be discarded). All is not lost, however! Yogurt can easily be substituted for the sour cream in this Stroganoff recipe, dropping the fat calories down to 30 percent. Eureka! We made the recommendation!

Of course it matters what else is eaten. So I checked out the fat calories in some vegetable combinations, as follows:

	Calories from fat
1 cup peas with 1 teaspoon butter.	32%
Green Giant Sweet Peas in Butter Sauce	36%
Birds Eye Green Peas with Cream Sauce	53%

Do not look to salad to help lower your overall percent calories from fat. The caloric value of salad greens is low, the fat in salad dressing is high and the percent of calories from fat is always high.

Dessert can be dangerous, with cookies, pies, cakes or ice cream — or very safe, with fruit, ice milk or yogurt:

Fresh fruit............ 4%
Ice milk.............. 30%
Oatmeal cookies 30%
Devils Food Cake 33%
Apple pie............. 39%
Ice cream............ 50%
Brownies............. 58%

Snacks may be dangerous or just dandy:

Raw vegetables (carrots) .. 4%
Pretzels 10%
Bread, no butter 12%
Saltines 24%
Butter crackers 35%
Snack crackers (Ritz) ... 51%
Potato chips 63%

A Palatability Fight?

These calculations have been sobering. Perhaps we are caught in a "palatability fight" with fat, hence the Ritz crackers instead of sodas, the Peas in Cream Sauce instead of plain peas. I think we need to consider what else is pleasurable in eating — the chewing, the subtle flavors, the sourness or bitterness of foods — and not be led astray by the all-too-easy sensory satisfaction of high-fat foods.

The complete report of the Senate Select Committee on Nutrition and Human Needs entitled "Dietary Goals for the United States, Second Edition" may be purchased by mail for $2.30 from the U.S. Government Bookstore, 450 Golden Gate Ave., Room 1023, San Francisco 94102. Checks or money orders should be made payable to the Superintendent of Documents.

IS PIZZA JUNK FOOD?

The answer is no if you indulge only occasionally, but pizza is a high-calorie, high-fat food and nutritionists are telling us that we shouldn't overeat on calories or fat, particularly animal fat. We took a recipe for pizza from *Joy of Cooking* and made some calculations. The recipe was for four or eight servings. One-eighth of the pizza had four hundred eight calories, a quarter supplied eight hundred fifteen calories. Forty percent of the calories were from fat.

The Senate's Select Committe on Nutrition and Human Needs recommends eating less fat: According to the committee, no more than 30 percent of our total calories should come from fat. Another goal recommended that no more than 10 percent of our calories should come from animal fats: The remaining 20 percent should be divided equally between mono- and polyunsaturated fats.

So, getting back to our hypothetical pizza, too frequent consumption of pizza gives us too many calories in one serving, making it hard to fit in the other foods we need during the other meals of the day. Secondly, the olive oil in pizza is largely monounsaturated and the cheeses and pepperoni contain only animal fats. Therefore, this pizza missed the goal of 30 percent calories from fats as well as 10 percent of the day's calories from unsaturated fat. However, low-fat foods with pizza would help lower fat calories for that meal.

Other goals recommended by the Senate Select Committee are: Eat more starchy food, eat less cholesterol, eat less sugar and far less salt. If you think about these goals a little, you will realize that true junk foods (soft drinks, candy, most desserts, cookies, potato chips and other chips) are ruled out for regular eating if you are trying to improve your food choices along the lines recommended by the committee.

WHEN A HOME ECONOMIST COMES TO SUPPER

I sang for my supper last week. I had invited myself to a friend's home and was pumped with questions. There are four kids in the family and my friends are bewildered about prices and food shopping like the rest of us. Here's a somewhat organized version of what we said:

Does Anthony Need Extra Protein, More Than Fred?

(Anthony is tall and lean and fifteen. Fred is his tall and lean father).

Just a little. The calorie needs of a teenager go way up, but the protein requirements don't climb proportionately. Even athletes or people doing heavy work need protein in proportion to their size rather than in proportion to their activity.

Is it Okay for Anthony to Fill Up on Carbohydrates?

Yes, if he gets his basic nutrient needs first and if the carbohydrate food is a reasonably good one that contributes other nutrients besides calories. Everyone should eat daily at least two servings of protein food, four servings of vegetables and fruits (one high in vitamin C such as citrus, one high in vitamin A such as carrots or greens), and four servings of breads or cereals. A teenager should have a quart of milk or its equivalent in cheese.

To fill in the calories it's okay to have thirds on spaghetti, fourths on potatoes, or five pieces of toast. But try to discourage filling up on soda pop, cupcakes, candy and other high-sugar foods. If possible, many of the "starches" should be whole grain — brown rice, whole wheat bread, plain oatmeal. Co-op Special Formula bread is a nutritious white bread with extra soy flour, dry milk and wheat germ.

Potatoes, especially baked or steamed, contribute vitamin C and iron. And of course all kinds of beans provide protein, B vitamins and iron as well as carbohydrate.

How Much Protein Do We Each Need?

You say in the *Co-op News* that the average adult needs from forty-five to fifty-five grams a day. How about the kids? The following amounts allow for a margin of safety to cover a wide variety of people.

Recommended Daily Allowances — Protein

Adult male, 154 lbs.	56 grams
Adult female, 120 lbs.	44 grams
Pregnant	+30 grams
Lactating	+20 grams
Children, 1-3 years	23 grams
4-6 years	30 grams
7-10 years	34 grams
Boys, 11-14 years	45 grams
15-18 years	56 grams
Girls, 11-14 years	46 grams
15-18 years	46 grams

Isn't it Hard to Get That Much Protein? Actually, no. Studies show that the average American eats about twice as much protein as he needs. Protein is the nutrient (besides calories and fat) that is best provided for in American diets. We keep talking about protein, maybe because we're obsessed with meat and meat prices, but it's very hard for Americans not to get enough protein.

However, because the vitamins and minerals that occur in protein foods are not easy to get in recommended amounts, nutritionists advise eating two or three servings of meat, fish, eggs, or beans and two servings of milk or milk products per day.

Before You Shop   55

In the *Co-op News* You List the Cost of Twenty Grams of Protein.

I Can't Visualize it. If you divide a pound of ground beef and make four patties, each one will yield about three ounces of cooked meat. Three ounces of cooked meat yields about twenty grams of protein. Some people don't realize that meat is not all protein. Beef is roughly 60 percent water, 20 percent fat and 20 percent protein.

How Does a Vegetarian Manage?

(She didn't ask this but I thought you would want to know).

This takes more thought and planning but it's not hard. Protein foods should be spread through all three meals. Also, either small amounts of animal foods (milk, eggs, etc.) should be eaten at the same meal with plant foods, or combinations that enhance protein quality, such as beans and grains, should be used. The recommended allowance might be met with these foods eaten in one day:

```
1 cup beans, cooked .............................. 15 grams
2 eggs ........................................... 12 grams
1 cup milk........................................  9 grams
1½ ounce cheese .................................. 11 grams
4 servings fruits and vegetables ..................  8 grams
4 servings bread or cereal........................  9 grams
   Total ........................................ 64 grams
```

Frankly, if I were a vegetarian I would be more concerned about getting enough iron and other vitamins and minerals than getting enough protein. I was rewarded with a banquet: A stew made with shank meat from the freezer (two pounds to serve eight, cooked long and slow, then cut up), lots of vegetables and a rich gravy. Shell noodles were cooked and added to stretch it all. We had sauteed zucchini slices from the garden topped with grated cheese, lettuce salad from my garden, and whole wheat blackberry muffins for dessert. Great!

I'M GONNA LOSE 20 POUNDS . . . IF IT KILLS ME!!!

So . . . How Are You Going To Do It?

Impulse I: By eating only grapefruit juice and bananas until I've reached my goal?

Impulse II: By eating one meal a day until I've lost twenty pounds?

Impulse III: By eliminating all breads and starchy foods until I've reached my goal?

Impulse IV: By cutting out rich desserts, junk foods, and eating smaller portions forever and ever?

On the Positive Side . . .

Becoming motivated to lose excess weight, making a plan and sticking to it is more than half the battle. But a plan that totals you out in the process will be short-lived. A good diet stresses basic nutritional foods during and after the period of dieting. Besides, who wants to make the same resolution next year?

On the Other Hand . . .

Impulse I: This diet is composed mostly of carbohydrates. You might lose weight on it, but a larger portion than normal of weight lost will be lean body tissue. Your own muscle protein will be wasted because your body needs a certain amount of circulating proteins that, in this case, is not available in the diet. This type of fad diet is deficient in most of the major nutrients and should never be followed more than a day or two.

Impulse II: There are two arguments against eating one meal a day: 1) Eating one meal does not necessarily mean you are eating fewer calories. It is possible to eat a day's supply of calories in one meal. In order to lose one pound a person must — over a period of time — eat 3500 calories less than his body burns up. 2) In animal studies one-meal eaters become more efficient in the use of food and have an increased capacity for fat synthesis. A correlation is made that an infrequent intake of large meals may predispose humans to obesity, elevate their cholesterol levels, and interfere with their metabolism of sugar.*

Impulse III: One slice of bread and one-half cup of rice or oatmeal contain about seventy to eighty calories. It is the fatty spreads we put over them that ruin our waistlines. A well-balanced diet will have three to four servings of enriched bread or cereal. The spreads are expendable. Breads and cereals are good sources of the B vitamins, iron and other essential nutrients.

Impulse IV: You guessed it. This solution is most logical if you were eating protein foods, fruits, and vegetables. Do not forget a good source of calcium such as milk or cheese.*

---

*Gilbert A. Leveille, *Lipogenic Adaptations Related to Pattern of Food Intake*, *Nutrition Reviews*, Vol. 30, No. 7, July 1972, p. 151.

WARNING: DRIVING A CAR MAY BE MORE 'FATTENING' THAN EATING POTATOES!

Ridiculous? Not really. Potatoes and some other very nutritious but starchy foods are often "put down" by labeling them "fattening." But have you ever heard of an automobile or an electric typewriter that was labeled as "fattening"? Think about it.

Fattening makes a negative impression. That word is vague but we get the feeling that it means something bad. We should avoid things so labeled. But, if we do give in and eat such foods, it's often done in grand style — we double or treble the calories by adding butter or other fat. This thoroughly convinces us that potatoes are "fattening."

To maintain a constant body weight, the number of calories taken in must equal the number of calories used up. For every pound of weight gain, we must take in three thousand five hundred more calories than our body uses; for every pound of weight loss, there must be three thousand five hundred fewer calories in our diet than our bodies require.

Suppose you used to walk to and from work but recently you decided to drive the 1¼ miles — about ten to twelve city blocks — both ways. Driving would use less than twenty calories, walking about two hundred fifty.

If you don't change any other activity and eat the same amount of food as before, you would gain about seventeen pounds a year. However, if you continued walking to and from work, your other activities remained the same, and you ate the same amount of food except for adding a cup of boiled potatoes daily, you would gain only twelve pounds in a year. That's what I mean when I say driving a car may be more "fattening" than eating potatoes.

You decided to replace your manual typewriter with an electric one. If you usually typed six hours a day, five days a week and everything else remained constant, you would use three hundred sixty fewer calories per week. This would amount to over five pounds weight gain per year from using the electric typewriter instead of the manual.

What you add to a food is important: You can increase the caloric content many-fold by adding varying amounts of fats:

Calories/cup

Boiled potatoes, salt added	118
Mashed potatoes, using some milk and fat	197
Boiled potatoes with 1 tablespoon of fat	220
Potato salad with salad dressing	248
Scalloped potatoes with milk and butter	255
Fried potatoes	456
Potato chips (4 ounces)	644

(Dancing, the "body language," for an hour would use up most of the calories in the potato chips. Is it worth it?)

Name Calling Does Matter

We are the losers if we eliminate a nutritious food such as potatoes from our diet because it's "fattening." A cup of boiled potatoes contains iron, B vitamins, almost no fat and furnishes almost half of the daily allowance for vitamin C. And all that for a little over one hundred calories. Is that too great a price to pay for a twenty-minute walk?

UNWANTED CALORIES, UGH!

Ever since water went out of style as a thirst-quencher we've had this awful problem of getting ugly calories with our beverages. Wine, soft drinks, fruit drinks and even fruit juice are high-calorie in the amount drunk to quench thirst. Water, of course, is calorie-free.

In our new enlightened state we drink wine with dinner in long-stemmed glasses. It is the American way of life! But alas, from a nutritional standpoint wine is just another junk food and the calories are substantial. Switching from water to two small glasses of wine (that's about two hundred calories) could result in a weight gain of more than two pounds per month, a whopping twenty-eight pounds a year!

That fruit soda is a horrid source of calories. One twelve ounce fruit soda with its eleven teaspoons of sugar has about one hundred seventy calories; a couple of those a day are even worse caloric hazards than wine. Gingerale, colas, quinine water, etc., are slightly lower.

Kool-Aid, Hawaiian Punch, Cranberry Juice Cocktail and Tang are yet higher in sugar and calories. They range from one hundred sixty to two hundred calories or as much as twelve teaspoons of sugar in a twelve ounce portion. Perhaps these drinks are not consumed as thirst quenchers, only as rare treats? I hope so.

Even apple juice, that lovable old standby, is a high-calorie beverage. If you drink twelve ounces of apple or orange juice instead of fruit soda, you get one hundred eighty calories. Orange juice is a good source of vitamin C, but apple juice is low in vitamins and minerals. Think of it as a wholesome treat, not as a substitute for water.

> **JACK SPRAT COULD EAT NO FAT**
> **HIS WIFE COULD EAT NO LEAN**
> **AND SO BETWIXT THEM BOTH, YOU SEE**
> **THEY LICKED THE PLATTER CLEAN.**
> *(Nursery rhyme. Author unknown)*

Somewhere out there among our Co-op shoppers are those who identify with Jack Sprat and want to gain weight, not lose it. Loud groans from most of us! But, indeed, it's true, and it strikes me that we're constantly suggesting ways to cut calories and hardly ever addressing ourselves to the thin ones who would like to pad their bones.

Calories and Calm

Weight gain or loss can be equated to calories taken in versus calories expended. If you eat more calories than your body can use, you will gain weight. If you eat more frequently you may be able to increase your calorie intake. The atmosphere in which you have your meals may be as important as what you eat. Try to eat in a calm, relaxed manner. This may mean eating before or after the family for a while if meal time is a bit hectic. In all this, we assume you are choosing foods from the Basic Four food groups, which have been discussed frequently in a variety of ways through our consumer information.

What's all the fuss about, you may ask? Just eat more and you will gain weight. No so easy, say the thin ones. We already eat as much quantity as we can manage and never seem to put on an ounce. Well, there's hope. First of all, we assume that you've had a recent physical exam and there's no medical reason behind your inability to gain. The calorie additions suggested below are generally high in fat so be sure your doctor says it's okay to make these dietary changes. Next step is to take a hard look at your eating habits, the quality of your diet and how much you eat.

Regular Meals and Snacks

Basic eating patterns of Americans emphasize three meals a day. Certainly if you're trying to gain weight, don't skip a meal. In fact, you may be able to up your calorie intake by eating several smaller meals. Have a snack in mid-morning: a peanut butter sandwich with a glass of milk, a cheese omelet, or sliced fresh fruit with half-and-half. Have you acquired the habit of a good breakfast? This means fruit in some form, possibly a citrus for the day's vitamin C. It means grain or cereal (preferably a cooked type for better nutrition and economy) made delicious and caloric with extra toppings of fruit and cream. For example, try oatmeal with sliced bananas, heavy cream and a dusting of nutmeg or cooked brown rice with stewed apricots, a dollop of butter and cinnamon.

If this seems like a lot to tackle, try a small portion at first and gradually increase the quantity. If you prefer bread, try a cheese sandwich dipped in an egg-milk batter, sauteed in butter until golden brown. Add calories by sprinkling sesame seeds in the batter for a crunchy texture.

Apply these kinds of suggestions to other meals as well. If after a few months of this effort you still haven't gained an ounce, continue to eat well and be grateful you're thin and not overweight which, according to most scientific information is hazardous to your health.

BEATING THE SWEETS: HOW MUCH IS TOO MUCH?

Once I ate a doughnut at the Co-op coffee bar to cries of "Shame! Shame!" from Co-op checkers, shoppers and other shocked spectators. Their reasoning was that Co-op home economists keep telling other people to cut down on sweets and therefore should never ever themselves eat sweets, especially in public. Now this is downright mean. Like anyone else, if it's there, I may eat it. Let me hurry to say that Co-op home economists do not counsel abstinence, anyway. Instead, following Nature's Law that things are always more complicated than we humans wish, we say, "Don't eat too many sweets!" And how much is too much? Well, that's the part that's complicated.

Sweets are bad because they replace nutritious foods, because they're terrible on teeth, because they add excessive calories, because they may be related to health problems in later life. A typical American diet has been described as including a sugared cereal, two soft drinks, a candy bar, cookies, a sweet dessert, sugar in coffee and jam on toast. Do you eat that much? More? It may be later than you think.

By most charitable estimates, the above diet includes about thirteen tablespoons of sugar or some seven hundred calories just from the sugar alone. A sweet-sweet, such as a serving of frosted cake, has three or more tablespoons of sugar; the sweetened cereal has one, soft drinks two or three. Custard or ice cream has about one tablespoon, a slice of cinnamon toast has only one teaspoon sugar.

They say our parents started it all using sweets as rewards, confusing them with love. Somehow sweets came to be prized above all other foods. Now some parents do things differently. They do not offer sweets to their young children. They let those eager appetites be rewarded with better foods. When the children are older and exposed to sweets, limits are put on them. It takes determined parents to do this! Honey, artificial sweeteners, even juices are not the answer. If the problem is one of expecting and wanting all foods to be sweet, then sweet substitutes are no real solution.

Teen-agers or others with urgent caloric needs, may stow away rich sweet-sweets with no noticeable over-weight. But the very big danger is the habit. It may persist long after the teen years.

Most diet plans do not cope with the problem of sweets, or they simply include none or minimal sweets. It is discouraging, accustomed as many are to eight sweets a day, to try for the ideal of no sweets. So we think one a day is a good compromise, though even this is too much for some people who are sedentary, or for small children. Why not try to: Put more distance between sweet-sweets! Eating two a day? Work toward one. Eating one a day? Try one every other day. Try less-sweet desserts. Try puddings, lightly sweetened fruits in place of candy, cake and cookies. Learn to love attractive non-sweets. Reach for the nuts, seeds, fruits, cheese, vegetables with dips instead of a sweet.

HYPERTENSION AND A BLACK CULTURAL PERSPECTIVE

Hypertension, commonly known as high blood pressure, is the result of an abnormal increase of pressure against the walls of the blood vessels that transport blood from the heart to all parts of the body. It strikes men, women, and children of all races. About twenty-three million Americans have it but only 10 percent of them know it.

High blood pressure is the major health problem in America today. It is the greatest single cause of death. Hypertension can induce stroke, heart attacks, heart failure, kidney failure, and other perils such as hardening of the arteries in the heart, brain and limbs, permanent loss of vision, and the senility of old age. It is a disease one can have and feel absolutely healthy. It is often unnoticed, painless, and symptomless. For these reasons, this disease is as dangerous as an assassin's bullet and two million Americans unnecessarily risk premature death because the incidence of the diseases associated with it is three to five times greater among hypertension victims than among normal individuals. It kills mainly because it is not detected and controlled.

What Causes It?

The actual cause of hypertension is obscure. However, researchers have shown that high blood pressure is caused by a number of factors: fear, anxiety, tension, stress, obesity, diet, and certain other psychological and physiological disorders.

Among black people, the incidence of hypertension is not only more frequent but also it develops earlier in life, is often more severe and causes higher mortality at younger ages. Studies have shown a prevalence of high blood pressure among blacks at a ratio twice as high as in the white population.

One authority states that there is a mosaic of causes for the higher rate of hypertension among blacks in America. Another suggested that "the United States itself may be taking its unhappy hypertensive toll on black people. Sociological rage, sustained emotional stress, economic worries, the daily psychic battles for self-respect . . . may all have induced high blood pressure in the black person." (*Ebony* magazine, June 1973)

Obesity and diet also play overwhelmingly important roles in controlling or triggering hypertension in blacks. For example, if a person is obese and black there is a good chance he has hypertension. Also, there is a positive correlation between salt intake and high blood pressure; therefore, a heavy or exclusive diet of soul food could be a major contributing factor since such foods as spicy barbecue sauces, heavily salted greens and beans, bacon, salt pork, ham and ham hocks (all of which are among soul food specialties) would not be restricted or limited. A selective diet consisting of a variety of foods as well as restricting the above foods considerably is recommended.

What Should You do About It?

Individuals who feel perfectly well should visit a doctor regularly or a health or hypertension screening clinic to determine if they have high blood pressure. Campaigns to find people with hypertension are now being conducted – contact your local heart association or health department for information.

If you are already aware that you have the disease, follow your doctor's orders – no matter how good you feel. The measures the doctor takes to control your high blood pressure may include drugs, diet, or changes in living habits. Obese persons are often placed on a reduction-type diet in which a normal amount of meat, chicken, fish, eggs and skim milk is eaten to supply protein. Fats, starches, sugar, cereals, cream, and foods made from these fat-producing substances are restricted. Often, the blood pressure comes down as the pounds go off.

A person with serious hypertension may be required to follow a sodium-restricted diet. No one should undertake a low-salt diet, however, except on the advice of a physician. The doctor will decide what type of diet is required, if any, and will see that the individual is instructed on how the diet should be followed. For the person on a low-sodium (low-salt) diet, there are more and more foods on the market that are prepared without salt. These include bread, canned vegetables, soups and meat.

SALT: ON LOVING IT LESS

And when did you learn to love salt? Not yesterday, I'll bet. More likely, when you were very young. Humankind learned to love it, and we mined it, fought over it, used it as money, and treasured it, starting at least three thousand years ago. The taste for salt is an acquired one. Primitive people who have never had it dislike it at first, but quickly overcome their dislike. In complex societies, the prestige value of salty, highly seasoned foods may be part of the reason such food is preferred.

For many years high blood pressure has been treated with low-salt diets. Now, doctors are suggesting that excessive salt in the diet, maybe from infancy, is the cause of high blood pressure in susceptible people.

Do babies need added salt? No. They get plenty of sodium because it naturally occurs in milk, eggs, meat, vegetables. Furthermore, babies do not have an inborn taste for salt, as they do for sugar. So it is practical to avoid salt in baby food. Let them learn to like it later. Baby food manufacturers have eliminated salt in their products in recent years. Parents who go the cheaper route of making their own baby food can leave the salt out too. When the baby is fed from the table, the food can be salted after the baby's portion has been removed.

Adults may be eating more salt today because more of our food is processed and preseasoned. About the only processed foods not salted are canned, dried or frozen fruits and juices, jams and jellies, and some frozen vegetables.

Most people know that salt is added to bread, even though it doesn't taste salty. We taste the salt in butter, margarine, canned vegetables, and it's listed on the label, anyway. But would you suspect salt in cottage cheese? It's there, and in buttermilk too. Such foods should be required to state all ingredients on the label.

Much saltier are catsup, pickles, prepared mustard, olives, potato chips, salted popcorn, soda crackers, corned beef, bacon, salt pork and ham. Some of these foods, used as seasonings, are not used in large amounts. Others, used as snacks, may be eaten in large amounts and may be adding much salt to the diet.

Some foods are much saltier in one form than in another. For example, processed cheese spreads are about twice as salty as natural cheddar cheese; prepared French or Italian salad dressing may be as much as four times as salty as mayonnaise; very thin stick pretzels may be twice as salty as thicker pretzels.

Among the very saltiest of foods are bouillon cubes and soy sauce. Soy sauce has four to six times the salt as the same amount of catsup.

When you shop, choose less salty foods. Buy unsalted peanuts in the shell, for snacks. At home, try easing up on the salt. You may be adding more than necessary. In becoming unaccustomed to salt, you will notice flavors frequently masked by saltiness. This is a very big plus for those who get along without, or with less, salt!

FIBER: INDIGESTIBLE AND INDISPENSABLE

What's fiber? Fiber is material that humans lack the enzymes to digest although the bacteria in the large intestine may break down some fiber. Most fiber passes through the body unchanged. It takes up water on this trip, making a very soft stool that is easy to evacuate. The time it takes for the food to pass through the gut is also speeded up.

Beneficial effects? Most of the evidence for benefits from fiber is based on the incidence of a given disorder in a relatively uniform population that, in this case, is consuming a low amount of fiber and relatively high amounts of fat and protein. Conditions known to be associated with low-fiber diets are constipation, diverticular disease of the colon, hemorrhoids and varicose veins. Unfortunately ownership of transistor radios is also – statistically – related to these diseases! So much for epidemiological evidence.

Cancer of the colon has not been found to be correlated with low-fiber diets. However, fiber from pectin, rolled oats or wheat bran is known to lower the blood cholesterol. Overweight can be helped by fiber since a high-fiber diet will contain fewer calories. Pectin and guar gum are thought to aid diabetics by reducing their need for insulin.

African diets very high in fiber are correlated with the absence of the disease conditions listed above. However, these people didn't live long enough to develop the diseases of old age, which is essentially what we are talking about.

Vegetables and fruits contain fiber but they are so high in water that they can't compete with wheat bran, shredded whole wheat, whole wheat bread, Wheaties or Grape-Nuts. It takes seven pounds of celery to equal the fiber contained in seven tablespoons of bran.

A word of caution to fiber enthusiasts. High-fiber foods have a lowered digestibility for the protein they contain. For example, the protein in white bread is 91 percent digestible, that in whole wheat bread is 87 percent and the protein in high-fiber breakfast cereals is 81 percent digestible.

Should cellulose from wood be added to foods? Some scientists in Germany found that eating a bread that contains wood cellulose allows the cellulose to get into the blood and to be excreted in the urine. The Canadian Food and Drug has banned the use of wood cellulose in Canadian foods. Branola bread contains bran, not cellulose, but we don't know whether the other nutrients in the bran (some vitamins and minerals) are actually capable of being absorbed from the human gut.

EATING FOR TWO

Pregnant and want a healthy baby? Eat! The health of you and your unborn baby depends upon a well-balanced and nutritious diet every day.

Beware of friendly advice because new knowledge has changed many of the traditional ideas of what and how much to eat when you're pregnant. Weight gain used to be a big issue. Women were scolded and given low-calorie diets if they gained beyond a certain magic number. A gradual and steady pattern of weight gain is the important factor, not whether the individual exceeds some established weight limit. A minimum weight gain of twenty-four pounds is now considered necessary for all pregnant women. This figure reflects the weight of the baby as well as the necessary weight increases of certain body tissues. Dieting to lose weight has no place during pregnancy because nutrient needs can't be met by low-calorie diets.

Ideas have also changed about salt restrictions and the use of diuretics. A certain amount of fluid retention is normal. It's called physiological edema and it's the body's way of dealing with the demands of pregnancy. Restricted salt intake and diuretics only interfere with delicate mechanisms for regulating fluids. Food should be lightly salted to taste (notice we're talking about lightly salted since many of us use too much salt) and diuretics reserved for other medical conditions.

While we usually don't recommend vitamin and mineral supplements, pregnancy is a special time when a well-balanced diet can't supply adequate amounts of certain nutrients. Iron is one such nutrient. Most women don't get enough in normal times, let alone when they are pregnant. Because the iron requirement is so high, the pregnant woman needs an iron supplement in addition to the iron obtained from a well-balanced diet. Folic acid supplements should also be prescribed as well as fluoride in areas where the water is not fluoridated. A well-balanced diet of nutritious foods can supply all the other important nutrients needed for a successful pregnancy and a healthy baby.

A well-balanced diet during pregnancy includes:*

Food Group	Serving Size	Number of Servings/day
Protein Foods		
Animal	2-3 ounces	4
Vegetable	1 cup cooked	
Milk, vitamin D fortified, and milk products	1 cup	4
Grain products, preferably whole grain	1 slice bread or ½ cup cooked cereal	3
Vitamin C-rich fruits and vegetables	½ cup orange or grapefruit juice (size varies with item)	1
Leafy green vegetables	1 cup raw or ¾ cup cooked	1
Other fruits and vegetables	½ cup	1
Oils and margarines	1 tablespoon	2

*This is a suggested food guide as discussed in the recently revised booklet *Nutrition During Pregnancy and Lactation*, developed by the California Department of Health, Maternal and Child Health Unit, 1975.

WHO WANTS TO BE PREGNANT?

If it's you who wants to be pregnant, whether this year or next, look to your food and drink today. Certainly, pregnancy is an enchanted state that will transform you! But it won't necessarily transform your food habits. It takes time and effort to do that. Now is not too soon to get psyched up; take charge and control those habits that are hard on babies.

Alcohol: An Old Wives' Tale?

No. The old wives were right. Alcohol passes through the placental barrier so that when the mother is drunk, so is the baby. Heavy drinking* has been linked to serious growth and nervous problems in infants, including a type of hyperactivity called Fetal Alcohol Syndrome.

So how much alcohol is safe? Some authorities recommend that pregnant women avoid alcohol entirely or, if they cannot,

*Heavy drinking is defined by the National Institute on Alcohol Abuse and Alcoholism as six drinks per day, each containing one ounce of whiskey or equivalent. The information on Fetal Alcohol Syndrome is from "Alcohol and Birth Defects," by Fritz P. Witti, FDA Consumer, May 1978.

limit it to two drinks per day, maximum. Unfortunately, it is not known whether a single drinking episode in the first month, before pregnancy is suspected, will cause some symptoms of Fetal Alcohol Syndrome. Women who hope for pregnancy should start limiting their drinking now.

Caffeine

Like alcohol, caffeine readily passes the placental barrier. Caffeine causes birth defects in animals, but its effect on human embryos has not yet been established. Some experts advise eliminating caffeine during the first three months of pregnancy. Caffeine is present in coffee, tea and cocoa, as well as non-prescription drugs such as cold tablets, headache pills, stay-awake pills, etc.

Don't Fool Around With Junk Food

The woman in good nutritional condition before pregnancy as well as throughout pregnancy has a better chance of having a full term, full-size baby. Difficulties related to smaller-than-normal babies can result from inadequate diets. Now is the time to start eating the good diet. Now is the time to reach your proper weight, not after pregnancy. Learn to appreciate whole grains, milk or cheese, beans as well as meats, dark-green leafy vegetables. If you start learning to fix and eat these foods now, you can drastically improve your diet by the time you're pregnant.

TWIGGY WAS NO FAT BABY

Research indicates that the number of fat cells that a person has throughout life may be determined during the first year of life. An overfed infant may become an obese adult. According to Dr. Derrick Jelliffe, professor in the UCLA School of Public Health, overfeeding of infants is an increasing problem due to 1) bottle feeding, 2) early introduction of solid foods, and 3) social pressure to "grow" a large child.

Breast or the Bottle?

Breast milk is easier for the baby to digest and, since mother cannot see how much milk her baby is getting, she is less likely to overfeed. Human milk has antibodies, which are passed by mother to child to protect the baby against infections. There are psychological advantages for both members of the nursing pair, also.

Before You Shop   69

Bottle-fed babies may be "pressured" to finish the bottle, and this insult may be compounded by feeding solid foods as early as the first few weeks of life by proud but misguided parents. It is important that the parents be able to "read the child's signals and not answer all discomfort signals with food." According to Dr. Hilde Bruch, professor of psychiatry at Baylor College of Medicine, overeating, as a way of life, may be taught the child who is fed by parents in response to his or her every cry of distress. So, love, burp, and play with the baby as well as feed the little dear.

Mothers who choose to use a bottle to feed their babies may wish to check that the formulas are not more concentrated than the doctor ordered (a little more is not better). Respect the baby's right to decide when enough is enough.

For the First Three Months
Unless your baby was premature or had a low birth weight, breast milk contains all the nutrients your baby needs except vitamin D, iron and fluoride. During the first three months, the baby uses the iron stored in his or her body before birth. Babies on formulas may require a vitamin C supplement unless the formula has added ascorbic acid.

Solid Foods
There is no nutritional reason to introduce solid foods sooner than three to six months after birth. After the first three months, an iron supplement should be started, usually a cereal fortified with iron. Pureed baby foods can be prepared at home, and by six to eight months foods from the family meals may simply be modified to suit the baby.

Usually the first solids are cereals and fruit. These foods are best fed to the baby with a spoon rather than diluted with milk in a bottle. The baby may not eat much the first time it is offered but he or she will soon learn that solid foods are to be eaten with a spoon. Spoon feeding usually leads to faster chewing and self-feeding by the baby. It is unwise to allow the baby to take a bottle to bed. Sleeping while sucking on a bottle prolongs the time food is in contact with the teeth and thus can increase the possibility of dental caries.

Studies on obesity show that infancy may be the critical time in the formation of the fat cells, both in size and numbers. Once acquired, fat cells are with us for life. A person with a large number of fat cells has a very difficult time controlling his or her weight. So, parents, give your baby a head start and let him or her "tell" you when enough is enough.

BREAST FEEDING THE BABY: A LOST ART?

A rekindling of interest is taking place among new mothers today in an ancient ritual called breast feeding the baby. Although this ritual has been successful for thousands of years, in only about two generations, a nourishment called "formula" has replaced breast milk as the prime food for infants and is considered the modern method. Yet, mothers and scientists are now learning from grandmothers and animal experiments that although a commercial formula allows an infant to grow, there are advantages to breast feeding that cannot be duplicated.

Breast feeding is the least expensive method if moderately priced foods are chosen for the extra five hundred calories per day needed by a mother. For about 43¢ a peanut butter and banana sandwich and a glass of whole milk will provide five hundred calories and twenty grams of protein. This compares favorably with the commercial formulas that cost between 68¢ and $2.10 per day. Formula made at home from evaporated milk would cost 48¢ a day. Special equipment costs extra.

Breast feeding is convenient. No special shopping is necessary and there is no need for special sterilized equipment.

Bottle Makes Bigger, but not Better

Bottle-fed babies do gain weight faster than breast-fed babies. Scientists are now concerned that bottle-fed babies may be accumulating extra fat cells that cannot be reduced in number later in life. A baby fed a bottle often is encouraged to finish it, while a baby nursing at the breast regulates the amount eaten.

Human milk contains antibodies, which protect against allergy and infections.

Ironically, if breast milk had nutrient labeling, it would not sell. True: The protein, calcium, phosphorus and sodium are much lower, while lactose, cholesterol, and essential fatty acids are much higher in human milk. The protein in human milk has a higher biological value and is better utilized than cow's milk. An excess of nutrients at an early stage in life may actually be harmful. A high calcium intake soon after birth may lead to greater loss of calcium later in life. High-salt diets (sodium) are thought to contribute to hypertension. Therefore, the high mineral and protein content of cows' milk may not be beneficial at all.

Isn't Cholesterol a Dirty Word?

No, cholesterol is a type of fat available in food and made by the body, which is distributed in all cells of the body. Adults prone to heart disease may have high blood levels of cholesterol and may be directed to follow low-cholesterol diets. Human milk has six to thirteen times as much cholesterol as the three most widely used formulas. However, laboratory studies indicate that a moderate amount of cholesterol may be important in early life to establish body mechanisms for using cholesterol and preventing atherosclerosis. More studies have to be done to verify these theories, but enough is known to reassure mothers to breast feed.

So wouldn't it be nice if: hospitals gave new mothers fruit rather than formula in the advertising "gift" package?; health clinics promoted breast feeding, rather than formula making?; government and doctors educated the public through television, radio, and pamphlets on the advantages of breast feeding?; employers allowed nursing breaks (liberate babies from bottles)?

Nutrition of Preschoolers

Preschoolers require the same nutrients as other children and adults in the household, but in varying amounts. Furthermore, the difference in needs between two children of the same age may be quite large as may be differences between the needs of two children of the same size.

The growth rate of preschoolers drops dramatically compared to the growth rate during the first year of life; the former rate is about one-fourth that of the latter. A two- to five-year-old child will grow two to three inches and gain about four pounds a year. About one-half of the total weight gain goes to muscle development. The growth of bone is slowed during this time, but deposits of minerals in the bone are high. The bones are becoming stronger to keep pace with muscle development and increases in activity.

Nutritional Needs

The amounts of nutrients listed here are given as a guide (allowance), not as an obsolute need. These allowances are generous for most healthy young children. So parents, do not fret. Your child may eat fewer nutrients than those in the "allowance" yet be in perfect health.

Calories: The calorie needs of a preschooler may range between one thousand and one thousand five hundred calories per day. Calorie needs are very much related to activity. During periods of low activity the preschooler's calorie needs may be quite low.

Protein: The protein allowance for one- to three-year-olds is twenty-three grams; four- to six-year-olds, thirty grams. Some of this allowance should be from high quality protein such as milk, cheese, eggs, fish, poultry or meat. This will insure adequate amounts and kinds of amino acids needed to build new tissues, especially muscles.

Calcium: The calcium allowance for preschoolers is eight hundred milligrams. This mineral as well as phosphorus, strengthens the bones. Although milk is an excellent source of calcium, it should generally be limited to three six-ounce glasses per day. Drinking too much milk could lead to low blood iron (anemia) if iron-containing proteins are not included in the diet.

Iron: The iron allowance for one- to three-year-olds is fifteen milligrams; four- to six-year-olds, ten milligrams. The larger allowance for the young toddler is most economically obtained from iron-enriched cereals, liver and eggs.

Vitamins and other minerals: The child should eat a variety of basic foods including fruits, vegetables, breads and cereals to meet these needs. Healthy children do not need to take vitamin or mineral supplements.

Food Struggles

In the family group, toddlers struggle to be individuals. They are willing to take chances, yet at the same time they want and need approval. Parents need to realize that children may use food in various ways in this struggle. The less importance the parent places on eating, at meal time, the less chance that there will be eating and nutritional problems then and in later life. After all, it's highly unlikely that the small child will waste away from skipping meals or from eating only tiny nibbles of bread and milk. However, for the three- to six-year-olds, this period is one of increased imitation of parents and peers at the dinner table. It is a "prime" time for parents to set good examples of eating.

Lifetime Food Habits

The incidence of specific diseases such as heart disease and certain kinds of cancer in various countries, when compared to the food eaten, seems to indicate a relationship with high fat, sugar or salt in the diet. Therefore, to develop good habits during these early years, it is recommended that foods high in sugars, fats, and salt be limited.

Use more starchy foods such as whole grain breads and cereals, dried beans and peas, and vegetables. Use more fruits, fresh or lightly sweetened instead of "sweet" treats. Use more fish, poultry, dried beans and peas; use less pork, lamb, veal and beef. Use more low-fat dairy products; use less cream, butter and full-fat milk.

Do not put the sugar bowl or salt shaker on the table at mealtime. (This would require cooperation from both parents as well as older children.)

FOOD PLAN FOR PRESCHOOLERS

(Remember that appetite and calorie needs will vary with activity.)

Protein foods providing calcium: Choose three servings per day.

¾ cup	milk, yogurt, tofu
1 slice or ounce	cheddar or other firm cheese
1 cup	ice cream occasionally

Protein foods providing iron: Choose two servings per day.

2 ounces	chicken, fish, beef, lamb
2	eggs
2/3 cup	cooked beans
4 tablespoons	nut butter

Fruits and vegetables: Choose three or four servings, two of which should be from A and B lists because these contain more vitamins and minerals.

½ cup	A Citrus juices, berries, tomato, cabbage, cantaloupe, for vitamin C
¼ cup - ½ cup	B Dark-green or deep-yellow fruits and vegetables, such as winter squash, carrots, apricots, spinach or other greens, for vitamin A and iron
¼ cup - ½ cup	C Other vegetables such as potatoes, beets, cauliflower, etc. Other fruits such as apple, banana, pear, etc.

Bread and cereal group: Choose three or four servings. Try to use the highly enriched iron cereals occasionally.

¼ cup	Cooked cereal, highly enriched with iron
½ slice	Bread, whole grain preferred
½ cup	Enriched rice, macaroni, spaghetti
1	Tortilla, piece of cornbread

Fats and oils: Choose one or two servings of vegetable oil, margarine or mayonnaise. One teaspoon is a serving. Limit use of butter, hydrogenated fat or coconut and palm oils.

HOW TO TELL THE TRUTH ABOUT NUTRITION

The Air Is Blue!

It's filled with words about nutrition flying at us from all sides! Words that are knowledge, words that are near-knowledge, and words that are downright doubtful. Pity us all, trying to tell the truth from the fiction. After these many years I have some thoughts about how to recognize a fact.

Personal Experience Is Not it

"I cured my hangnails by eating green cheese!" Very interesting. It may be a fact that the hangnails did clear up. The non-fact is that the green cheese was responsible. This does not prove that green cheese was *not* involved, either. It simply proves nothing. That's why personal experiences are at the low end of the totem pole for credibility. But sometimes a shrewd personal observation followed by careful research does indeed lead to real facts.

Clinical Experience Is Not it

"My doctor cured my warts with garlic!" Doctors may seem successful with nutritional treatment, often combined with drugs and other therapy. Clinical experiences of doctors are important indications of areas that deserve follow-up in careful research. But until this research is done, forget it. Here are possibilities. Not facts.

Newspaper Reports Are Not it

Clinical studies or experiments reported in newspapers are exciting! The newspaper may even sell better if the reports are sensational! But wait. Think. Be skeptical. Often such reports are premature conclusions of preliminary studies. Alas, too often such research cannot be duplicated in another laboratory!

Population Studies Are Not it

Researchers see different disease rates in different countries, and tie them statistically to eating habits. This points the way to promising areas for research. But until the research clarifies and confirms such relationships, we've got possibilities again. Not facts!

Money, Money Everywhere, and Hardly a Cent for Nutrition

Well, that's not quite true. But it's vital to know who pays. Did the sugar industry pay for research on the safety of artificial sweeteners? Are such sweeteners competing with sugar on the market? That research needs repeating in another laboratory not funded by the sugar industry.

Controlled Studies Are it, Sometimes

In a controlled study, part of the subjects receive a nutritional factor while others do not. All other factors are kept exactly the same! Even so, a well-controlled study may be possible only in limited aspects of the nutritional problems. In humans, with our complex emotional responses, great care must be taken that the researchers themselves do not influence the results. Double-blind studies are necessary, in which neither the subject nor the researcher giving the pill knows who gets the vitamin C!

Duplication in Another Lab . . . Eureka!

Sometimes after painstaking, carefully designed studies done by conscientious people, their results cannot be duplicated in other laboratories. Why? Perhaps some inadvertent bias had crept in. Perhaps the subject is more complex than originally thought. When research is duplicated, a giant step toward establishing fact has been taken.

But We've Got Plenty of Areas of Non-Fact

Nutritional studies of humans are hard to do, require great skill, scientific acumen, piles of non-suspect money, and the most cautious interpretation. From us, the public, a little patience is required.

OUR DILEMMAS

We nutrition types may give the impression we're know-it-alls. We speak in certain tones. But nutrition education is fraught with many dilemmas. Here are just a few:

How much should we push, scare, cajole people to get them to improve their diets? Does instilling guilt make people less sure they are in charge of their own eating? Or, on the other hand, are our messages too wishy washy?

How does our mental attitude interact with metabolism? Here we know next to nothing. But I'd like to know how our psyches affect the way our bodies make use of food — beyond the strict vitamin-mineral-protein content.

How do we balance ecology and a good diet? Advocating eating less meat and using less packaging is easy. But what about our urging people to eat an abundance of fresh vegetables and fruits when some of these take lots of energy and land to produce? (For most fruits and vegetables it takes more than a calorie of energy to produce a calorie of food).

Should we demand fresh tomatoes in January? Do we expect too much of a "good" fresh diet year-round? What responsibility do we have toward the people of Mexico, whose economy and lives are being turned topsy turvy by large-scale production of produce for the United States in winter?

Are fresh fruits and vegetables much superior to processed? We have assumed so. But some "fresh" food such as the tomatoes mass-produced in Florida are engineered way beyond anyone's conception of a garden tomato.

How much do we muddy the waters of our nutrition messages by telling all we don't know? How many "ifs," "ands" and "buts" can people take before they're completely confused?

3

Planning for Eating

Eat Low on the Pyramid, Not High on the Hog

The consumer cooperatives in both Norway (NKL) and Sweden (KF) are concerned with the rapid increase in the cost of food in their countries during the past six years. In order to help their members shop economically and still select a nutritious diet, the nutritionists at KF devised a "food pyramid" consisting of three layers of foods.

The base or bottom layer consists of the basic foods. For an adult the following foods in these amounts will provide a good nutritional balance, although they are low in some vitamins and minerals:

Food	Calories	Cost
6 slices bread	390	11¢
2 ounces cereal products (flour, oatmeal, shredded wheat)	150-200	2, 6, or 10¢ (average 6c)
1 ounce cheese, cheddar or jack	114	10¢
1 tablespoon margarine	100	3¢
3-8 ounce glasses of low-fat milk	363	26¢
4 potatoes	360	8¢
Total	1527	64¢

These are all staple foods in the Scandinavian diet and choices and amounts were worked out by nutrition experts. They supply most of the essential nutrients, about two-thirds of the needed calories, and a day's supply in the United States costs 64 cents. The protein in the milk, cheese, bread and potatoes adds up to fifty grams and is of high quality. According to international standards set by the Food and Agriculture Organization and the World Health Organization, this amount of protein is clearly above the safe level.

Scandinavians, like Americans, eat less bread, less potatoes and less cereals than the portions recommended as basic. They also consume considerably more fat and protein. These basic foods, if used as recommended, will change dietary patterns radically. We don't need so much fat with its high calorie count and, in adults, protein over and above the daily fifty grams or so is burned as calories; the body cannot store it. Children under ten, persons with weight problems and old people can reduce the portions a little. Persons doing heavy work will need to increase them.

The middle section of the pyramid includes fruits and green and yellow vegetables. No portions are specified because one can eat as much as desired of these low-calorie foods. The basic foods are a bit low in vitamin C, folacin, iron and perhaps other nutrients. Therefore, it is important to choose fruits and vegetables that will supply these nutrients in sufficient amounts. Dried beans and legumes are also in this middle group. They supply good, quality protein when eaten with cereal foods at a cost per gram of protein that is one-fourth to one-third that of meat and fish.

The top section of the pyramid consists of animal foods rich in protein, of which we need far less than most Americans eat. Unfortunately, even though we don't need these foods for complete nutrition, our eating habits are such that many people eat large amounts. Meat is a high-status food, but just one steak can cost as much as all the basic foods. In 1977 on the average each person in the United States ate ninety-five pounds of beef and all meat eaten accounted for about 40 percent of the total fat in the American diet. From a nutrition point of view, most of us would be better off eating less meat.

Fish and poultry are not high-fat foods. However, the fish crop is limited. If overfished, any particular species could be endangered. (At present, it is estimated that we are harvesting fish at about the maximum amount possible without overfishing).

Raising poultry directly for food uses substantial amounts of grain. Egg production is lower down on the grain usage scale, so the more efficient method would be to use chickens for egg production and the old laying hens for human food.

Beef is not acceptable to most of us unless it has been grain-fed before slaughter to "finish" it with a layer of fat. Any animal fed on grains before slaughter will be expensive in terms of total calories from grains available to us as food. Milk can be produced by herds grazing on grasses only, but heavy buying can raise the price of both milk and cheese because of the time needed to increase production and the limiting factor of the amount of pasture land available. In general, it is very inefficient from the point of view of both total calories and total protein to process grains through animals.

The emphasis in the nutrition education put out by both the Danish and Swedish consumer co-ops (both have test kitchens and staff home economists) is now aimed at encouraging people to eat more of the basic foods and less of the expensive animal proteins. The object is not to eliminate animal foods totally, as strict vegetarians do, but to aim for a lacto-vegetarian eating pattern. Because of the high cost of food in these countries, people are more easily persuaded now than in 1974 when the food pyramid was first introduced in Sweden. Here at home it is easier now to persuade our Co-op's food merchandisers to feature basic foods in ads and in the food stores.

Gunnar Myrdal in his 1975 Nobel speech said, "In particular, people in the rich countries should be challenged to bring down their lavish food consumption." The Scandinavian food pyramid is an excellent educational tool for helping to achieve this goal.

Most of the information in this report came from a speech by Anna-Britt Agnsater, head of the test kitchen in the Swedish Cooperative, KF, to a meeting of the International Cooperative Alliance in October 1977. I also discussed the use of the food pyramid with Ann Aandaven from NKL's test kitchen when she visited our Co-op recently. Three well-known books that expand further on the general theme of efficient use of the world food supply are *Diet for a Small Planet* by Frances Moore Lappe, *Food First: Beyond the Myth of Scarcity* by Francis Moore Lappe and Joseph Collins, and *Laurel's Kitchen* by Laurel Robertson, Carol Flinders and Bronwen Godfrey.

CALORIE NEEDS

Recommended by Food and Nutrition Board, National Research Council, National Academy of Sciences, 1979.

FEMALES	MALES
120 lbs. - 5'4"	154 lbs. - 5'10"
15 to 22 years . . 2100 calories	15 to 22 years . . 2900 calories
23 to 50 years . . 2000 calories	23 to 50 years . . 2700 calories
51 to 75 . . . . . . 1800 calories	51 to 75 . . . . . . 2400 calories
76 and over . . . . 1600 calories	76 and over . . . . 2050 calories

The easy way to be sure that one is obtaining all the necessary nutrients is by following a *food guide*. A food guide groups together foods of similar nutrient content and figures out how many servings of each group must be chosen each day to meet nutrient needs. Single meals or whole-day menus may be planned around the food guide. It is a simple solution to an everyday headache.

The food guide in most common use in the United States is quite old and many consider it out-dated and inadequate to meet nutritional needs. While nutrition authorities work on a new and better guide, Co-op home economists have worked out an interim food guide that should meet nutrient needs of most people.

Interim Food Guide

The list below has been enlarged from older food guides to allow for nutrients about which more is known today. A variety of choices within food groups helps ensure balanced nutrient intake.

Eat These Foods Every Day:

Milk products (protein foods providing calcium) . . . . **2 Servings**
One serving is a cup of milk, yogurt or tofu; 1½ ounces of cheddar-type cheese or 1½ cups ice cream. Caloric range: 80 (nonfat milk) to 375 (ice cream).
Meats, eggs, beans, nuts (protein foods providing iron). **2 or 3 Servings**
One serving is 2 or 3 ounces cooked (4 or 5 oz. raw) lean, boneless meat, fish or poultry; 2 eggs; 1 cup cooked dry beans, lentils, or tofu; 4 tablespoons peanut butter; ½ cup tuna or nuts. Caloric range: 140 (2 eggs) to 400 (peanut butter).
Grain products (breads, rice, cereals) . . . . **4 to 6 Servings**
One serving is one slice of bread or ½ cup cooked cereal, noodles, rice; ¾ cup dry cereal; 4 crackers; 1 pancake; 1 roll. *Whole* grain

cereals are preferred because of higher levels of trace nutrients. Caloric value: 70 calories.

Vitamin C-rich vegetable or fruit.................... 1 Serving
One serving is one orange, ½ grapefruit or ½ cup orange or grapefruit juice, 2 tomatoes, 1½ cups tomato or pineapple juice, one stalk broccoli, ½ cup green or red pepper, ¾ cup raw cabbage, greens or chili peppers. Caloric value: 40 calories.

Dark-green vegetable............................. 1 Serving
One serving is 1 cup cooked broccoli, cabbage, greens, Brussels sprouts, asparagus; or 1½ to 2 cups raw dark-green lettuce, spinach, or scallions (including tops). Caloric value: 40 calories.

Potato or other vegetable or fruit .... 1 or 2 Servings
One serving is ½ cup corn, beets, potato, yams, peas, onion squash, green beans; ¼ cup raisins; one peach, apple, small banana, pear or 4 prunes. Caloric range: 40 (fruits) to 70 (starchy vegetables).

Fats.. 1 Serving
One serving is 1 tablespoon oil, margarine, mayonnaise. Caloric range: 100 calories (margarine or mayonnaise) to 120 (oils).

Plus other foods .... **in limited amounts**
Use limited amounts of sweets (candy, cookies, cake, sweet rolls, presweetened cereals, soft drinks, etc.); fatty foods (fat crackers, potato chips, sauces, gravies, butter, margarine, sour cream, etc.); and alcoholic beverages (beer, wines, hard liquors).

Note: The food list above provides between one thousand one hundred and two thousand two hundred calories per day, depending on the choices within food groups. Persons who need more calories should choose more or larger servings. Persons who need fewer calories should consider increasing caloric expenditure through increased activity, rather than reducing food intake.

ABOLISH DRY CEREAL!

by Nancy Bratt

"But Nancy, I like my kids to be able to get up and get their own breakfast."

What ever happened to the old custom of somebody fixing breakfast and then a family sitting in a group and celebrating the beginning of a new day over some kind of nutritious fuel?

I see two tragic things happening in our culture: 1) To feed a family is becoming just a way of satisfying taste buds and appetites as quickly and painlessly as possible. People aren't thinking of eating food as a way to grow and maintain and regulate healthy bodies. 2) Meal time is becoming extinct. Besides being a time to keep in touch with the people we live with, it's probably healthier to sit down for meals rather than to eat on the run.

Do your kids have to make their own breakfast? The least we can do, as adults, is to have foods available from each of the four food groups. Not only people are interdependent; so are nutrients. That's why we keep encouraging groups of foods instead of just a bowl of cereal.

For each meal, have at least three of the following: fruits and/or vegetables, grains, protein foods (meat, eggs, legumes), milk or milk products.

There are lots of quickie breakfasts that are okay: tomato, cheese and bread; hardboiled egg, orange juice and milk; peanuts, grapefruit juice and cheese, yogurt, bananas, toast.

Lots of children enjoy cooking. Wheathearts or Zoom take only a few minutes to cook. Add milk and a glass of juice and you have an okay meal. Or a blender breakfast — milk, fruit, egg whirled in a blender — can be fun and quick.

Start the Day With Breakfast

If you could help all the members of your family attain better health, be more efficient in their daily activities (including school studies and work projects) and be more relaxed as well just by preparing a meal, wouldn't you do it? On the assumption that many of you would, we are suggesting an emphasis on better breakfasts.

Many nutritionists consider breakfast the most important meal of the day. Since twelve hours, or more, have passed since the previous meal, the body's need for calories and nutrients is great.

Among reasons given for not eating breakfast, the two most often heard are "not enough time" and "can't face food the first thing in the morning." The lack of time is a feeble excuse. A few minutes spent the previous evening in setting the table, getting out any necessary dishes and utensils, and planning the menu can be a tremendous help in slowing down the morning "rush hour." The actual preparation and eating time can be as little as fifteen or twenty minutes.

Overcoming the "can't face food in the morning" hurdle may be a bit difficult at first, but why not start with a simple menu such as fruit, toast and beverage, and then gradually add to it as morning appetites improve, which they will for many. Incidentally, omitting breakfast as a means of losing weight rarely, if ever, works. Evidence shows that the calories not eaten in the morning are almost inevitably made up later in the day or at other meals or with snacks.

For some, the solution is to forget so-called breakfast foods such as eggs and cereal and think "lunch." Why not a grilled cheese sandwich? Why not a fruit and cottage cheese salad plate? Why not a mug of hot tomato soup and peanut butter on raisin bread? Try these or similar foods to see whether they appeal to your family.

A good breakfast is *not* a doughnut or sweet roll with a cup of coffee. A good breakfast includes fruit or juice rich in vitamin C, such as orange, pineapple fortified with vitamin C, tomato juice, berries or melons; it includes a protein food such as eggs, meat, fish or milk; it includes whole grain or fortified cereal products such as bread or breakfast cereals.

THE LONESOME EATER

Old Ms. Nature has designed us to crave company while we eat. Eating goes well with conversation, conviviality, chortling and jollity. Also with grousing, grouching, blowing off steam and other necessary evils. Some people would rather go hungry than eat alone!

Unfortunately, there are people who must eat alone. Too many of them grab a doughnut here, crackers and soda pop there, or any easy-to-eat calories. As for the other nutrients, everybody figures on making it up at dinner or tomorrow or sometime, whenever that is. It happens over and over. It is the stuff of poor nutrition.

Who Eats Alone?

Well, there's the teenager, facing breakfast alone, the parents having gone to work early. There's the housewife, eating lunch alone. There's the single office worker, eating dinner alone. And the elderly retired? They may eat every meal alone.

The Most Awful Crimes

The alone eaters' frequent offenses include: . . . skipping fruits and vegetables, so they don't get enough vitamins A and C *or* enough roughage; skipping milk or cheese, so they don't get enough calcium *or* that B vitamin, riboflavin; glutting on sweets or fat foods, so they get too many calories.

Eating alone seems to bring out the worst food habits. Therefore, one must outwit nature with a clever plot: Planning! To plan is to decide in advance what to eat.

For example, you decide on Wednesday (or even before!) to eat one-half chicken breast baked with lemon juice and herbs, for Thursday's dinner. And you decide on Wednesday to have some French bread and stir-fried broccoli to go with the chicken on Thursday. And you decide on Wednesday to have a ripe d'anjou pear with cottage cheese for dessert. Then on Thursday afternoon, you experience a curious exultation, just knowing the decisions are already made. Just thinking about dinner whets your appetite.

A young shopper gave me this charming idea: She relishes her dinner alone eating each food in sequence as it finishes cooking. The potato bakes, the artichoke boils, the meat patty fries, while she eats a tossed salad. Next, she enjoys the meat patty. Next, a leisurely session with the artichoke. Finally, the potato, in all its buttery glory. For all these courses she provides herself with fascinating company: some good reading, or an absorbing program on radio or television.

Equipment need not be new. Check the second-hand stores, flea markets and garage sales. To start, we suggest this minimum:

1 Frying pan 8" or 10" with cover. Cast iron is excellent
1 Paring knife
1 Pancake turner or spatula
1 Glass pitcher or jar (with lid) for mixing juice or milk powder
Measuring cup and measuring spoons
Mixing bowl
Grater
1 Saucepan (1 quart) with cover
1 Baking dish of 1 or 2 qt. size with cover
1 Long knife
1 Can opener
1 Coffee pot or teakettle
2 Pot holders
Cutting board (a piece of plywood can be used)

Cooking With Minimum Equipment

Consider Irish stew, New England boiled dinner, fish chowder, etc. A series of dishes can be prepared on one burner. If you have a heavy, cast-aluminum or cast-iron pot, it can keep one food hot while another is cooking.

A double boiler is useful for preparing a meal on one burner. Foods such as creamed fish can be kept warm in the upper section while a vegetable cooks in the lower. Or boil a potato, ear of corn or an egg in the lower pot and warm a roll or heat leftover meat in the upper.

If your budget will stretch that far, you might think about buying a toaster-broiler oven which sells for $25 or $35. It's quite versatile. Or, it is possible to buy a used stove from such outlets as the Salvation Army or Goodwill for about the same price. Be sure it's in good condition and that your landlord will allow you to intall it.

OCCASIONALLY HAVE A MEAL REQUIRING NO COOKING AT ALL!

Salad Meals

Combine diced, leftover cooked meat, fish, poultry, hard-cooked eggs, tuna, sardines, canned mackerel with canned garbanzos or other cooked beans. Add raw or cooked vegetables, such as spinach, mushrooms, jicama, turnips or rutabaga. Or add fruit, such as diced pears, apples, mandarin oranges and water chestnuts to add an Oriental touch. Toss the salad with any preferred dressing. Serve with whole wheat, rye or pumpernickel bread. Add milk and an oatmeal cookie; you have a nutritious, delicious meal.

Alternatively, a no-cook meal can be based on two or three pieces of raw or stewed fruit topped with plain yogurt. Raisin bread spread with peanut butter is a delicious accompaniment. With the meal have nonfat milk or cappuccino (half hot coffee and half hot milk).

HAVE FUN WITH YOUR MEALS

Create many different atmospheres or settings. Candlelight dinners are always nice; fresh, cut flowers on your table or tray add a happy touch. Eat in different places: breakfast in bed, picnic-style on the floor, in the park or in your backyard.

EATING HABITS WHEN YOU'RE OLDER

Senior citizen? Mature person? Golden years? Whatever the euphemism, when we enter the fifth, sixth, seventh or eighth decade of life, many of us tend to eat more poorly than we did when we were younger. That's too bad. It really is important to eat well all your life. Older people, for example, often neglect to eat calcium-rich foods, like milk. Food requirements are about the same no matter what your age, with the exception of calorie intake. As one becomes more sedentary, the body's need for fuel decreases — and calories are the body's fuel source.

This message came across to me loudly and clearly recently. For about three months, I had not been spending two active days a week at the El Cerrito Co-op as home economist. In that period of time, I gained three pounds. It may not sound like much, but it is. Had I continued at that rate, the year's accumulation could have been twelve pounds! Happily, I'm back on schedule determined to shed the three pounds.

Problem 1

Perhaps the biggest problem is consumption of empty calories. As we need fewer, the necessity for making sure that each calorie provides important nutrients becomes more important. If you "breakfast" on a two-ounce doughnut and black coffee, you've consumed two hundred twenty-five calories and few nutrients. Substitute one slice of whole wheat bread spread with one tablespoon of peanut butter and a cup of skim milk. Caloric intake?: two hundred fifty calories plus a good start on the day's need for protein, calcium, vitamins and minerals.

Problem 2

An older person often shops for one, which presents the problem of quantities. However, produce items can be bought by the each. Dairy products come in small containers. Frozen foods are in single serving size or can easily be divided. If the packages of meat are too large, ask the meat department for less. They will package one or two chops, or a smaller amount of ground beef if needed.

There are juices in six-ounce cans, vegetables in buffet sizes. Of course, it's an expensive way to go. Try to use the large sizes in two days or share with a friend.

Problem 3

Most serious for last. Lack of motivation to prepare a meal. Many older people tell us that they just don't feel like bothering. All we can do is urge you to try. Invite a friend. Put a flower on the table. Light a candle and dine by its light. Turn on the radio or play a record. Other ideas? Let us know.

FOOD FOR BACKPACKING

How to Package

Backpackers need lots of food but remember, it's the cook's vacation also! The time required for meal preparation in camp can be greatly reduced if the food is prepackaged at home. This may save weight, as much of the bulky packaging can be removed.

It is important to group the food by some system, such as a day's supply or by meals. This will prevent the supplies from running low in the latter part of the trip when appetites have greatly increased.

Plastic bags, jars and bottles can be used in place of the original packaging for nearly all items. Canned goods with meat must be kept sterile in the unopened can and freeze-dried foods should be kept in the foil-wrapped packages. Soft or liquid items such as peanut butter, jam, honey or lotion can be transferred to plastic jars or bottles. Dry supplies and foods such as cereals, mixes, coffee and sugar can be placed in plastic bags and secured with rubber bands. Insert a small paper label in each food bag to identify it and to indicate the amount of water to be added or any other important instructions. Place the individual food bags in a larger and stronger plastic bag to minimize punctures and food losses.

Foods to Take

Foods for backpacking should be light, relatively moisture-free and of high caloric and nutritive value. Before shopping it's a good idea to make menus for all the meals to ensure that *enough* food, but *not too much*, will be available on the trip. It's worth trying to plan well-balanced meals but even so, the diet will probably be low in vitamin C (ascorbic acid). Take ascorbic acid tablets (50 mg./day) if you are worried about your daily intake or if the trip will be longer than two weeks.

Most of the food can be regular foods, not special backpack foods. Some freeze-dried meats, vegetables and fruits will help round out the menu and lighten the load for the backpacker taking a long trip. Individually-wrapped hard candies may relieve dry throats on the hot, dusty trail and will enthrall the little ones. Include foods from the following groups in each day's menu:

Breads and Cereals: Breads should be dense (buffet rye or pumpernickel) to reduce bulk in the pack, and crackers, hard (rye crisp or pilot bread) to lessen breakage.

Dry mixes prepared at home are often less expensive than commercial ones. Make your own trail mix or for breakfast, prepare the homemade Granola-type cereal.

Take the precooked or quick-cooking cereals or rice if you will be camping at eight thousand to ten thousand feet altitude. Water boils at a much lower temperature at high altitudes and wholegrain breakfast cereals and rices may never get tender due to insufficient heat. However, spaghetti, macaroni and noodles will cook tender but may take five to ten minutes longer at high altitudes.

Dairy Products: Nonfat dry milk, premeasured in usable amounts, can be used as a beverage either alone or mixed with flavorings. Dry milk can also be added to pancake and biscuit mixes or puddings. Natural cheeses such as cheddar, Swiss, provolone and other firm cheeses will keep for about two weeks if kept cool. Where temperatures are very hot, use processed cheese foods, which mold less readily and in which fats separate less quickly.

Vegetables - Fruits: Fruits and vegetables available for pack trips include instant mashed and hash brown potatoes, dehydrated onions, dried mushrooms, regular dried fruits and freeze-dried fruits and vegetables. On the whole, the freeze-dried fruits are very good. They are available either with sugar (RichMoor) or without (Mountain House). It is a good idea to try the freeze-dried vegetables at home before the pack trip, some may not cook to a desired tender stage.

Meats, Nuts and Eggs: Freeze-dried meats such as beef patties, pork chops, sausage, diced beef or chicken are *expensive,* but very lightweight and relatively well-flavored. Dried egg powder may be used in pudding and pancake mixes for color, flavor and additional protein. Two tablespoons of the powder is equivalent in food value to one fresh egg. Dried egg powder may be rehydrated, lightly salted, and served as scrambled eggs. (For variation, season with dried spinach, dried chives or other herbs). Mix the egg powder with a small amount of water to make a smooth paste, then add the remaining water. Cook over low heat with constant stirring; remove from heat before eggs are set. *Don't overcook!*

Serve immediately.

Peanut butter and nuts are valuable additions to the menu for variety and their high protein and caloric content.

Fats: Don't forget margarine or canned butter; fats provide twice the calories per ounce when compared with protein or carbohydrate. Some one thousand to two thousand *additional* calories per day may be needed when hiking is strenuous.

Dishes to Take

Most menus require only a couple of cooking pots since backpackers usually eat by "courses." A pot may be reused once or twice to prepare food that will be eaten later in the meal. Check the menus to determine the utensils needed to prepare each meal. The only eating utensils needed are a large cup and a spoon per person.

Dishwashing

Never, never wash dishes (or anything) in streams or lakes; it will pollute the water supply. Use a *clean* pot to gather water and wash some distance from source.

Carefully scrape food from dishes and cooking pots. (A metal scratcher hastens the process and can be cleaned by soaking in the hot dish water). Separate cooking pots may be used to heat wash and rinse water. Soap or detergent will make dishwashing easier, rinsing afterward in hot water. (If soap or detergent is not used, rinse the dishes in boiling water to remove grease). Allow dishes to air-dry.

Leave a Clean Camp

Burn all burnables. Pack out all non-burnable materials such as glass, cans and any foil or foil-wrap packaging.

Shopping List for Backpacking Trips

Bread and Cereals: Quick-cooking rice, wheat and oat cereals; pancake, biscuit, cornbread or gingerbread mixes; Spaghetti, macaroni, noodles; rye hardtack, Rye Krisp, Swede Krisp; pumpernickle, Norwegian flat bread, Finn Krisp; granola.

Fruits and Vegetables: Freeze-dried fruits and vegetables; dried fruits; dehydrated onions; instant mashed and hash brown potatoes; dried mushrooms; trail mix (make your own).

Dairy Products: Dry milk powder (nonfat or buttermilk); Cheddar, Swiss, Provolone or other firm cheese; grated Parmesan or Romano cheese, processed cheese food.

Meats, Nuts and Eggs: Freeze-dried meats; canned hams requiring *no* refrigeration, canned liver paste or Vienna sausage; sardines or kippered snacks; canned chicken and tuna; dry salami chubs; beef jerky; dried egg powder, omelet or other egg mixes; peanut butter; canned, shelled nuts; roasted soy beans; miso; nutritional yeast.

Sweets: Honey; sugar, white or brown; chocolate bars (no milk chocolate); hard candies, individually wrapped; cookies (dry types and fruit bars); marshmallows.

Miscellaneous: Margarine or canned butter, oil; non-dairy powdered cream substitute, salt and pepper; herbs and spices; bouillon cubes; dehydrated soups; instant pudding mixes, fruit gelatin; instant coffee or tea, flavored instant drinks; Tang or Wyler's drinks; popcorn.

Other Supplies: Powdered detergent or soap flakes; hot pad or heavy glove, small wire beater; aluminum foil; metal dish scratcher; plastic quart measure, matches; cooking spoons, forks or pancake turner, as needed.

Personal Items: Soap; toothbrush and powder; toilet paper; pocket knife, flashlight, extra batteries; chapstick and hand lotion or cream; first aid kit including moleskin; aspirin; sunglasses; sunburn cream or lotion; hat; insect repellent.

THE PERFECT HOSTESS THANKSGIVING COUNTDOWN

7 Days Before . . .

Serious housecleaners should complete all major waxing and polishing before today. As for the rest of you, Co-op home economists do not recommend taking a swipe at the windows on Thanksgiving morning.

6 Days Before . . .

Count your dishes, silver, tables and chairs. Will you be using your fine china from Richfield or decorator colored paper plates? Figure your turkey size: allow three-fourths to one pound per serving for birds under twelve pounds, and one-half to three-fourths pound per serving for larger birds. Do you have a big enough roasting pan?

5 Days Before . . .

Buy your staples. Don't forget such trifles as salt or paper towels! Have you ever run out of coffee on Thanksgiving? Beginners, pick up some canned cranberry sauce or ask Aunt Rosie to bring it. No need to make everything from scratch.

4 Days Before

Dream of your centerpiece . . . something gorgeous with persimmons, perhaps? Are you getting the refrigerator ready, by using up (or throwing out) leftovers?

3 Days Before . . .

Let it thaw, let it thaw! in the refrigerator, not on the kitchen counter. Turkeys over twelve pounds may take three days to thaw.

Before You Shop 91

2 Days Before . . .

Shop for perishable groceries. By now, your frig is empty and waiting for all the Thanksgiving goodies. And when you've done this twenty times, dear, you'll agree that tonight's dinner can come out of cans.

1 Day Before . . .

Make the pies, wash the lettuce, make the salad dressing, fix the ingredients for the stuffing . . . but don't stuff the turkey until tomorrow! You want to poison your mother-in-law? Fix the centerpiece instead.

Thanksgiving, The Day . . .

Stuff the turkey and throw it in the oven. Let your guests help with the rest of the work . . . it's such a good time to pick up tips from the relatives! But most of the work is already done, anyhow. So here's to your fun, food and family on Thanksgiving!

Contemplating Calamities

All of you with emergency food and water supplies at home may now stop reading. The remaining 99 percent of us should consider this lugubrious topic. Because if it's awful to think of earthquakes, fires or floods, it's much worse to be unprepared for them.

Water Is More Important than Food

You can last a long time without food, but water you must have. Usually one half gallon per day per person is considered a minimum. Include more for washing or food preparation if you like. In an emergency, water in hot water tanks and toilet tanks is safe to use, though intakes may have to be closed to protect such water.

Choose Canned Foods, Mostly

Partly because of water problems, plan foods that are ready-to-eat, such as canned foods that already contain water. Don't store dried foods unless you plan to store extra water for them. Use canned milk, single-strength canned juices and soups.

Forget the Leftovers

Can sizes should be right for one meal; you don't want leftovers that you can't store safely.

Expect To Be Powerless

Emergency foods should be foods that can safely be eaten cold or with little heating; power and gas may be unavailable. Your camp stove and supplies could be invaluable, including fuel, matches, candles, can opener, flashlight. Certainly you can cook over a hibachi with charcoal, too. Just remember it isn't safe to use in a closed room.

Make it Nutritious and Tasty

Plan your food stores around the Four Basic Food Groups, including protein foods; fruits and vegetables; crackers, prepared cereals or breads; canned milk. Snacks are nice, preferably not salty ones, which will increase your need for water. Essential for morale are coffee or tea.

How Much and For How Long?

They used to say, store a two-week supply of food for each member of your household, against an atom bomb attack. That could be a strain on your storage capacity and your organizational capacity. Because you've got to use up and replace this food supply every six months to keep it from getting too old! So my advice is to keep your supply at a reasonable size, and make it foods you like well enough to use for unexpected company. That's an emergency that can happen to anyone!

IN 1978 WE ATE STANDING UP

Certainly, we did a lot of eating in 1978. More than ever, it seems, we did a lot of eating while standing up, even moving around. Everywhere I look I see people walking along, eating.

Mostly people walk along eating doughnuts, or popcorn, or potato chips, or hamburgers, or drinking secretly out of paper bags. But not always. Once I watched a man pawing through the green beans in the produce department. He picked out a couple that pleased him and walked off munching the beans, appearing gratified.

Margaret Mead would be fascinated by this specter of the single, mobile eater: using, but not participating in and oblivious to the vast human ingenuity that produced horticulture, food preservation, cooking and baking, menu planning, graceful table settings and food serving, and innumerable vivacious and elegant mealtime conversations.

What does the stand-up eater think about? Does he laugh over some comic happening? Does he sigh with satisfaction? With hunger satisfied, does his mind turn to wondering? Or to planning the next stand-up feeding?

As children, we had to sit down to eat. Walking while eating could cause us to choke! Fall blue-faced onto the floor, in mortal agony! But of the walking eaters I've seen, none have choked. All seem unconcerned about such hazards.

There's an aimlessness about this type of eating.

There's no plan to it, no combining of foods to meet nutritional needs. It's a matter of eating what's handy; a sort of adaptation, thousands of years later, of our early days as food gatherers before agriculture existed. Perhaps we're completing some dimly discernable cycle of food habits.

We could eat sitting down. Have meals, sometimes with others. Give ourselves the value and beauty of combining foods to compliment and complement each other. Relish that moment of relaxation, that building of anticipation, that musing over which food to taste first. Have that blessed unwinding of the mind, that putting aside of vexation, the laughter, the arguments that are part of eating together with people.

In 1979, let us give ourselves the pleasure of eating sitting down.

4

As the Twig Is Bent, So Grows the Tree

START WITH THE CHILDREN

According to the American Heart Association, 54 percent of all deaths in the United States are due to heart or blood vessel disease. The expected cost of these diseases in 1978 is $28.5 billion (not counting pain and grief). Good nutrition plays a large part in preventing these diseases. Basically, we need more fruits and vegetables and whole grains and a sharp reduction of fat and sugar in the American diet.

Middle Age Is a Little Late

We must start with the children, perhaps by offering alternatives to junk food snacks (candy, chips or soft drinks). The average child gets as much as one-fourth to one-third of the day's calories from snacks. So it's very important to see that snacks have food value other than fat or sugar.

Beat the Hunger Alarm

When the child comes in hungry, it's too late. If nothing better is handy, the hungry child succumbs to junk food. So the first rule is to plan and prepare alternatives that are ready when the child is ready.

Vegetable or Fruit Ideas

Prepare a tray of favorite raw vegetables cut in finger-sized pieces to eat with cottage cheese dip (carrots, jicama, broccoli stems, etc.) Fruit is good as is, but try freezing some so it can be eaten frozen (seedless grapes, pieces of melon, apricot halves, peach quarters, strawberries). These frozen fruits can also be blended with milk for a tasty drink (about one-half cup fruit to three-fourths cup low fat or nonfat milk).

The Measured Snack

Control overeating by storing snacks in measured amounts — offering a whole bowl of even a nutritious snack may encourage the child to eat too much.

When You Shop, Plan Leftovers

Leftovers make good snacks. Think about it when you shop. Cold pizza or quiche makes a delicious snack. Cold beans (perhaps sprinkled with vinegar) or even cold potatoes taste good to some people.

Children's Snacks

There's a funny thing about food. Everyone must learn to enjoy plenty of different nutritious foods, but eat sparingly of very enjoyable non-nutritious (junk) foods. The trick is to get children to see this.

Why Use Snacks?

When children reject important and needed foods at mealtime, snacks may help to solve the problem. They can be the means of adding vitamin C to the diet of the child who refuses juice for breakfast. Or they can add protein for the child who refuses meat or beans at dinnertime.

A new food may be accepted eagerly when offered as a snack, but rejected in favor of familiar foods when offered as part of a meal.

Some children eat poorly at meals because they are too excited by the gathering of the whole family. Yet, at more relaxed times, when food may safely be picked up by the fingers, when they are not overtired, children will eat the same food they might reject later. If Johnny eats tuna chunks and carrot sticks at 3 o'clock, who cares if he eats only potatoes, milk and fruit for dinner?

Make the Most of Hunger!

Children who experience acute hunger within two or three hours after eating, as when they are growing fast, may satisfy their hunger with soft drinks or candy. Hunger can be a powerful motive.

Use it to your advantage by making good foods available. Satisfying hunger with nutritious food will leave a pleasant memory that will help to establish preference for good foods. Timing is important. The snack must be offered at the time of hunger but not so late that the appetite is spoiled for the next meal.

A Reminder: Snacking Should Not Replace Meals

Though snacks can be useful, there are good reasons for eating meals. Some nutrients may be absorbed better when several foods are eaten at once. Calories are used more efficiently when food is eaten in a few meals instead of in many snacks. But also, a child learns about the society in which he or she lives, through the social give and take at mealtime.

Make a Snack Plan

First, decide what your family needs. Which foods should be added to their diets by means of snacks? When is the best time to offer them? How much of your limited time are you willing to spend on snacks in addition to meals? If fixing something special that is not eaten makes you frustrated and angry, why not stick to simple foods that may be put away if not eaten? Perhaps a "snack spot" in the refrigerator may be the answer.

Some Suggestions for Snacks That Supplement Meals

To add protein: Offer some hardcooked eggs, chunks of tuna, pieces of cheese, slices of leftover roast. Let them use their fingers. Or stuff celery sticks with peanut butter or with tuna and mayonnaise. Offer nuts, seeds, toasted soybeans or a peanut butter log.

To add vitamin C: Strawberries, melons, tomatoes, citrus fruits are the best sources; other berries, mangos, nectarines, papayas and raw pineapple are good sources. Serve as is or skewer on a bamboo stick. Try cherry tomatoes, cold cooked potato or sliced jicama. Cut the rind off melon and serve wedges that may be picked up with the fingers. A squeeze of lime adds flavor. Make frozen juice bars.

To add vitamin A: Dark green or bright yellow fruits and vegetables add vitamin A. Arrange carrot sticks, green pepper rings, chunks of broccoli or dark green lettuce leaves (dark green veggies also may add vitamin C) on a plate. Serve plain with a dip made from cottage cheese mixed with onion salt, celery salt and chives.

Or try cottage cheese mixed with drained, crushed pineapple, or tuna and mayonnaise. Put cheese and carrot spread on whole wheat bread or crackers.

Many children prefer raw vegetables to cooked, and they may particularly resist cooked vegetables at dinner. If these youngsters will eat raw vegetables at snack time, then they need not be served cooked vegetables at dinner. Besides the raw ones mentioned above, you might try raw green beans, turnips, broccoli, Brussels sprouts, spinach, chard, green peas or zucchini.

To add calcium: Dairy products are well-known sources of calcium. Try frozen yogurt sticks, cheese chunks, custard, or cottage cheese and fruit. Tofu (soybean curd) is also a good source of calcium and children may enjoy cold cubes of tofu that have been dipped in an egg batter and fried in margarine or butter.

To add B vitamins and minerals: Use whole grain and enriched breads and cereals, dairy products, nuts. Put out a big bowl of unshelled mixed nuts and let them crack their own. Warm tortillas with butter or cheese.

Homemade cookies, especially when they contain oatmeal, raisins and nuts may be more nutritious than store-bought cookies. For extra measure, try substituting whole wheat flour for part of the white in your favorite cookie recipe and decrease the sugar.

Snacks to limit: Candies, very sweet or rich desserts, commercially prepared cookies, cakes, doughnuts, soft drinks, potato and corn chips, pretzels and crackers are foods to limit. Usually it is difficult if not impossible to restrict these foods entirely; keep them in their place by making rules about when and how often they may be eaten. Or don't buy them.

SNACK ON THE RUN

Bother!

You have to return the shirt you bought in haste last Saturday. And you have some other things to pick up. So you pile the kids into the car and off you go.

First, Susie's thirsty so you stop for a soft drink, then you buy a snack for Kevin and Michael at the candy counter as you pass through the next store. At 1 o'clock you have still one more stop to make and everyone's hungry. You zip into the nearest fast food outlet and load up on hamburgers, fries, cola and shakes.

You Don't Gather Moss, Just Fat

Your fast-paced lifestyle is what McDonald's, Colonel Sanders and the rest appeal to. Now you are out $10 for high-calorie, refined snacks. Does this contribute to one-third of Americans being overweight? Do you need that kind of help? You don't need them to "do it all for you."

Next Time

Grab yourself before going out the door and assemble some easy traveling snacks. Fill a thermos with water or fruit juice. Take raisins, nuts and fruit. Throw in some crackers and cheese or peanut butter or canned sardines and a knife. Some relatively nutritious cookies that travel well are oatmeal-raisin cookies, fig bars or peanut butter cookies. If you have leftover chicken or salad that needs to be cold take a couple containers (i.e. coffee can or leftover margarine or cottage cheese container) of ice to keep things cold. As it melts you have extra drinking water.

If You Think Ahead

Slice vegetables the night before for dinner and put the remainder in a plastic container with water. For extra crispiness put a couple of ice cubes in before you leave.

Stop at a Park

Enjoy your lunch. Listen to the birds. Then finish your shopping with a clearer mind and as you pass give old Mac a wink for me.

Grandma Did It

Feeding the Baby Using Foods Prepared at Home

Co-op home economists get questions about feeding babies without using commercial baby foods. It isn't difficult. We think many people may want to prepare their baby's food at home, possibly for reasons of economy, for better flavored food, and to be able to feed baby foods that contain the amount of salt, sugar and other seasonings or thickeners you choose to add.

The suggestions that follow as to when to introduce new foods to children, as well as amounts to give, are made as general guides and will normally vary from child to child, and even from day to day.

Baby Foods for the First Nine Months of Life

Newborn to About Three Months

Breast-fed infants need a vitamin D supplement; formula fed babies need a vitamin C supplement if evaporated milk is used. (Some breast-fed babies need extra vitamin C if the mother's diet is not adequate in this vitamin). All infants and children need fluoride, which must be prescribed by a physician if it is not available in the water supply. Phone your water company to find out if your water is fluoridated. No additional foods are needed.

Three to Four Months

This is soon enough to start supplemental foods, beginning usually with cereal. Use iron-enriched baby cereals (Gerber or Pablum brands of oat and barley are best), Instant or Quick Cream of Wheat, or Quick Malto-Meal, twice daily. Other regular cereals do not contain enough iron. Then add cooked fruits pureed or put in a blender; fresh fruits such as apple, pear, banana or peaches can be scraped, mashed or strained. If you want to use commercially prepared fruits as desserts, stick to the straight fruits. Avoid the elaborate combinations such as Blueberry Buckle and Peach Cobbler, since they are more likely to contain additives, including sugar, you may want to avoid.

Four to Six Months

Any fairly lean meat, fish or poultry plus vegetables can be cooked and put in a blender, the resulting puree put into an ice cube tray, sandwich or ziplock bag, and frozen. When ready to use, place frozen pureed food in a four-ounce Pyrex custard cup, set cup in pan of water, and heat slowly until food is thawed and warm enough to serve. Or you may use a blender or baby food grinder to make small amounts using the foods the family will be served.

If you do not have a blender or grinder, cooked meat can be cut *very fine* and cooked vegetables rubbed through a sieve. Cook in small amount of water and save any excess cooking liquid (though not for more than two days) to use for diluting the pureed vegetables and meats since the water contains dissolved nutrients.

Six to Seven Months

The transition to finger-fed table food is confusing for the Gerber or Heinz-dependent parent. Ease off on pureed foods and substitute finger foods as the baby is able to handle them. Babies often like ground beef (cooked medium), tuna, liverwurst, cheese, and tiny avocado or creamy peanut butter sandwiches. Also, many like a chicken drumstick with a little bit of meat left on, scrambled eggs, breadsticks and graham crackers or zweibach. Some like peeled fruits and vegetables, such as cooked string beans or cooked carrot strips, slightly cooked apple or pear plus other foods from the basic food groups.

Nine to Ten Months

The baby is usually able to eat foods served to the rest of the family.

Raw carrots, nuts and popcorn are really hazardous finger foods for babies and small children because they might not chew them thoroughly. Bits of them might get inhaled into the lungs.

New Ideas on Food for Preschoolers

Your two-year-old dawdles at the table, mixes the noodles with the broccoli, takes one bite of noodles, pushes the plate away and says, "What's for dessert?"

Your four-year-old eats everything on the plate after skipping lunch, but insists that no two foods touch each other on the plate and crumbles into tears when the broccoli falls off the fork onto the floor.

Preschoolers vary tremendously in their food habits. Some children will be messy; some will be finicky. There will be cycles of rigorous activity and passive thoughtfulness. Yet their nutritional needs are high in relation to the calories they require. Because children's requirements fluctuate, parents need to be creative in introducing new foods to a child. Preschoolers may not eagerly try new foods. They may only like the foods most familiar to them.

Hints for Successful Food Acceptance: Be Models

Try to get an agreement with the adults in your family that all will try a new food. If one parent eats greens and carrots, but the other does not, the message that greens and carrots are questionable food comes across loud and clear.

If you shop with the kids, avoid pacifying your own hunger with candy, doughnuts, soft drinks or other sweet foods. Plan ahead for hungry children: Bring snacks from home, such as vegetable sticks, cut up fruit or a peanut-butter-and-banana sandwich.

The Setting

Children need a time for rest before the evening meal. Overly excited children find it difficult to settle down to eating.

Keep junk foods (foods that offer little nutrition other than calories) out of the house so that they do not become a point for argument.

Children are influenced by other children in group eating situations. Urge your child's preschool to offer nutritious foods, if food is part of the program.

Keep the television off while eating. It is distracting enough to the young child to try to join a dinner conversation with adults who may have been away all day and to manipulate eating utensils at the same time.

Involve Preschoolers

Preschoolers Want To Be Boss, so Let Them

Grow it: A garden plot of fast-growing vegetables, such as lettuce, peas, radishes, carrots, and even onions may become a snack center for preschoolers.

Prepare it: Let children peel or grate carrots, assemble sandwiches, tear lettuce into a salad, or decide what vegetables to put into a vegetable soup.

Play with it: Sometimes when children are not very hungry, they may play with their food; they are learning more about the texture of broccoli or fish; be patient.

Offer opinions: Do not coax, force, or bribe your child into trying new foods. Treat your child as you do other family members without letting him or her be the center of attention. Children have food preferences, too. Continue to offer different foods even when they have been rejected before. Show no disappointment when they are not eaten. Be sure to reward your child with a compliment if one bite of a new food is taken.

Other Approaches

Serve one of your child's favorite foods at the meal with a new food or recipe. Try only one new food at a time. Children have a keen sense of taste, and strong or spicy flavors such as onions, cabbage, curry, garlic, ginger may be disliked. A plainer version of a spicy recipe may be served to children. Portions need to be small. Some children get fat because they are taught to eat more than they need. A teaspoon of various foods is reasonable. A child can always ask for more. Bite-sized pieces and finger foods are suitable for small hands.

If practically no vegetables are eaten, but starch is eaten, use vegetable cooking water to cook rice and macaroni.

Take advantage of timing: When children are the hungriest (often just before dinner), offer raw vegetable sticks or finger foods from dinner.

Part Three
About Foods and Buying

5

Beverages

TO QUENCH A THIRST

Long ago, people drank water. After a hot, sweaty hunt for saber-toothed tigers, they loved the feel of cool, sparkling water in their parched throats. Later, they learned to make wine. How thrifty, to save the grapes for winter use! And what a thirst quencher.

And after the passage of a thousand years, give or take a few, what hath science and industry wrought? Soft drinks! It became possible to get your water nourishment in a sweet, prickly soft drink. Little children blamed their parents if they suffered thirst, when there was no cola in the refrigerator.

Finally came the present, and a great clamor about water pollution. People now worry about phosphates, nitrates and plain old sewage in the water sources. After all, babies' formulas are made with water; fish grow in water, and even soft drinks are made from water. Some people yearn for the good old days, and think about drinking water to quench their thirst. Some even buy bottled water! It may become the fashion to serve water at dinner parties, and to argue the flavor of Mokelume River over Hetch Hetchy water.

BOTTLED WATER

Sales* of bottled water reached $36 million in 1977, a 23 percent increase over 1976. It is estimated they will increase at least that much again in 1978. (In 1970, the sales were a bare $8.7 million). Bottled water carries one of the highest gross margins of any liquid refreshment.

Perrier, an imported, naturally-carbonated water, is in the lead. For a three-month period in 1978, the Co-op sold nearly sixteen thousand bottles of the twenty-three-ounce size of Perrier. We sold nearly twelve thousand gallons of Black Mountain Spring Water (a natural spring water) and four thousand six hundred gallons of Napa Valley Spring Water (a natural mineral water).

What are some of the reasons for this increasing use of bottled water? Some people just like the taste. Others are concerned about possible health hazards from environmental pollutants that may get into municipal water supplies or substances like chlorine and fluoride that may be added to it. Still others prefer not to drink beverages that are colored, flavored or sweetened with compounds they feel may be unsafe to drink in large amounts.

It is essential that we take in the daily equivalent of eight glasses of water (more when the weather is hot). We need it to keep our bodies functioning right, take the nutrients out of the food we eat and excrete the wastes we produce. But bottled water may carry as many questionable minerals as the municipal water supply. Any water that comes out of the ground as a spring or geyser will carry minerals picked up from the soil it travels through — not to mention pesticides and industrial wastes that may have gotten into the water during its travel to the surface. Some of the minerals dissolved in drinking waters we are now finding to be essential nutrients in tiny amounts, but, like fluoride, are toxic in larger amounts.

The dilemma is that we don't know enough about what is needed and what can harm us. And we are continuing to pollute our environment more all the time.

*From *Chain Store Age/Supermarket*, November 1978.

APPLE JUICE, HUMPH!

"Apple juice is a waste of money!" said the wicked, mean, establishment-type Co-op home economist.

About Foods and Buying 109

And everybody fainted. Their sensibilities were badly bruised. Because, isn't all apple juice unsweetened? True. Isn't it so that apple juice, being pasteurized, never contains preservatives? Oh, yes! Isn't it more wholesome for kids than colas? Indeed, yes. Isn't it the loveliest refreshing cool drink on hot days? Yes, yes. Isn't it the fastest moving grocery item of any at the Telegraph Avenue Co-op? So true. Don't Co-op shoppers buy an average of five thousand gallons a week? Yes, yes, yes it's all true. So how could anyone attack apple juice?

Well, these virtues do not change the fact that in nutritive value, apple juice is forgettable. Apples themselves, though admirable for their crunchy, juicy, tooth-scrubbing, gum-exercising action, are very low in vitamins A and C, for which we usually depend on fruits and vegetables. B vitamins[1] in apples are even lower than in apricots, bananas, cherries, grapefruit, melons, and oranges, most of which are low also. Apples, like most fruits, are also low in iron.[2] Even mildly processed, unfiltered apple juice does not have more nutrients than the apple itself.

Juices that would contribute more nutrients to a meal or snack than apple juice include orange, grapefruit and tomato juices.

This wicked, mean, establishment-type Co-op home economist has quit lugging home gallons of apple juice (regularly) for another reason. I had discovered that one of my offspring would drink anything between meals to quench his thirst, except water. I should exert my labor and pocketbook to support his extravagant tastes? A pox on such food habits! Anybody drinking apple juice — or soda pop, beer, wine, etc. — just to quench thirst between meals, is spending more money than necessary on food.

In these sad days of shocking food prices, every purchase needs sharp scrutiny. Even, dear friends, apply juice!

1. Thiamine, riboflavin, niacin, pantothenic acid, pyridoxine.
2. However, canned apple juice contains a respectable amount of iron, possibly picked up in part during the canning process or from the can itself.

THE 'GUESS THE JUICE' GAME

With the decline of water as a drink (pity!) there came Kool-Aid, juice drinks, nectars, cocktails, punches and others to quench your thirst. Some, not all, contain certain amounts of juice. Juice, as you know, is the fast, modern way of drinking an apple or orange. To heck with that old tedious biting, chewing and swallowing! The game is to find out how much juice is in these thirst quenchers. Match your wits with the labels on the cans.

The Name Is the Tip-Off

You can tell a real juice, because by law the label name, with a few exceptions, is "juice." That's all, just "juice." Not juice-drink, not cocktail, not punch and not any other fancy name that sounds juicy. The label of a juice may or may not say "unsweetened" or "100 percent" or "pure," which comforts some people.

A few drinks are 50 percent juice; the other 50 percent is water, sugar, citric acid, etc. But good news! Some products say "50 percent juice" right there on the front label! Others are 35 percent or 45 percent juice.

Many products are only 6 to 12 percent juice. A few say so, right on the front. Others conceal it. Clue: try the ingredient statement on the back in small print.

Some are no juice, but how can this be? No juice at all? Actually, it's easy, starting with sugar, citric acid, cellulose gum or modified food starch, salt, artificial flavor and color, etc., etc., etc. A few of these products say "Contains No Fruit Juice." And some products give no information at all about the percent juice. Should there be a law? Well, there is, sort of. A regulation recently finalized by the Food and Drug Administration will soon require that products containing no juice must say so on the front panel of the container. Alas, low-juice products can still maintain their mystery. So we'll still, by playing games, be guessing the juice content when we buy.

Calorie Count of Beverages

Fruit sodas and collins mix 114
Root beer 100
Cola. 96
Ginger ale 76
Quinine water. 70
Soda water 0

HOMEMADE FRUIT DRINKS

Many fresh, frozen and canned fruit drinks have appeared on the market in recent years. They may be called fruit drinks, juice drinks, breakfast drinks, fruit-ades, etc., but they should not be confused with true fruit juices, which are 100 percent juice. Fruit

About Foods and Buying 111

drinks contain other ingredients, which, as required by law, are listed on the label. Generally, these products are mixtures of water, fruit juice, sugar, coloring agents and citric acid. Some (but not all) contain added vitamin C.

Judging from the increasing consumption of these drinks, they are being substituted for carbonated and cola-type beverages for children who like a between-meal drink. This substitution could be accidental — the mother does not realize that these are not pure fruit juice, or she may think these are more healthful than the carbonated products. In any case, they are expensive in terms of the actual amount of juice present in this diluted form. They are also relatively high in calories, since they average 12 percent sugar. The vitamin C content ranges from zero to about half the amount in pure orange juice.

You may prefer to make your own fruit drinks, since these are less expensive than the commercial ones and you will know what is in them. However, remember that these homemade drinks, as well as the commercial ones, should not be relied upon to supply very much of the recommended daily allowance of vitamin C. They should not replace the usual good sources of this vitamin in the daily food unless they are made with orange juice, the most concentrated source of ascorbic acid of the usual fruit juices. Three ounces of orange juice supplies the daily allowance of vitamin C for children and adolescents and adults.

To mix a drink comparable to the better commercial recipes, use the following proportions:

Fruit Juice	**Water**	**Sugar**
2 cups	4 cups	¼ - ½ cup
1 quart	2 quarts	½ - 1 cup

Citric Acid	**or Lemon Juice**
¼ teaspoon	1 tablespoon
½ teaspoon	2 tablespoons

Suggested fruit juices might be orange, pineapple, grape, grapefruit, tangerine, lemon juice, etc. Fruit nectars are often used in combination with the juices mentioned above for variety and flavor. Pineapple juice, particularly, may need the addition of some other fruit juice for a more appealing flavor. A little lemon juice added for taste may be used in place of the citric acid. The smaller amount of sugar in the above recipe yields a drink with a 5 percent sugar content; the larger amount is equivalent to 10 percent sugar.

Since fruit juices vary in sugar content, it is wise to begin with a small amount of sugar and add more if necessary.

The sugar content should be kept as low as is compatible with the "sweet taste" preferences of the children. The aim should be to create a thirst-quencher rather than a high-calorie drink.

Citric acid is the most plentiful acid in citrus fruits and is either extracted from them or prepared by the fermentation of glucose. It adds a tangy flavor to the drink. It may be purchased at most drugstores or may be sold as sour salt in some grocery stores, often with the canning supplies.

Drinks made from this recipe will keep for several days with little loss of quality or nutrients, if tightly covered and refrigerated.

Caffeine in Foods and Beverages

Colas, 12-oz., average	45 mg.
Coffee, 5-oz. cup	
Instant	65 mg.
Regular	100-150 mg.
Cocoa, 5-oz. cup	15 mg.
Decaffeinated coffee,	
5-oz. cup	3 mg.
Tea, 5-oz. cup	45 mg.
Baking chocolate,	
unsweetened, 1-oz.	25 mg.

WHEN YOU GRIND YOUR OWN COFFEE BEANS

Whole bean and ground coffee should be kept in a tightly covered container and stored in a cool, dark place — not in a refrigerator. A storage limit of one month after roasting is recommended for whole beans. After grinding, coffee should be used as soon as possible.

Different kinds of coffee beans owe their special qualities in part to the area of the world in which they are grown. Here are descriptions of some of the important types of coffee beans. We are indebted to the late Jim Hardcastle from Capricorn Coffees, supplier of Co-op Coffee Beans, for preparing this information.

Straight Coffees

Each distinctive coffee is selected and roasted after many samplings, testings and tastings. Checks are made for flavor, taste, body, aroma and acidy quality. Incidentally, the word "acidy" is misunderstood and misused by most people in reference to coffee.

In the coffee trade, the term simply means that the flavor is sharp and pleasing to the taste, that the coffee is smooth and rich and has snap and life. It does not refer to the actual amount of acid in the cup, nor does it carry the chemical connotations of sour, caustic or bitter. Coffees low in acidy flavor, by comparison, are sweet, heavy and mellow. The range in the list here is from mild and mellow to the very liveliest.

South American

Brazil Santos: The finest coffee grown there is one developed from Mocha seed – Bourbon Santos. It is smooth, has heavy body and a bittersweet taste that adds to blends, but, because its own flavor is "light," it does not detract if richer flavored straights are mixed with it. By itself a most palatable cup; it is essential in blending.

Colombian: Because of its extensive promotion, Colombian is probably the best-known coffee in the United States. However, there are many varieties and grades, and only the better varieties measure up to the claims of richness, body, flavor and aroma attributed to straight Colombian coffees.

Peruvian: Coffee from Peru compares favorably to the coffee from Colombia. This coffee is dark in color, mild in strength.

Central American

Costa Rican: This sharply acid coffee with its heavy body is particularly adaptable for use in blends.

Nicaraguan: These beans are good roasters and have fine acid. Though somewhat like the Mexican, it is difficult to make comparisons because the Nicaraguan stands apart in its own special way.

El Salvador: Noted for its good acidity and body and its mild taste, this coffee is a splendid blender. There is just enough of a winey characteristic to make this a remarkably fine cup by itself.

Antigua: This is a real treat for coffee lovers because it is considered to be one of the choicest coffees grown anywhere in the world. It is grown on table land at an altitude of between five thousand and six thousand feet in a district just west of Guatemala City. The essentials of good coffee – fine acidity, body, flavor and aroma – are indescribably combined in the Anitgua.

Guatemalan: This mountain-grown coffee makes a wonderful brew with a full, heavy body. As one would expect, this coffee is much like the Mexican in its character. More acidy, its distinction is its nutty flavor – rich and sweet.

Mexican: The bean we use is from the west coast area of Mexico and is selected because it is less acidy than some of the current varieties. Mellow, it has wonderful bouquet and rich, full body. Mexican is the preferred straight coffee of most of our customers. We use this sweet, fragrant coffee extensively in our blends.

African and Middle Eastern

Ethiopian Mocha Harrar: The coffee is remarkably spicy and aromatic, quite acid and flavorful with a taste that seems slightly sweeter than the Arabian Mocha coffee from Yemen.

Kenya: This African coffee, one of the world's superior coffees, is grown on beautiful plantations in this east African country that borders the Indian Ocean. Quite strong, it leaves a distinctive *dry* taste on the palate, a quality suggestive of the finest burgundy wines. It has a pleasing caramel-like taste. The kind of Kenya coffee we buy is difficult to obtain since it is almost all consumed in the European market.

Arabian Mocha: Our Mocha coffee comes from Yemen, a country along the Red Sea known for its superior grade of coffee. After it is roasted, this coffee has a bouquet much like sun-dried wild berries. But a taste that is reminiscent of bitter chocolate is its real claim to fame. Naturally acidy, this chocolate-like flavor, so easily detected by coffee lovers, enhances the taste and aroma of any blend into which Mocha is added.

Far East and Oceania

Celebes Kalossi: A rich, full flavor, slightly acidic with mellow, velvety undertone.

Java: Only coffees of the *Coffee Arabica* variety grown upon this island of Indonesia can be labeled "Java" in the United States, although other varieties are grown there. Partly because of this regulation, Java coffee is fast becoming rare in the United States. The fragrance released when the beans are being ground is a remarkable prelude to the spicy bouquet of a coffee in the cup.

Sumatra Mandheling: This coffee has a heavy body with a unique "smoky" flavor and aroma. The bean has a dull, flat, brown color when roasted — not at all the appearance one usually associates with good coffee. Yet this Indonesian Arabica bean is one of the world's best and truly unique.

New Guinea: Our high-grown New Guinea bean is smooth and mellow, rich in flavor and a great favorite of people who prefer a medium-strength coffee.

Roasts

Light French Roast: This French Roast is a combination of three coffees, roasted darker than the usual American type so that the natural oils come to the surface. We have blended Brazil for its bittersweet taste and for its body, Mexican for its sweetness, Colombian for its flavor.

Dark French Roast: This is the darkest of all coffees. Roasted almost to the burning point, it is quite oily in appearance. Excellent to serve with cheese, fruit, pastries and rich desserts of all kinds, it also makes a superb cafe au lait. Try it with brandy or cognac, or with liqueurs.

Italian Roast (Espresso): In color it actually lies between the two French Roasts. This is a combination of four coffees, roasted dark and heavy to make a fragrant, thick and creamy cup. Though designed for use in espresso machines, its excellent flavor is maintained when made at home using any method.

Brazil New Orleans-Type Roast: This is a darker roast, falling between Light French Roast and Italian Espresso Roast for a New Orleans-type coffee that is tasty alone or when used with the addition of chicory imported from France.

Blends

When one coffee is mixed with another, or several others, to achieve a different and desirable taste, the process is called *blending.* We consider blending both an art and a science. Behind the blend that makes a satisfying cup is the specialized knowledge about each coffee used. And just as colors are put together considering tone, intensity, hue, depth, brilliance, etc., so are coffees put together to produce the utmost in fullness, fragrance and flavor. Of the many blends possible, here are two famous ones.

Mocha-Java blend: Everyone seems to have heard of the combination of Mocha with Java. These coffees were available before coffees were produced in many other parts of the world, and it was learned years ago that when these two were combined, the product was a delightful and unforgettable taste experience. Blenders vary their proportions, so a Mocha-Java blend can vary in taste considerably from place to place.

New Orleans blend: A tradition in the Mississippi Delta country and extending throughout the Appalachian area. In recent years the substitution of inferior coffee to cut production costs has tended to downgrade this famous old blend. As originally made, chicory imported from France was combined with Bourbon Santos, which had been brought up to a French Roast; that is, the beans had been roasted high enough to bring the natural oil of the coffee to the surface. We have turned back to this traditional blend, bringing it back to its old standards, hoping to restore it to a pungent, strong, rich and creamy drink.

Others

French Chicory: The root of a plant grown in France, chicory is cured, roasted, ground for export and used as a coffee enhancer. It adds a rich, bittersweet flavor to coffee. Chicory is used for blending only. Use one-fourth chicory to three-fourths coffee.

TEA, A PLEASURABLE BEVERAGE

Tea is the world's most popular beverage next to water.

The story of tea is so ancient that its origins are lost in time. It most certainly has been refreshing palates and quenching thirsts for at least four thousand years. Tea is crucial to the economy of many of the countries of the world. India, Ceylon and China, among others, count on tea for a large part of their export income.

A wide variety of tea is available on the market, and a tea drinker must make his or her choice on the basis of flavor, fragrance, color and cost. The following descriptions and glossary of tea terms may help you find your way through the maze of tea choices. If you have always bought only one kind, be daring and try another.

Black, Green and Oolong

Black tea has been allowed to ferment before drying; Green tea is dried immediately after plucking. Oolong is different; it's between green and black in flavor. It's partially fermented (and sometimes flavored with jasmine blossoms). All come from the same plant. A cup of tea of moderate strength contains about one-half the caffeine in a cup of coffee of moderate strength.

Tea should be stored in an airtight container to preserve its freshness.

Black and Green teas are classified according to leaf size. The larger the leaf, the "poorer" the quality. About 97 percent of the tea drunk in the United States is black. Black teas in order of increasing size of leaf: Flowery Pekoe, Orange Pekoe, Pekoe, Pekoe-Souchong, Souchong. Very small and broken leaves called Fannings are usually used in tea bags. The word "Pekoe" refers to the downy appearance on the underside of young leaves, and the word "orange" to the color of the tips of still younger leaves.

Some other terms describe the geographic source of the tea. They indicate flavor differences, not quality necessarily.

Assam: These teas from the Assam province of India are "robust." Growing at a relatively low altitude probably contributes to their characteristic flavors.

Ceylon: Teas from this area are grown at four thousand feet or higher; their strong aroma probably relates to the slower maturation of leaves at this altitude.

Darjeeling: Teas from this area in northeastern India grow at an altitude of seven thousand feet; it is considered by many to be the best of Indian teas.

Keemun: Refers to a tea originally coming from the province of that name in China; its flavor is described as sharp or winey.

"Herb Teas": There are, of course, dozens of herb teas available. These are not true teas, but are dried herbs, which are steeped in boiling water to make a hot drink. Two of the most popular are Peppermint and Camomile. As with tea, herb drink preferences are personal. Experiment until you find your favorites.

A Glossary of Other Tea Terms

These terms have come into common use for various reasons:

Earl Grey. This mixture of Indian and Ceylon black teas originally referred to a special blend made up for the private use of a British nobleman, an importer of teas over one hundred years ago. There is no longer a copyright on the name, so any blend of teas can legally be called "Earl Grey." One's choice depends on individual preference.

English Breakfast. This term usually refers to black tea from China or of the Chinese type. The term is an American term, not used in England.

Lapsang Souchong. This strong tea has a smoky flavor due to the baking of the tea leaves over smoking fires. It is black tea, usually from Taiwan.

Brewing Teas and Herbs

Tea is unlike coffee in that there is only one good way to prepare it as far as devoted, orthodox tea drinkers are concerned.

1. Use a preheated pot, preferably earthenware, as it retains the heat well.

2. Allow about one teaspoon tea leaves per six-ounce cup of water (three-fourths of a measuring cup). If you prefer a weaker brew, use less tea.

3. Heat freshly drawn water just to the point of a brisk boil. This is important to prevent the driving off of dissolved air and carbon dioxide.

4. Add the tea to the pot and pour water over leaves; allow to steep for three to five minutes.

5. Serve immediately, or pour into a heated teapot, removing tea leaves in the process. Longer steeping extracts the tannins in tea, which make it bitter, and drives off the volatile oils that are responsible for the aroma.

CAROB OR COCOA?

Carob powder is a brown powder that tastes surprisingly like cocoa. It comes from pods of a large evergreen tree that grows in any climate suitable for orange trees. The pods, which look like a large insect, may have been the "locusts" that St. John the Baptist ate in the wilderness. So, the carob pods are also called St. John's Bread.

Carob Versus Cocoa

Carob powder is a welcome substitute for those who are allergic or sensitive to chocolate and cocoa. In addition, since cocoa is one of the sources of caffeine (and a related compound called theobromine) carob can be used by those who wish to avoid these stimulants.

Carob powder is about 1½ percent fat, while cocoa is from 8 to 24 percent fat. Chocolate, from which cocoa comes, is 53 percent fat.

Carob powder can be used to make a milk drink like cocoa, using the same recipe. I find the carob drink pleasant and quite acceptable, though chocolate freaks may notice differences. Carob is lower in fat than cocoa, but when made into a beverage with milk the difference in calories and fat is slight.

Carob in Junk Foods

Carob used in candies in place of chocolate or cocoa has no nutritional advantage, to my knowledge. In order to make a candy

About Foods and Buying

of acceptable texture, fat must be added to make up for the lack of fat in carob. The chocolate-like coating on malt balls and various nuts has hydrogenated vegetable oil as its largest ingredient, followed by sugar, then whey, and finally carob. These products are essentially high-fat, high-sugar junk food and the shrewd shopper should be wary of them.

6

Beans and Nuts

DRY BEANS, ANCIENT AND HONORABLE

Since prehistoric times, new bean recipes have been emerging from the kitchens of inspired cooks in every corner of the world. Because their flavor is bland, beans can be agreeable even when combined with the most preposterous ingredients. Consider sweetening with molasses, brown sugar or fruit, adding tartness with vinegar, wine, tomatoes or sour cream; adding pepperiness with mustard, chili or curry; thickening with cornmeal or rice; combining with meat, fish or cheese — to mention only a few! Join the hosts of anonymous cooks of history, and make up your own recipe.

Dry beans can be substituted for meat to make an economical meal. Figure about one and one-half cups cooked beans as equivalent to three ounces of cooked meat. To improve the quality of the protein in the beans, include in the same meal a cereal food or a small amount of animal protein food. Many bean recipes include some meat or cheese. A cottage cheese salad or custard for dessert accomplishes the same thing. Beans also provide calcium, iron, and B vitamins.

Cranberry, pinto, pink, red, and kidney beans are similar and can be used interchangeably in recipes. White beans, including Great Northern, small whites, navy or pea beans are similar enough to be interchangeable. Mung beans are similar to split peas. Black beans are whitish inside, cooking up to a gray color if broken. Lima beans, blackeye beans, garbanzos and soybeans have somewhat more distinctive textures or flavors than the others. Soy and mung beans are both commonly used for bean sprouts.

Packaged dry beans need only be rinsed and any imperfect beans removed. Beans purchased in bulk many require more careful picking over before rinsing.

Beans may be soaked overnight. Or, boil one cup dried beans in two to three cups water for two minutes. Set aside. Soak one hour before cooking. Then proceed with your favorite recipe. Some people like to use the water in which the beans have been soaking to cook the beans. Note: lentils and split peas do not need soaking.

How long to cook: Blackeye peas, lentils, split peas, lima beans, and whole peas: one-half to one hour. All others: one and one-half to two hours. Do not cook beans at a rapid boil, because they tend to break up. Gentle cooking, or simmering, helps prevent this. Beans that have been stored several months take longer to cook.

Adding seasonings: Do not add acid foods such as tomatoes or vinegar until beans are almost tender, as the acid delays the softening of the beans and so makes longer cooking necessary. Salt may be added at any time after soaking. Figure about one teaspoon salt per cup of dry beans if no other salty food is being added, such as salt pork. Meats, onions, celery and herbs add more flavor if added during cooking rather than after beans are cooked.

To help prevent foaming during cooking: Add about one tablespoon fat per cup of dry beans. This will not help much to keep large limas from foaming, however.

Using a pressure cooker: Foaming may clog the cooker vent tube; see above. In addition, fill the cooker no more than one-half full, including the water. Follow directions that come with the cooker. Pressure should rise and fall slowly so as to prevent the breaking of beans.

At high altitudes or where water is hard: Increased cooking time is required.

Freezing bean dishes: Cooked beans freeze well and will keep four to six months in a freezer.

More Beans: Soybeans, Black Beans and Mung Beans

Soybeans differ from other dry beans in that they are higher in protein, lower in carbohydrate and higher in fat. The caloric value is only slightly higher than that of other beans, however. Soy protein has the highest quality of any vegetable protein.

Soybeans are an important crop in the United States as animal feed and as a source of many important food products for man, including soy sauce, soybean curd or tofu, miso, soy oil, soy protein, and lecithin. Soy flour, used in the proportion of one-sixth cup with five-sixths cup wheat flour in place of one cup of wheat flour, improves the nutritive value of breads and other baked goods. This is because the soy flour has more protein, calcium and certain B vitamins than wheat flour, and because the proteins of the two flours complement each other as well.

Dry soybeans can be cooked as are other dry beans and substituted for them in most recipes. Because of their higher percentage of protein, they tend to foam somewhat more than other beans and take longer to cook. They are firmer than most other beans and have a delicious, nut-like flavor. To make them as tender as other beans, they should be cooked in a pressure cooker.

Black beans are also called turtle beans or turtle soup beans. These small black beans are whitish inside. They are used extensively in South America. They should be soaked and cooked as are most other beans. Cook at least two hours after soaking to make tender.

Mung beans are small dark green beans native to India. They are used for bean sprouts or can be cooked into a thick soup or mush. Botanically they are related to the more common beans, such as limas and white beans, and their chemical composition is similar. If mung beans are not available, split peas can be substituted for them in recipes.

Tofu

This low-cost protein backbone of the East Asian diet (for more than two thousand years) was discovered by a Chinese prince in 140 B.C. Tofu, also known in the West as bean curd or soybean cake, is the most important soybean food for more than one billion people, and is prepared fresh each morning in thousands of shops in Japan alone. Now widely available in many parts of the United States, tofu is becoming popular among a growing number of nutrition and cost-conscious people.

Tofu is white in color, bland tasting, rather cheeselike in consistency. It is added to soup or combined with meat and vegetable dishes or eaten as is, seasoned with soy sauce. It is versatile enough to become an indispensable ingredient in many of your favorite Western dishes including dressings, spreads, dips, and hors d'oeuvres; salads, sandwiches, soups and sauces, egg, vegetable and grain preparations; barbecued and deep-fried specialties; casseroles and even desserts.

Tofu is prepared from soybeans that are soaked overnight, then ground, boiled and strained through a cloth. The addition of either calcium chloride or calcium sulfate to the liquid results in the precipitation of the white curd, which is cut into blocks, covered with water, and sold in cartons in the refrigerated sections of the produce departments in supermarkets. The residue from the preparation of tofu, called kirazu, is also eaten but is not generally available in stores.

A quarter pound of tofu has about eighty-five calories, has eight to ten grams of protein and five grams of fat, most of which is unsaturated. Since it comes from vegetable sources, the fat contains no cholesterol. Tofu is a fairly good source of iron and quite a good source of calcium (13 percent and 19 percent of the U.S. RDA, respectively, in one-fourth pound).

MISO

Miso might have been used in that tasty soup served to you as a first course in a Japanese restaurant. It is a fermented blend of rice, soybeans and salt. It has the consistency of peanut butter and has a flavor all its own. Because it is so high in salt, it keeps well without refrigeration for long periods of time. Once opened, it should be refrigerated. It comes in several varieties from light colored to almost black. Do not add salt to recipes in which you use miso until you have tasted them — one-fourth teaspoon salt equals one teaspoon soy sauce or two teaspoons miso.

Miso has a pleasant, rather nutty flavor that complements a wide variety of foods. The Japanese use it mainly in soup and as a preservative for pickled vegetables. However, it can be used as a flavoring for fish, shellfish, fresh vegetables (raw or cooked), and meats. Experiment with it, mixing it with cream cheese for a dip or spreading it thinly on raw vegetable slices for a snack or hors d'oeuvre.

Peanut Butter

Does your child demand peanut butter on his toast for breakfast? If so, please keep cool. He is making a most nutritious choice!

About Foods and Buying 125

Peanut butter is a good source of protein, as are other members of the bean or legume family, and can be used as a substitute for meat. Protein quality is improved when bread or other grain is eaten at the same meal, or when small amounts of animal protein food such as milk, eggs or meat are included in the meal. Unlike other legumes, peanuts and peanut butter are very high in fat, about 50 percent. One tablespoon of peanut butter is almost one hundred calories.

Early in the 1900s, peanuts were developed as a crop to enrich depleted soils in the South by the famous black scientist, George Washington Carver. Of the more than three hundred by-products of peanuts developed by Carver and others, peanut butter is certainly one of the best known and loved. Strangely enough, the use of peanut butter has not spread much beyond the United States. Most other countries grow peanuts mainly for the oil.

Any product called "peanut butter" must conform to government standards. This means that it contains at least 90 percent peanuts, with the remaining 10 percent limited to sweeteners, hardened vegetable oil (stabilizer) and salt. Products containing less than 90 percent peanuts may call themselves "peanut spreads." Added vitamins, artificial sweeteners or flavorings, etc., are not permitted. If hydrogenated vegetable oil is added, the peanut oil does not separate from the peanut butter. The product spreads easily. Such peanut butters are often called "homogenized."

Another type of peanut butter on the market consists of just peanuts and salt or even of peanuts alone. Sometimes called "old fashioned" or "natural," these products have a stronger peanut flavor, and the peanut oil tends to rise to the top of the jar upon standing. They are harder to spread and do not keep quite as well, but true peanut better fanciers love them. In blind taste tests, people can easily tell one type from the other and tend to have decided preferences. For best quality, stir in the oil and store in the refrigerator. Remove a short time before using to let it soften.

BROWSING AMONG THE BEANS

In the cheap old days, about two years ago, you could take ten cents worth of dry beans and make a marvelous old-fashioned toy called a "beanbag." This device for amusing kids and old folks alike could be made into all kinds of shapes, even like a clown, with arms and legs! It could be hurled gloriously into the air, or perched rakishly on top of the bookcase, with one leg dangling over the edge.

But no more. Beanbags can no longer be classed as inexpensive. And it is even urgent to browse among the beans, dry or canned, comparing prices before buying. For food, that is! It's a good idea, too, to compare the cost of beans with meat or other high-protein foods. Then decide which to buy.

When comparing cost of raw food versus cooked food, such as canned, consider the changes that take place during cooking. For example, meat shrinks in size and weight when baked or broiled, due to dripping of fat and evaporation of water. The protein is thus more concentrated in cooked meat than in raw. Canned tuna provides more protein per pound, and so more servings per pound, than fresh fish.

On the other hand, beans and rice or other grains take up water during preparation. So the protein in cooked beans or rice is less concentrated than in raw beans or rice. To compare the costs of the amount of raw beans that provide equal amount of protein with that of canned beans, the change in protein content must be taken into account.

It addles my brain to try to remember, when shopping, how much meat shrinks or beans swell on cooking. Therefore, I like to use rules that compare yield, or equivalent protein values such as are listed here.

This rule-of-thumb takes into consideration the liquid added to the canned beans in processing: One pound dry beans equals about three and one-half pounds canned beans (five and one-half cups, cooked).

The easiest way to compare dry or canned beans with meat, fish, etc., is by number of servings per pound, with each serving having about the same amount of protein. The servings below each have about twenty grams protein, about one-third the recommended daily protein intake for an average size adult:

>1 pound dry beans = 5 servings
>1 pound raw boneless lean meat = 4 servings
>1 pound raw fat and bony meat = 1-2 servings
>1 pound canned beans = 1½ servings

It was most illuminating! By the above rules, dry red beans were more expensive per serving than canned kidney beans, and just about the same as regular ground beef. Try it yourself. You, too, will be amazed!

A GASSY SUBJECT

Shoppers keep asking the home economists which beans produce the smallest amount of gas, medically called flatus or flatulence. Well, the scientists are working on this problem and now have a few answers for us. This is important economically in light of the protein shortages worldwide, because beans and legumes are the cheapest sources of protein we have available to us.

Beans contain some complex carbohydrates. Humans do not have the enzymes needed to digest these compounds. However, when these substances reach the large intestine, some of the millions of bacteria present in this portion of the gut can break them down. The result is that gas is produced — largely hydrogen and carbon dioxide.

Scientists at the USDA Western Regional Research Laboratory in Albany, California, tried to isolate these offensive carbohydrates and breed a silent bean. So far, they have failed.

Dr. Michael Levitt, whose research was done at the University of Minnesota Medical School, has determined that the average person on a normal diet passes between 400 and 1200 milliliters of gas daily. If one assumes as an average 800 milliliters per person, then 280 trillion milliliters of wind are broken around the world each day. That's more than enough to fill several Goodyear blimps!

However, Dr. Louis Rockland at Western Regional Research Lab has come up with a "flatulence rating." He says his list is a preliminary one and might prove incorrect after further tests are completed. So take it with a grain of salt. Number one is the gassiest and number ten the least:

1. Soybeans
2. Pink beans
3. Black beans
4. Pinto beans
5. California small white beans
6. Great Northern beans
7. Lima beans, baby
8. Garbanzos
9. Lima beans, large
10. Blackeyes

Dr. Rockland says that cooking soybeans with an equal portion of rice eliminates about two-thirds of their flatulence. Also rumor has it that peppermint will control flatulence, and that is why there is often a dish of peppermint candy next to the cash register in restaurants.

A San Francisco nurse writing in the American Journal of Nursing recommends headstands on the theory that gas rises. "The methods usually recommended to relieve gas pains proved either inappropriate or ineffective. Walking, though popular with the hospital staff in cases of stubborn and intractable flatulence because it gets the patient out of bed and out of sight and hearing, provides only temporary relief," nurse Ardith Blackwell wrote.

References: The list of beans is from *"The Books of Lists"* by Wallechinsky and Wallace, 1977. The rest is from an article by Donald Zochert in *The Calgary Herald* for July 2, 1977.

NEWS ABOUT NUTS

A favorite snack in my family is walnuts in the shell. When hunger pangs strike at 9 p.m. after a small dinner, the bowl of walnuts gets attacked by hand, hammer and nutcracker. Every so often, the shelled nut reveals a dark, dried, mysterious lump only remotely resembling a walnut kernel. A fossilized walnut? No, a mistreated one. Nuts have a high oil content and unless they are handled with tender loving care, they tend to get rancid, shrivelled and otherwise unappealing. So, cover them tightly and store in the refrigerator or freezer for the months ahead. Family, friends and neighborhood squirrels will thank you.

Nuts in the shell are about $1.25 per pound. About half is waste, bringing the cost of the kernels to $2.50. Shelled walnuts are $1.66 for six and one-half ounces or $4 per pound. Pecans are $1.63 for six ounces or just over $4 per pound. At today's prices they are interchangeable. Normally, pecans are a lot more expensive. In that case, try substituting walnuts. They work in most recipes. And how about some of the soybean products that are similar to nuts? An eight-ounce jar of Soy Nuts is 99¢ — half the price of tree nuts. Try grinding toasted ones in a blender or grinder for a few seconds to coarsely chop them, and use in cookies and breads. Their flavor is distinctive, so be sure you like it before tossing them into the chocolate chip cookie batter.

Peanuts, not botanically a nut but a legume, are probably the least expensive "nut" and are good in some cookies, homemade trail mix, or for the evening "quick, my stomach is empty" snack. A twelve-ounce bag of peanuts in the shell costs 69¢.

About Foods and Buying 129

As noted above, nuts in the shell are generally less expensive than shelled nuts. One pound in the shell will yield approximately one-half pound of kernels. Try to avoid nuts with cracks, holes, mold and discoloration or stains. Soft, rubbery or shrivelled kernels indicate a definite lack of that TLC we talked about before. Discard moldy nuts, as they are not safe to eat.

If preservatives are used on packaged nuts, the label will so indicate.

IS THERE A GREAT ANTI-VEGETABLE-PROTEIN-BALANCING CONSPIRACY?

"Why don't you tell people how to balance vegetable proteins?" "Why do you discourage eating vegetable protein?" "Why?" "Why?" We've gotten many such letters, some quite angry.

Some of these responses were to a line in our ad under beans. "Add a little animal protein for better utilization of bean protein." I'm getting rather defensive on this issue because I see no way that such a sentence indicates an anti-vegetable protein conspiracy.

We haven't said much about balancing of amino acids by mixing vegetable proteins because it doesn't seem to be a practical problem with many people in this country. We do encourage eating vegetable protein: We include vegetable proteins in Lifeline, we publish low-meat and no-meat recipes, and we encourage eating less meat. Here is our position:

Americans eat too much meat. And Americans eat almost double the protein they need. Where does the extra protein go? It becomes calories just like carbohydrate and fat. It is hard not to get enough protein if you eat a varied diet that meets your calorie needs and which includes grains, beans, dairy foods, eggs, and vegetables.

Eating most of our protein and much of our calories in animal form and eating more protein than we "need" is very wasteful of resources. *Diet for a Small Planet* by Frances Lappe is a very important book because it awakened many people to this possibility.

My family's personal response in the last few years (and maybe the response of the Co-op home economists and other nutritionists) has been to cut way down on meat and to increase use of grains and beans but not to cut out meat altogether. Many people are vegetarians for moral, religious, health or ecological reasons. I think the home economists have been supportive of people who've decided to cut out meat completely. From a practical standpoint we probably end up with more "protein saved" by convincing many people to cut down on meat and excess protein than to convince a few to be vegetarians. But I feel: to each his/her own.

Protein balancing should be no problem for vegetarians who eat milk, cheese and eggs. "Having a little animal food at each meal" is good advice. (Example: milk complements protein of oatmeal.)

Strict vegetarians (no dairy products or eggs) may need some advice on balancing proteins. The main thing to remember is that grains and beans (or other legumes such as peanuts) complement each other. Also, a wide variety of food is important. Protein balancing becomes more important when protein intake is very low. I don't think the detailed balancing advocated by Ms. Lappe is necessary in this country.

Protein may be the least of your problems if you are a vegetarian. In the average American diet meat, milk and eggs provide one-third to two-thirds of the major vitamins and minerals, except vitamin C. Milk is important for calcium and riboflavin. Meat provides iron, niacin, zinc. Vitamin B-12 is found only in animal foods. As we decrease the sources of our food, we decrease the chance that we will meet all our nutrient needs. This doesn't mean it's impossible, but strict vegetarian diets need careful planning for all nutrients, not just protein.

Experimental evidence seems to indicate that it's possible to plan an adequate strict vegetarian diet for healthy adults. I don't think we know enough to say such diets will be adequate for children, pregnant women or people in poor health.

(From the Idaho Bean Commission)

7

Breads and Cereal Foods

GRAINS ... ODD AND INTERESTING

Who eats grains? Who eats all that corn, wheat, oats, barley, rye, millet, rice?

Well, everybody. All of us chickens, cows, hogs, and humans eat grains. In fact, 70 percent of what we humans eat is grain! Either we eat it directly, or we eat the chickens, the cows, the hogs who eat it.

We're on quite intimate terms with processed grains such as flour, bread, breakfast cereals. But now the Co-op is carrying the whole grain seeds — merely harvested, threshed and cleaned — in the bulk sections of our produce departments. These are strange, unfamiliar. How does one cook these hard kernels of barley, rye, wheat? Searching for answers to this question and others, we stumbled over odd and interesting facts about whole as well as processed grain.

In some parts of the world people get 60 percent of their calories from grain or grain products, eaten directly. Here we get only 21 percent of our calories from such foods. We used to eat more! In 1969 we each ate one hundred fourteen pounds of grain foods; fifty years earlier it was three hundred nine pounds per year. Now, we spend only 13 percent of our food dollars for grains, though from grains we get 20 to 40 percent of our protein, iron and the three major B vitamins.

Some processing, such as refining wheat into white flour, results in loss of important nutrients, which is partly compensated in the enrichment of white flour and rice. Other processing is less damaging: Parboiled rice is more nutritious than regular white rice. While both are enriched with iron, thiamine and niacin, parboiled rice such as Uncle Ben's Converted Rice contains over twice the vitamin B_6 that ordinary white rice contains and almost three-fourths of that of brown rice. That's because this process involves steaming the rice before milling, during which some of the water-soluble nutrients are absorbed into the white kernel.

Microflaked wheat or rye are whole grains. They have been briefly heated (five seconds at 220 degrees) and then rolled to crush them slightly. The nutritive value of these whole but slightly crushed grains should be good, and they are fairly fast cooking. Because they are more tender, too, when cooked, they may be more acceptable to people unaccustomed to the chewiness of relatively hard-to-digest wheat berries.

Cooking guide for whole grains: Start with one cup of grain in two cups of water or broth and one-half teaspoon of salt. Cook until done. Here is a rough guide for time:

15-30 minutes: Cracked wheat, bulgur, white rice, buckwheat, microflaked wheat or rye (millet thirty-five minutes); 45-60 minutes, sometimes more: Brown rice, barley, whole oats, triticale, rye; two hours: Wheat berries. Pressure cooking works well for long-cooking grains; brown rice cooks in eight minutes.

WHEAT AND WHEAT PRODUCTS

Wheat is the grain of a grass that probably originated in the Euphrates Valley thousands of years ago. It is the most widely grown of all cereal grains. In the United States, the colonists brought wheat to our country quite early but, because the climate on the East Coast was unfavorable, it was not until the Midwest was opened to homesteading that wheat became a major crop.

The wheat grain has three main parts: 1) the outer covering, the bran, 2) the inner part, which is largely starch, called the endosperm and 3) the tiny nucleus within the endosperm, the wheat germ that is responsible for the sprouting of the wheat kernel. If the entire wheat kernel (also called the wheat berry) is ground, we have whole wheat (or graham) flour. If only the endosperm is ground, we have white flour. Hard or soft wheats are used for making various kinds of flour: soft wheat for pastry, cake and all-purpose flours, and hard wheats for bread flours and pasta. Many all-purpose flours are mixtures of hard and soft wheats and so contain enough high-quality gluten (found more abundantly in hard wheat) to make satisfactory bread when well-kneaded.

Store flours at cool room temperatures in tightly closed containers. Whole wheat flour should be stored in as cool a place as possible and not kept for more than three months unless refrigerated. The whole wheat products all tend to become rancid due to the presence of fat in the wheat germ. Because the germ is missing in white flour, it can be stored much longer than whole wheat.

In most states, the law requires that all white flour and products made from it must be enriched — the levels of thiamin, riboflavin, niacin and iron are restored to about their original levels in the whole grain. (Nutrients *not* added back include zinc, vitamin B_6 and others.) These products must also be nutrition labeled and also have an ingredient statement. You may wonder why malted barley is added to most white flours. It is added to standardize the enzyme level so the yeast action will be more uniform from batch to batch of white flour.

Besides the various types of wheat flours, wheat is marketed as the whole wheat berry, cracked wheat, which is the berry coarsely ground; hot and cold breakfast cereals, bulgur (parboiled wheat), wheat flakes, wheat germ and various kinds of crackers.

A Pasta Primer

Simply defined, pasta is a dough made from semolina and water. Semolina is the heart of the durum wheat; high in gluten, it contributes the protein to grains. Much pasta, of which there are more than one hundred varieties, is made from this basic dough. The different shapes are produced either by forcing the dough through a variety of perforated metal plates, forming in molds, or pressing through rollers before drying. Egg noodles are made from the same basic mixture, to which at least 5.5 percent of egg solids must be added. Vegetable macaroni is pasta to which not less than 3 percent vegetable solids have been added. These vegetables may include tomato, artichoke, beet, carrot, parsley or spinach, either fresh, canned or dried. It is difficult to analyze the precise nutritive value of these vegetable pastas. Both the egg solids and vegetable solids contribute a small plus to the diet, but probably not of any great significance.

Some of the more imaginative Italian names for pasta include farfalloni (big butterflies), linguini (little tongues), occhi di lupo (wolf's eyes), rigatoni (little fluted ones), vermicelli (litte worms), and stelline (little stars). Not all of these are widely available, but many are fun to use for a change.

DELIGHTFULLY DIFFERENT: BULGUR

Bulgur is a food that may be made from several varieties of wheat. The bulgur is processed by boiling whole grain wheat, drying it, removing some of the outside bran particles and cracking the kernel. For many centuries, bulgur has been produced in various countries of the world where hand methods are used.

Today, modern food technology has provided methods for mass production of bulgur, making it widely available. It may be of fine, medium or coarse grain, depending on the need for different granulations for various cooking uses. Bulgur is a versatile, nutritious product roughly comparable to brown rice in nutrients. It may be used as a cereal, an ingredient in soup or salad, a side dish with the main course, or as the main dish when a small amount of meat, fish, poultry or cheese is added. It can be substituted for rice in most menus and recipes. Some people may find that the roughage in bulgur is more than their digestive systems can easily tolerate. If so, we suggest combining bulgur with enriched white rice for a colorful, tasty combination.

Questions and Answers on Bread Enrichment

Q. What does enrichment of breads and cereals mean?

A. It simply means adding to refined flour, bread and cereals the most important vitamins and minerals lost in the milling. Specifically, this means restoring thiamine, riboflavin, niacin and iron to the level present in the whole grain products.

Q. If extra fat, milk solids, sugar, eggs, etc., are added to give richness, why is it necessary to add vitamins and minerals?

A. While these ingredients improve the flavor, and some of them may improve nutritional qualities somewhat, they do not add thiamine, riboflavin, niacin or iron in sufficient amount.

Q. Why don't you forget about adding things to white bread and promote the use of whole grain cereals only?

A. For years nutritionists have tried to do this. However, the widespread acceptance of white bread and refined cereals makes it

About Foods and Buying 135

imperative that these products be made nutritionally as close as possible to the whole grain products.

Q. Do foods made with unbleached flour need to be enriched?

A. Yes. White flour needs enrichment whether it is bleached or unbleached. It is the milling of flour that takes away the B vitamins and iron.

Q. What about white rice? Should it be enriched?

A. Yes. However, enrichment of rice differs in that riboflavin, a yellowish vitamin, is not added because of technical problems. Note: The added vitamins and iron will be washed off.

FLOUR POWER

A Question Often Asked by Shoppers

I see many kinds of flour in the store. What are their basic differences and how can I use them?

1. Whole wheat flour: Made from the whole kernel of wheat and contains the bran as well as the germ. It has more minerals, vitamins and slightly more protein than enriched white flour. Because of higher fat content, whole wheat flour does not keep as well as white flour.

2. All-purpose flour: Usually made from fairly hard wheat and is satisfactorily used for quick breads, raised or fermented breads, and pie crust. It may contain too much gluten to make delicate textured cakes but can make successful cakes that have a high fat or high sugar content such as butter cakes, pound cakes, fruit cakes and cookies.

3. Cake and pastry flour: These flours are both made from soft wheat and have a low gluten content. Cake flour is bleached and is the most finely ground of all the flours. It is soft and satiny. Chief use is for cakes and pastries but may be used for quick breads. These flours may be more desirable for waffles than all-purpose flour because they make a more tender product.

4. Bleached and unbleached: Both whole wheat and white flours may be bleached or unbleached. Bleached is chemically treated to age it and unbleached is aged naturally. Because the "age" of unbleached flour varies, the handling of yeast doughs may not be consistent from batch to batch. Aging improves rising power.

5. Self-rising flour: This is refined bleached flour that contains leavening and salt in proper proportions for home baking. The leavening will lose its potency if stored too long. This is not recommended for making bread or pastry.

Wheat flour is the most extensively used flour because of its high content of the protein gluten. The only other flour that contains much gluten is rye. Gluten is important for its binding and stretching qualities, making it possible for yeast breads to have a high volume and a fine texture. It stretches and forms an elastic frame-work to enclose bubbles of gas produced by the yeast. In other baked products, fat and/or sugar cut the gluten strands, thus making a more tender product.

Whole Wheat Bread Has More: True or False?

1. Whole wheat bread has better protein, more vitamins and more minerals than enriched white bread, other ingredients being equal.

True. Several essential nutrients in whole flour are largely lost in the milling and are not added back in the enriching, including magnesium, calcium, potassium, phosphorus, manganese, molybdenum, vitamin B_6, pantothenic acid and vitamin E.

2. The darker the color of bread, the more whole wheat flour it contains and the more nutritious it is.

False. Many breads have caramel color added, including some "wheat" breads and many rye or pumpernickel breads. Some very dark breads have less whole grain wheat or rye than lighter colored breads. Egg breads or rolls frequently have yellow color added. Read the ingredient statement.

3. Breads called "Wheat Bread" and those with fancy names such as "Natural," "Ecology," etc., are just as nutritious as whole wheat bread.

False. We advise you to regard fanciful names with suspicion. The magic in a name doesn't extend to transforming ingredients! "Wheat" breads and breads with seemingly wholesome names often have less whole wheat flour than enriched white flour. They are usually less nutritious than breads made with all whole wheat flour.

4. Cakes and cookies made with whole wheat flour are just about as nutritious as whole wheat bread.

False. Sorry about this! Whole wheat cookies and cake still have much larger proportions of fat and sugar than bread does and so less whole wheat. Therefore they are lower in vitamins and minerals than just good old whole wheat bread.

WHAT DO YOU SAVE BY MAKING BREAD AT HOME?

To find the answer to this question, we took recipes for two of our Co-op label breads and costed them out at current, regular prices. When we compared the cost of the homemade breads with their store equivalents, we found:

Co-op Special Formula Bread, 1½ pounds
    Store-bought $.83
    Homemade   .39 (a 53 percent savings)

Co-op Whole Wheat Bread, 1 pound
    Store-bought $.73
    Homemade   .25 (a 66 percent savings)

Further savings can be achieved if ingredients such as flour and non-fat dry milk are purchased when they are on sale. The yeast, instead of being purchased in individual packets, can be purchased in larger amounts and stored in a closed container in the refrigerator.

How much time does it take to make bread at home? Depending on the amount you make, how long you knead it, the temperature of the proofing arrangement (rising of the dough) and how many times you let it rise, the total time for the entire process will vary a bit. However, it seems reasonable to allow at least four hours. So you need to plan to be home for this length of time. Of course, you can at the same time do the ironing, house cleaning, sewing or whatever.

To make the best use of your bread-making time, make three or four loaves at once and freeze the extra ones. If you have a small family, you might make smaller-sized loaves. Larger families or those that take bag lunches with sandwiches will be able to use the larger-sized loaves easily.

TRY IT – YOU'LL LIKE IT

Working with yeast doughs can be an exhilarating and satisfying experience. This is dedicated to those who exclaim over home-baked breads, but have never tried making them.

I can still remember so clearly, and it was long ago, shivering in the hot summertime while making mud pies. How I loved to mix and shape the muddy mixture into "pie shells" that would later be filled with assorted flower petals and leaves. But, how I hated the feeling when the mud dried on my hands and left me shivering!

A decade after mud pies, I discovered yeast doughs. How delightful the dough felt while kneading and what fun it was to make it into various shapes and forms by braiding, tying, twisting, stretching, rolling or cutting. And, if I used a little flour, the dough didn't stick and then dry on my hands. That was even better than mud pies. There's no excuse, but some people keep trying. Such as:

Excuse No. 1: There's no time to make bread because of the forty-hour work week. That's a matter of priorities. All you need is to be available for small periods of time when the dough needs attention — it doesn't need to be watched every minute. For instance, on a Saturday morning, you can garden, saw, plant, clean, paint, sew or even run short errands to the store while the dough is rising. And, after a few tries, the whole process will probably take no more than three and one-half hours from start to finish.

The time schedule runs like this:

Assembling ingredients and mixing	20 minutes
First rising	45 minutes
Second rising	30 minutes
Shaping dough into loaves	10 minutes
Rising of dough in pans	60 minutes
(pre-heat oven the last 10 minutes of rising time.)	
Bake at 375 degrees	15 minutes
Bake at 325 degrees	25 minutes
Total	205 minutes
	(about 3½ hours)

Excuse No. 2: It takes an expert to make good bread. No way! Experienced bakers accept the fact that the bread will vary from time to time because of the protein content of the flour, the freshness of the yeast, temperature variations while doughs are rising, or just plain differences in mixing techniques from one batch to another. You can do the same.

Helpful suggestions for the beginner: (1) Keep the dough warm but not too warm. Growing yeast (in the dough) prefers a temperature about 80 degrees — this is slightly warmer than the usual

About Foods and Buying 139

room temperature. However, avoid a temperature above 90 degrees because it will kill the yeast; if that happens, the dough will rise no more and, if baked, will be "as heavy as a ton of lead." (2) Use unbleached all-purpose white flour or half all-purpose flour and half whole-grain flour. Until you get the "feel" of yeast doughs, it is better not to use only whole-grain flours. The latter, though more tasty in breads and more nutritious, will produce a coarser and heavier product than white flours. And it would be all too easy to equate the "heavy" product with failure.

To this day, I am envious of the potters shaping clay with their hands (likening it to making mud pies), but I revel in the fact that they cannot boast of a wonderful fragrance when "baking" their wares.

WHY LIME IN CORN TORTILLAS?

The ingredient statement on La Tolteca Corn Tortillas is very simple: corn, water and lime (calcium hydroxide). We have had objections from shoppers to the lime, which they fear might be harmful.

Let's talk about it. Corn tortillas are the ethnic "bread" from old Mexico, using the native corn. It was the "staff of life" for most Indians in Mexico long before the white man introduced his favorite foods. Whole corn is soaked in a weak solution of lime (originally derived from birdlime prepared from holly bark or from limestone) to loosen the outer hull. When this is removed, the germ remains with the kernel and small traces of lime are present in the corn. The corn is then ground, mixed with water, pressed into flat cakes and baked on a flat, hot surface. This limed cornmeal has a characteristic flavor.

Nutritionists tell us that the small amounts of calcium from the lime remaining in the corn tortillas contribute appreciable calcium to the Mexican diet when lots of tortillas are eaten and practically no dairy foods. Jack cheese is about the only dairy food eaten by Mexicans even today in sizeable amounts.

Lime (calcium hydroxide) is caustic in concentrated form and can cause skin burns. However, in the small amounts found in the finished tortilla, it is perfectly harmless and probably beneficial.

Scientists have now come up with another "educated guess" as to why the corn tortillas were such a vital part of the traditional Mexican diet. This diet was low in animal protein and corn was one of the main sources of protein. In our southern states pellagra was endemic in the poor population in the early 1900s; they were eating a diet high in cornmeal and low or lacking in animal protein. This cornmeal was not treated with lime as the Mexican corn was and it did not contain the germ. Unfortunately, corn is rich in an antivitamin that knocks out the vitamin, niacin. Corn is also low in tryptophan, one of the amino acids in proteins that the body cannot make and that therefore must be present in sufficient amounts in our foods. Tryptophan can be converted to niacin if there is enough present in the diet to first meet the protein need. But since the cornmeal was low in tryptophan, this couldn't happen and the poor people developed pellagra.

Native American Indians living in the plains of the United States and Mexico did not develop pellagra because they used wood ashes in their cooking. The ashes added lye that, like lime, produced alkaline conditions in the foods. This, so the present theory goes, inhibited the antivitamin, allowing the niacin present in the corn to be used by the body. Thus the niacin plus the tryptophan was available in sufficient amounts in the Indian diets to prevent the development of the deficiency disease, pellagra.

We need to have respect for native foods. They have been developed over many thousands of years of trial and error. They are, for the most part, beautifully tailored to meet the nutritional needs of the people eating them.

Cereals:

Champion of Breakfasts?

Q. Is cereal enough breakfast every day?

A. It is if you add orange juice and milk and maybe toast — and, if it's a "good" cereal.

Q. So, what's a good cereal?

A. One good cereal would be any whole grain in milk. A poor cereal is a high-sugar cereal such as Sugar Pops (which have up to half their weight in sugar — and sometimes more sugar is added at the table). Also not recommended are those super-fortified cereals with 100 percent of the Recommended Daily Allowance for vitamins (Kellogg's Concentrate, Total, Product 19 and many others) because you can get too much of some vitamins, especially A and D.

What You Should Expect of a Cereal

This is hard to decide, Joan Gussow states well the argument for whole grains. Cereal should contain the minerals, vitamins, protein, carbohydrate and fiber of the original grain. And of course it should taste good.

We have been exploring and pondering the criteria for rating cereals. We have finally agreed on these:

- Whole grain cereal is best.
- Hot cereal is generally more nutritious than cold.
- Added sugar is bad, especially at the levels of 30 to 35 percent found in the sugared cereals.
- Fortification, if done at all, should be at moderate and uniform levels (about 25 percent of the Recommended Daily Allowance).

Joan Gussow, professor of nutrition education at Columbia Teachers College, has this comment on cereal fortification. "The question is whether it is okay to enrich garbage. We simply don't know enough to keep someone alive on enriched garbage. The fact is that at present we take out of cereal grains all kinds of vitamins and minerals and then we "enrich" them by putting back in only those that science in its infinite wisdom has shown to be 'essential.'

"The obvious answer to what a cereal ought to contain is that it ought to contain those nutrients normally found in cereal grains, i.e., most of the trace minerals, the whole B-vitamin complex, naturally unsaturated oils, iron and protein, leaving it to other foods (e.g., fruit, fruit juices, milk, butter) to supply calcium and vitamins A, C and D at breakfast.

"Moreover, I am waging war on the side of 'natural' foods because we just don't know enough about nutritional requirements — especially where the trace elements are concerned — to take the chance of not eating natural foods."

Whole Grains Are Best

When grains are milled, many of the nutrients are removed in the outer layers and germ. When grains are fortified, some of these nutrients are added back but others are not. With the American diet becoming increasingly refined, these "minor" nutrients may be in more critical supply in our diets.

While it is true that the natural balance of nutrients in a grain has evolved for the growth and reproduction of that grain, not for the benefit of animals and man, we favor the likelihood that whole grains, with their original nutrients, are superior foods to highly refined grains with added nutrients.

'Hot' Cereal Is Generally More Nutritious Than 'Cold' Cereal

When cold (ready-to-eat) cereals are manufactured, they are subject to a lot of processing including hot, dry heat to make them crisp. This hot, dry heat is more destructive of nutrients such as thiamin and protein than is the moist heat at which hot cereals are cooked at home. (Some hot cereals such as Wheatena are toasted so we can't make a blanket statement that all hot cereals have been processed in a nutrient-saving manner.)

We suggest that you cook hot cereals in milk. We have found that people put much too little milk in a bowl of cooked hot cereal (it's already moist) than they do on a bowl of dry cereal. So, unless everyone is drinking some milk for breakfast, why not simmer the cereal in milk? (Example: Add two-thirds cup dry milk and one-half teaspoon salt to two cups water. Then add one cup rolled oats and simmer five minutes.) Other longer-cooking grains can also be cooked in milk, but you may want to use a double boiler. Another advantage: Milk consumed at breakfast sticks with you through the morning so you are less hungry than with a predominantly carbohydrate meal. The protein in the milk also complements the protein in the cereal.

Presweetened 'Cereals' Have as Much Sugar as Cookies or Cakes

We think that "cereal" is not a proper term for presweetened cereals that contain 30 to 55 percent sugar and sometimes more. A serving of cereal is about one ounce, so 50 percent of this is about a tablespoon (three teaspoons) of sugar.

While it's possible (but not likely) for someone to add this much sugar at the table to any cereal, it's impossible to separate out the sugar in a high-sugar cereal. Besides, some people add no sugar to cereal, and many add just a little.

How Much Sugar?

When we first printed *Cereal, Champion of Breakfasts?*, we wrote to every cereal company asking for their product's composition, including approximate percent of sugar. Most told us it was a trade secret, although testing for sugar is a simple matter for those with a laboratory. Finally, in the spring of 1976, Kellogg's started listing the amount of added sugar and the other cereal companies eventually followed suit. The problem is that sugar is stated as grams per ounce, which is less meaningful than percentage of added sugar by weight.

When reading labels keep in mind that one ounce of cereal weighs about twenty-eight grams and one tablespoon of sugar weighs about twelve grams. So, Cap'n Crunch, which lists twelve grams of sucrose and other sugars per ounce contains one tablespoon sugar in an average serving or approximately 43 percent sugar (12 divided by 28). Some consumer groups suggest that any cereal with a sugar content above 25 or 30 percent should not be called cereal but "sugared breakfast food."

What's so Bad About Sugar?

The average American eats more than one hundred pounds of sugar a year, for which he or she gets no nutritional benefits other than calories. Regular white sugar is 100 percent carbohydrate with no vitamins or minerals. (Brown sugar, raw sugar and honey aren't much better.) Most nutrition authorities say that one hundred pounds of sugar per person is too much. Why? 1) Sugar definitely contributes to cavities, especially in children; 2) high sugar consumption means that there isn't as much room in the diet for better foods; 3) current research has found a relationship between high sugar intake and high blood fat levels, which is suspected of contributing to heart disease.

The high-sugar cereals are mostly low in protein and without fortification they would be low in other nutrients. Sugar simply replaces the grain with its protein, vitamins and minerals.

High-sugar cereals are often eaten as snacks. This is even harder on teeth than is sugary cereal eaten with milk for breakfast because the milk and other foods help wash the sugar away from the teeth.

Percent Added Sugar

There is no added sugar in most hot cereals, or in Shredded Wheat, Puffed Rice and Puffed Wheat.

Sucrose and other sweeteners in one ounce of cereal (Divide grams sugar by 28, multiply by 100 to get percent).

Grams

1 - 11%

Cheerios 1
Corn Flakes. 2
Grapenuts 3
Product 19 3
Rice Chex 2
Rice Krispies 3
Wheat Chex. 2
Wheaties 3

12 - 20%

Life 5
Team 5

21 - 30%

All Bran. 6
Cinnamon Life 6
Corn Bran 6
C.W. Post. 7
Fortified Oat Flakes 6
Granolas . . . . approx. 9
Most 8
40% Bran. 7
100% Bran. 6
100% Natural 8

30 - 55%

Golden Grahams 11
Kellogg's and Post Raisin Bran . . . . .9 and 13
All sugar cereals. 10-16

Fortification Should Be Moderate

This is a complicated subject. Ideally our diet of food would contain all the nutrients we need. But even on a "good" diet it is hard for some people to get enough of certain nutrients — such as iron. Most ready-to-eat breakfast cereals are fortified with about eight nutrients, added at levels higher than in whole grains. This could be good for those people who are low in these nutrients and a waste for others. When we have listed hot, whole-grain cereals

About Foods and Buying 145

above refined, fortified, ready-to-eat cereals, it is based on our judgment from an accumulation of data rather than on specific research showing one is superior to the other.

You can get too much especially of vitamins A and D, which accumulate in the body. We see no reason for a single bowl of cereal to carry 100 percent of the vitamins and minerals listed as mandatory on nutrient labels. These "cereals" are essentially vitamin pills in a sugar-grain flake, puff or blob. A child of five eating two one-ounce bowls of cereal a day would eat four times his Recommended Daily Allowance of vitamin A. When you add vitamin A from milk, other foods and a vitamin pill, the child could be getting a toxic level of vitamin A over a long period.

While the hazard of too much vitamin A or D is well documented there are potential problems with imbalance of other nutrients. Examples: Increased consumption of one mineral may change the need for another mineral. Calcium and phosphorous should be consumed in approximately equal quantities daily, according to the RDA. The need for certain B vitamins is proportional to calories consumed.

Very high protein diets may increase the need for other nutrients. Long-term consumption of high levels of vitamin C may increase the need for that vitamin. These are just some of the examples of why fortification and vitamin supplementation are tricky business.

Fiber

Fiber is the indigestible carbohydrate that does not provide calories but which helps move everything along inside your digestive tract. There has been an increased interest in fiber recently.

Some nutritionists question whether Americans in their highly refined white-sugar-white-flour diets are getting enough fiber. They speculate that lack of fiber may be related to increases in colon cancer, diverticulosis and other intestinal diseases. Whole-grain cereals contain much more fiber than refined cereals. Bran cereals contain the most fiber of all but often they contain added sugar and/or fat.

Recently, eating unprocessed bran has become a popular way of adding extra fiber to the diet. We don't have much information on the long-range effects of this practice but we have been told that eating excess bran is probably not dangerous. Large amounts of bran generally cause gas, diarrhea and discomfort so that a person tends to eat only what he/she can tolerate. We recommend that people get fiber by eating unrefined basic foods such as beans and dried peas, fruits, vegetables and whole grains. These foods provide fiber as well as being good sources of a wide variety of nutrients.

Fat

Many cereals are low in fat, containing less than one gram in a one-ounce serving. But that pattern and the type of fat added are changing. Some of the cereals contain coconut or palm oil. Even though these oils are from vegetable sources, they are as saturated as some animal fats. This is a problem because diets high in saturated fats are thought to be one of the causes of heart disease. Granolas contain considerable added fat: about 20 percent or six grams per one-ounce serving. While the oil is usually not coconut or palm oil but one of the unsaturated vegetable oils, the fat does add many unnecessary calories and substitutes for the grain. We recommend selecting cereals with little or no added fat.

Additives

Some people want to avoid artificial colors or flavors or other additives such as preservatives or stabilizers. Most hot cereals, most granolas and a few other ready-to-eat cereals do not contain additives. To be sure, read the label.

Premiums

We've seen recommendations not to buy cereals with premiums. This is rather hard for a cereal-eating family to do because, except for granolas, Co-op cereals and Kellogg's Concentrate, most ready-to-eat cereals have some kind of a "premium" or offer.

8

Fruits

THE FRUIT SEASONAL HEARTBREAK

You succumb to the glowing peach. Or invest in a melon. You fetch it home, slavering. You cut, you bite it . . . and have nothing. No juiciness. No sweetness. No aroma, flavor, melting texture. It is awful!

It is our misfortune that large-scale farming and long-distance marketing make such summer fruit available when it is not really ready to eat. It becomes a matter of skill and forbearance to know, first, when fruit is worth buying and, second, how long to wait before eating it.

Chemists study the ripening of fruit in marvelous detail and still say they don't know the whole of it. One of the important happenings is a color change. The green banana turns yellow, because its chlorophyll has broken down, letting yellow pigments show through.

Softening is important. As fruit ripens, complex pectins break down to mere pectin and with over-ripeness to pectic acid. For jelly-making it is important to avoid over-ripe fruit, for the whole pectin has become pectic acid.

With sweetening, sugar increases, sometimes due to the change of starch to sugar. There may also be a decrease in acids and in puckery or astringent substances.

Aroma, that heady, characteristic fragrance of fruits, develops with ripening. Other gases form. Ethylene gas, present in all plant tissue, builds up in the fruit and at a certain stage of maturity it stimulates ripening. In some fruits this does not happen as long as the fruit is still on the tree.

Avoid seasonal heartbreak by following these rules:

1. Buy at the peak of the season. Early fruit and late fruit tend to be poorer in quality and higher in price.

2. Learn the signs of ripeness. In general, ripeness is judged by background color, fragrance and changes in texture from hard to firm to soft. Each fruit has its own typical color, odor and texture that must be recognized.

3. Ripen at home at room temperature. Don't eat until fruit is fully ripe, judging by the signs typical to that fruit. Fruits capable of ripening after harvest include peaches, pears, plums, bananas, apricots and melons.

HOW CAN I TELL IF THE FRUIT IS GOOD UNLESS I TASTE IT?

Look at the background color in muskmelons, peaches and nectarines. It should be yellow or creamy, not green. Grapes, plums and berries should have good, bright, uniform color. Pears are ripe when the flesh will yield to gentle pressure of the fingers. Depending on the variety, they may be yellow-green, green or brown when ripe.

Hard squeezing or pinching of fruit may bruise or cause spoilage. Someone must pay for fruit lost by careless handling. Smell the fruit too. When ripe, many fruits will smell like you want them to taste.

Fresh fruit in the store may only be "firm ripe" which is not quite ready to eat. Let fruit stay at room temperature for a couple of days in a bowl, or in a paper bag. It is not good to leave fruit closed in a plastic bag; it may get moldy. Don't ripen fruit directly in the sun. It will shrivel, sunburn and rot.

How to Pick a Melon

Melons, besides being delicious, are noteworthy for other reasons. They are low in calories — an average slice has about thirty. Cantaloupes and other netted varieties are good sources of vitamin C, an average serving (one-fourth of a two-pound melon) providing about one-half of an adult's recommended daily allowance. The same amount of honeydew would provide about one-third; watermelon and casaba, about one-fifth of the allowance.

About Foods and Buying

The accompanying chart should help you to get a good melon. All of the melons listed, except watermelons, may be ripened at home. Keep them at room temperature out of the direct sunlight until ripe, then store in a plastic bag in the refrigerator until ready to eat. A few melons, such as a very green honeydew, may never ripen.

Softness at the stem or blossom end of a melon may indicate ripeness in a melon that has never been handled, but may also merely mean that many people have been pressing it to see if it is ripe. This is properly a valid test only where the melon is purchased green to be ripened at home. Aroma, while an indication of ripeness, is not necessarily an indication of good flavor. Aroma is not significant in watermelon.

	APPEARANCE	TOUCH
CANTALOUPE	Thick, raised netting; yellowish color underneath. Scar should be "full slip" (smooth scar at stem end).	Should not be hard. Heavy for size. Softness around stem end.
HONEYBALL	Creamy, yellow; thin netting at blossom end. Scar should be full slip.	Slightly soft. Heavy for size.
HONEYDEW	Larger melons are usually best. Creamy white to pale yellow.	Should not be hard; slight softness at stem end. Heavy for size. Sticky rather than slick.
PERSIAN	Covered with fine netting. Color underneath should be light-green or brownish.	Surface yields to slight pressure. Heavy for size.
CRANSHAW	Smooth, golden-yellow, pointed at end.	Surface yields to slight pressure. Heavy for size. Sticky rather than slick.
CASABA	High ridges. Deep yellow; round rather than pointed.	Heavy for size. Blossom end yields to slight pressure.
WATERMELON	Yellow ground color (sometimes white).	Heavy for size; well shaped with rounded ends. Skin peels easily when scraped gently with fingernail. Should be dry rather than moist or oily. Sound when thumped is not always reliable indication.

Fruit Cocktail

In case anybody thinks canned fruit cocktail has been around forever we hasten to say that this is not quite true! Fruit cocktail required the development of some rather amazing machinery, and only became a reality in the late 1930s when one machine for chopping fruit and one for stemming grapes were invented. Considering that the stemming is done by machine, isn't it remarkable to find so few stems in the finished product?

However, when a stem does get through, it is considered a defect. Two grades for quality have been set up by the U.S. Department of Agriculture: Grade A and Grade B. Anything below this is "substandard." Quality is judged by clearness of syrup, number of defects, brightness and uniformity of color, uniformity of size, and firmness of texture. Flavor, unless it is definitely "off," is not considered because it is so hard to evaluate.

In addition, Standards of Identity were established by the Food and Drug Administration in 1942, so that any product called "fruit cocktail" must meet these standards. The amounts of different kinds of fruit that may be used are specified:

>   30 - 50 % peaches, diced
>   25 - 45% pears, diced
>   6 - 20% seedless grapes
>   6 - 16% pineapple, diced or sectioned
>   2 - 6% cherries, halved

Usually, these fruits are all fresh when canned except for the cherries and pineapple. The standards of identity also state that the sweetener added may be a syrup made with sugar, corn syrup, or dextrose in various combinations. Corn syrup is present in the syrup of practically all canned fruits.

Are private label brands of fruit cocktail a good buy? Because fruit cocktail is standardized to a degree far beyond that of most canned fruits, there is little difference between brands. When private label brands are priced below the national brands, you save when you buy them and you get about the same quality. In can cuttings performed by our home economists, Co-op fruit cocktail has compared well with Del Monte, Libby, Townhouse, and other brands. All are USDA Grade B; very little Grade A fruit cocktail is on the retail market.

Dried Fruits

Dried fruits, while not cheap, can still be considered a good buy for certain uses. They are easy to store and transport because of their concentrated form. They are a very good dessert for lunches — straight from the package. Dried fruit stewed with small amounts of sugar or no sugar at all make simple dessert or breakfast fruits and help add variety during months when fresh fruits are not plentiful. Hikers and campers find them almost a necessity where foods need to be carried in concentrated form.

Dried fruits are fully ripened fruits that have about 75 percent of their moisture removed by dehydration or sun drying. These fruits are allowed to ripen longer in the orchards than those used for other purposes. Therefore, their natural or fruit sugar content is higher.

To appreciate the food value in dried fruits, consider that each one pound is concentrated from several pounds of fresh fruit: apricots represent six to eight pounds, figs about three pounds, prunes from two and one-half to three pounds, and raisins represent four pounds of grapes. Naturally, the caloric count has a similar jump in proportion: One pound of dried apricots has one thousand two hundred calories to two hundred twenty per pound of fresh.

During the drying process, light-colored fruits are exposed to sulfur dioxide fumes for several hours to preserve the natural color and their vitamin A and C content. When sulfur isn't used, the dried peaches and apricots are brown in color rather than the expected golden orange. These unsulfured fruits are available in our Co-op Natural Food store and many other stores. Whether sulfured or not, they are a good source of vitamin A and a fair source of iron.

Tips on Buying and Storing Dried Fruit

Dried fruits come in handy, protective cartons and in bags. Both may be used for storing the fruit, even after opening. Close the box or fold the bag tightly. Dried fruits should be stored in a cool, dry place. On very warm days, keep them in the refrigerator.

Usual Dried Fruit Sizes

Prunes: Prunes are USDA graded as follows: Small - not more than 85 prunes per lb; medium - not more than 67 prunes per lb; large - not more than 53 prunes per lb; X-large - not more than 43 prunes per lb. Sometimes one sees a "jumbo" size prune (20 to 30 per lb.)

Raisins: 1½ oz. pkg. - "Snack-packs"; 15 oz. pkg. - 3 cups (approx.); 1 lb. bag - 3¼ cups (approx.); 2 lb. bag - 6½ cups (approx.). Apricots, peaches and mixed dried fruits are usually sold in 11-oz. boxes or 8- or 12-oz. bags.

Preparation of dried fruits: Packaged dried fruits are ready for cooking. They do not need to be washed. Soaking shortens the cooking time and tends to give a richer juice, but is not necessary. Time of cooking is approximately one-half hour. If fruit has been soaked, use the same water for cooking. Cook slowly. If sugar is used, add one-fourth to one-third cup per pound of dried fruit.

9

Meat, Fish and Poultry

THE NIGHT THEY STOPPED EATING MEAT

"That does it!" yelled Ooga the Caveman, throwing down his club in disgust. "It's too blasted much work hunting game for protein every day! If I'm lucky, which isn't often, I get to drag home some huge beast that takes the tribe two days to skin, clean, carve up and hang. Then half of it spoils before we can eat it. I'm sick, sick, sick of the whole lousy system!"

Ooga was really worked up this time! So Goona the Cavewoman, who was cleaning a jackal for dinner, said:

"And I'm sick of hearing you bitch about it! I keep telling you, we don't have to eat meat, fish or fowl for protein. Why don't we go out and discover agriculture? Maybe we could invent bread, too. We'd get eight or ten grams of protein just from four servings of bread and cereal."

Ooga started counting on his fingers. "That's true," he said. "And we could try storing some milk in a goat-stomach bag, to see if it'll make cheese. Three ounces of cheddar would give us twenty or so grams more." He unwrapped his feet and started counting toes. "Let's see, that makes . . ."

"Don't forget beans and nuts," put in Goona. "Two or three handfuls of beans would add another twenty-five or thirty grams . . ." and she unwrapped her feet too.

Ooga started a second time around on his fingers and toes, saying, "I suppose we'll want some fruits and vegetables, too, and four servings of them will add in five or ten grams . . ."

That's it!" interrupted Goona joyfully. "Eureka! That's fifty-five to sixty-five grams of protein and that's all we need per day! Ooga, we can do it!"

They were so excited that they couldn't eat the jackal, so they took it out and gave it a decent burial and afterwards Ooga sank down on the bed and said solemnly:

"Goona, this is a great truth that I've discovered. We don't need to eat meat at all! Why didn't I think of it before?"

Protein

The amount of protein is about the same in:
- 3 oz. cooked, boneless meat; poultry, fish
- 4 oz. boneless, lean meat; poultry, fish (before cooking)
- 3 oz. cheese
- ¾ cup cottage cheese
- 2½ cups milk (skim or whole)
- 1½ cups cooked beans*

*Protein from beans is better used by your body if some animal food (as a glass of milk) or some cereal food (as a slice of bread) is eaten at the same meal.

BEEF

What are needs in beef research? A dry subject perhaps, but I got pretty involved when I was asked to give the consumer view for a symposium in 1977. After much pondering I settled on three areas: producing beef that is lower in fat, eating less beef, and being sure that the beef we eat is safe.

Lower fat beef is needed. Why? Because most Americans eat too much fat, especially saturated fat. Actually, beef marketed today is leaner that a year ago because new federal grades permit the inclusion of more lean beef as "Choice" grade of beef.

How can we move toward eating less beef? Beef consumption has almost doubled in twenty years. Production of beef uses lots of resources — not just grain but energy. Beef is an expensive way to get calories and protein. A modest amount of beef fills a need for many people — for pleasure as well as for protein, iron, etc.

But the great amount of meat and animal fat we eat is a suspected contributor to heart disease and maybe to intestinal diseases.

The Senate Select Committee on Nutrition and Human Needs says Americans should get fewer calories from fat and sugar, more calories from complex carbohydrates, and the same calories from protein. If we did this we'd be bound to eat less meat because more of our protein would come from starchy foods. (Senator George McGovern, who chairs the Select Committee, seems to have backed away from the "less meat" suggestion because of pressure from cattle people. Too bad.)

Is there enough thought to safety? Probably not. New food additives get pretty thorough checking. But existing additives or processes are used without enough assurance of safety. Examples: Antibiotics and DES are used to fatten cattle despite serious warnings. Other problems: use of nitrites, accidental contaminants such as PCBs (polychlorinated biphenyls), use of chlorine, effectiveness of inspection, food poisoning bacteria.

After the symposium I wondered whether we should go slower and not always jump to apply "modern" methods. Today we can bring a steer to maturity in less than twelve months with corn, supplements, hormones, antibiotics. It used to take four to five years when cattle just ate grass. When our eye is only on "efficiency" we may not look for long-run ramifications. There is a maxim among ecologists that any change in the ecosystem will have ramifications greater than anyone could have imagined.

Many of our problems and health hazards have surfaced lately because their consideration wasn't on our agenda. I think eating large amounts of meat and other energy-intensive foods is part of our over-consuming society, which also uses too much fuel, steel, plastics, medicine, and produces mounds of garbage.

We're all in it – industry, government, consumers. To have a more ecologically balanced and healthier food system, consumers must be willing to eat more grains and smaller portions of meat and to have that meat less marbled and less dripping with fat.

How to Buy Beef

Two things are important when you buy beef – the quality grade and the cut. Different cuts vary in tenderness. But for any one cut – like a rib steak – the higher the U.S. Department of Agriculture (USDA) grade, the more tender, juicy, and flavorful the meat will be. (Meat grading is voluntary — paid for by the processor.)

Look for the quality. These marks, stamped on the meat, are a dependable guide to quality. The meat must first be inspected for wholesomeness before it can be graded. (Inspection is mandatory — required by law before meat can be sold.)

Prime grade beef is the best and most expensive. Most cuts of this grade are very tender, juicy, and flavorful.

Choice grade beef is high quality — and this is the grade sold in most stores. It is produced in such large amounts that it is often a very good buy. USDA Choice steaks and roasts will be quite tender and juicy and have a good flavor.

Good grade beef is not as juicy and flavorful as the higher grades — it is somewhat more lean, but it is fairly tender.

Look for the cut. Any cut of beef makes good eating if it is cooked properly. Use dry heat — roasting in the oven, broiling, or pan frying — for the most tender cuts and the higher grades. Use moist heat — pot-roasting or braising — for the less tender cuts and the lower grades.

The most tender cuts are rib roasts and steaks and loin cuts, like porterhouse, T-bone, club, and sirloin steaks. These may be cooked with dry heat in any grade. These cuts are the most expensive, but are no more nutritious than less-tender cuts.

Moderately tender cuts, which are usually a good buy, include rump roasts, sirloin tip roasts, blade chuck roasts and steaks, top round roasts and steaks, and shoulder clod roasts. Cook these with dry heat in the Prime and Choice grades; use moist heat for lower grades.

Less-tender cuts are often the best buy. Such cuts include shoulder arm chuck roasts and steaks, flank steaks, bottom round and eye-of-round steaks and roasts, and brisket. Cook these with moist heat in any grade.

FOUR RECIPES FROM ONE ROUND STEAK

By all the market reports it looks as if beef prices are high and going higher. Here's a couple of ways to enjoy beef and beat some

About Foods and Buying   157

of the cost. One is to buy a large piece and cut it up to make several recipes. The other is to plan smaller servings of beef and make it up with other less expensive protein foods at the same meal.

Check prices and when you see a good buy in a roast or large steak, grab it. Allow yourself time to cut it for cooking, refrigerating or freezing. You can save money and a lot of time this way on later meals. A good, thick chuck roast is a favorite for this, but other roasts, even steaks, can be used with great success.

Here's How

Recently, I tried the cut-up method with a round steak, which has practically no waste. The plan was for four meals for the four people in the family from two pounds of meat. I cut the steak into fourths to prepare for beef stroganoff, stew, stir-fry, and shish-kabob. Half the round steak was cut in quarter-inch strips, browned and simmered until tender with a large, sliced onion. Half of this was put in the freezer for stew which would be finished later with vegetables and thickening. To the other half of the cooked meat, I added a can of mushrooms, some sour half-and-half and served it for dinner over noodles as beef stroganoff. The third section of meat was frozen raw. At a later date, this will be partly thawed, cut paper-thin and cooked as Asian-type stir-fry with tofu and vegetables. The last part of the meat was cut in one and one-half-inch squares and put in the refrigerator with meat tenderizer and marinade. Two days later it was broiled on skewers with vegetables, and served as shish-kabob on bulgur wheat.

On Protein

You're right, two pounds of meat can't furnish enough protein for four meals for four people. You will have to add other good protein sources, such as tofu in the stir-fry, extra milk, cottage cheese, bean salad, cheese, etc. If you add these high-protein foods with your low-meat meal, protein needs can be met.

MEAT'S HIGH

No, it's not fair to say "eat less" when you scream about meat prices. And eating less is no long-term solution to drastic inflation. But it's all we can suggest practically. Eating less meat should help your pocketbook, might help your health (because you eat less fat), could help the ecology of our country (by devouring less grain and energy) and might help bring meat prices down a little.

We've said it before: Many people in this country eat more meat and more protein than they "need." This gets expensive because extra protein above physical requirements is burned for calories. Protein is probably the best supplied nutrient in the American diet, except for calories.

Getting protein from several sources means that a variety of other nutrients can be provided. Beans, meat, and eggs are good sources of iron. Milk and cheese provide calcium and riboflavin. By not counting on meat too much for protein and by eating more beans, tofu, poultry and fish you also eat less fat.

Vegetarian? This is a solution for some, for a variety of reasons. If your primary source of protein is from plant foods (beans, seeds, nuts, grain) the usability of the protein will be improved if you mix several foods, especially grains and beans. Or you can add some animal food such as milk, cheese, eggs, or fish at the same meal.

Cutting down, not cutting meat out altogether is the answer for many. You might have several no-meat dinners a week and use small amounts of meat stretched with vegetables, grains and beans most of the rest of the week.

WHAT ELSE FOR PROTEIN?

What does it cost to get your day's protein? Well, that depends. If you get it from turkey legs, beans and peanut butter it costs about 39¢ per person. If you get it from bologna, T-bone and bacon, it costs about $2.69. Quite a difference. With meat prices high and going higher it's a good time to look for alternative sources of protein.

The amount of protein and the number of servings vary with the kind of food, the amount of bone or fat in the meat, etc.

Eight servings per pound — Includes soybeans (uncooked) and nonfat dry milk.

Six servings per pound — Peanuts, peanut butter, eggs (per dozen).

Five servings per pound — Includes most beans (uncooked), canned fish, cheese.

Four servings per pound — Includes lean, boneless, raw meat, fish or poultry.

Three servings per pound — Whole raw chicken or turkey, chicken breasts and thighs, roasts and chops with some bone or fat, bologna, frankfurters and cottage cheese.

About Foods and Buying 159

Two servings or less per pound — Includes meat with much bone or fat such as bacon, spareribs, chicken wings and backs, pork sausage, lamb shanks, etc.; also, milk (per quart).

Hams and Other Cured Pork Cuts

An old legend tells us that the curing of pork was discovered when an injured pig ran into the ocean and died of its wounds in the briny deep. When its flesh was cooked, the flavor was enthusiastically relished by the ancient Sumerians in whose time this event is alleged to have occurred.

Today a wide variety of hams is available to consumers who want to know, among other things, the differences between smoked hams and fully cooked hams, between shank and butt halves, between picnics and hams.

Curing is one process for preserving fresh meat. To do this a solution of water, salt, sugar and sodium nitrite is pumped into the ham mechanically to preserve the meat, develop the flavor and pink color. After curing it may be smoked.

Smoked ham is the hind leg of the hog. It has been smoked to an internal temperature of 140°F. This is hot enough to kill trichina but not hot enough to completely cook the meat. These hams need additional cooking.

Fully cooked or ready-to-eat ham is heated to an internal temperature of 150°F in addition to smoking. It does not need further cooking but may be reheated if desired.

Ham, water added, may contain up to 10 percent added moisture. If the finished ham contains more than this amount, it must be labeled "Ham: up to 20 percent added water" or "Ham: up to 25 percent added water," etc., as appropriate.

Shank Half is the lower portion of the ham. It is more pointed in shape, has a smaller proportion of meat to bone, and is usually slightly lower in price than ham butt.

Butt Half is the upper part of the ham (the part nearest the hog's body). It is more rounded in shape, has a higher proportion of meat to bone, and is higher in price.

Note: If the center slices are removed from either half of the ham, the remaining portions must be labeled butt or shank end or portion; these are higher in bone.

Canned hams are boned and trimmed of most of the fat. They are then properly called "skinless and boneless." They are cured in a brine solution and may or may not be smoked before canning. The label should make this clear. If the label says "smoke flavored," it means just that; the ham has not undergone a true smoking process. If the ham to be canned is not smoked, the cured, raw ham is vacuum sealed with a small of dry gelatin, in a can. It is then fully cooked. During this process the ham juices combine with the gelatin. The label must say "Fully Cooked Ham with Natural Juices, Gelatin Added." The juices plus gelatin are edible and are included in the net weight marked on the can.

All canned hams are "fully cooked"; however, not all are "fully processed," meaning that although they are cooked, they are not sterile and must be kept refrigerated at all times. Canned hams weighing less than three pounds are usually sterile and need not be refrigerated. Read the label and follow instructions for refrigeration. All canned hams, of course, should be refrigerated after opening.

Some meat departments will open a canned ham for you, slice it to desired thickness, and tie it back together for convenience in heating. Be careful not to overheat such presliced hams, or the ham will dry out too much.

Smoked Shoulder Butts and Picnics are smoked pork cuts with characteristics similar to ham. They are from the shoulder, are somewhat less tender than ham, and are less costly. Smoked shoulder butt, a boneless cut weighing one to four pounds, should be cooked before eating. It may be baked, simmered in water, or sliced and then pan fried or broiled. Picnics are available as either cook-before-eating or fully cooked products.

RECOMMENDED BAKING TIMES FOR CURED PORK

	Internal Temperature	Minutes/lb. 325° F oven
Cook Before Eating		
Whole Ham	160°F	18 - 20
Half Ham, Butt or Shank	160°F	22 - 25
Rolled, Boned Ham	160°F	30
Shoulder Butt (boneless), Picnics	170°F	35 - 40
Fully Cooked		
Whole Ham	140°F	10 - 15
Half Ham, Picnics	140°F	14 - 18
Rolled, Boned Ham	140°F	12 - 15
Canned Ham, 6 lbs. or under	140°F	15 - 20
Canned Ham, 8 - 13 lbs.	140°F	10 - 15

To bake a ham, place the meat, fat side up, on a rack in a shallow roasting pan. Do not add water or cover, and do not baste.

About Foods and Buying 161

Insert a meat thermometer into the center of the thickest part of the meat, making sure it doesn't touch any bone. Center slices can be baked, broiled or pan-fried.

Glazing a ham. Half an hour before end of cooking time, stud the ham with cloves and glaze with one cup of red jelly mixed with one-half teaspoon dry mustard and two teaspoons horseradish. Or use your favorite glaze.

MEAT FOR BREAKFAST – NO NITRITES

Bacon and eggs, pancakes and ham. For many, this is the American breakfast. One problem with this meal is that bacon, ham, lunch meats and cured meats, like corned beef and pastrami, all contain nitrites, which, in recent years, have become suspect as carcinogens. Some consumers would like to avoid nitrites completely. Others would like to cut down on their intake, but not necessarily eliminate them entirely. Based on the best available current information, it is difficult, if not impossible, to set specific limits. Much more nitrite is microbiologically developed in our intestines and saliva than is consumed in foods with added nitrite.

However, if you're eating a lot of foods containing nitrites, it may be prudent to cut down. This is especially important for young children, since they will have more years for the nitrite to be working as a carcinogen, if indeed this proves to be the case. It's probably a good idea for pregnant women to cut down as well.

So What Meat Is There For Breakfast?

1. There's fresh and frozen sausage, both in bulk and in links. The bulk is for breakfast patties.

2. In the "deli" case, I spied Leo's Breast of Turkey, oven baked, which would be good between two slices of bread, dipped in egg and milk and sauteed for a French toast sandwich.

3. How about bratwurst or bockwurst, uncured veal and pork sausages packed in random weights? Simmer or fry slowly until well cooked and serve with hash browns.

4. Frozen ground turkey and turkey sausage are naturals for the innovative cook. Slice the plain turkey roll into half-inch slices, saute and season with herbs or spices of your choice. The sausage is already seasoned.

5. The freezer case offers several soy protein "meats" such as

breakfast patties, strips and grillers that may be reasonable facsimiles of comparable animal products.

6. There are, of course, several suitable fresh meats such as chicken livers, beef liver, chicken parts or, considering today's prices, a very small hamburger patty or cubed round steak.

This is not an exhaustive list. For other choices, read the labels for the ingredients contained in the foods you're considering.

Vary Your Meals With Variety Meats

Variety meats is the term used to designate the following edible portion of meat animals: liver, heart, kidney, tongue, tripe, brains, and sweetbreads. Liver, heart, and kidney are very flavorful, while brains, sweetbreads and tripe are delicate in flavor. Heart, liver and kidney are much more nutritious than other meats. Iron and B vitamins are much higher; vitamin A is much higher in liver and somewhat higher in kidney. Except for liver, these meats are in less demand than other cuts. This usually means lower cost. There is no bone waste to contend with when figuring costs, and prices do not fluctuate greatly.

Most of the variety meats are slightly more perishable than other meats, and should be used within two days after purchase. Liver, heart, kidney, brains and sweetbreads are best purchased fresh. Tongue is sold fresh, pickled, corned or smoked. Tripe may be fresh, pickled or canned. Fresh tripe is partly cooked before selling. Variety meats, like other meats, are cooked according to their tenderness. Liver and kidney from young animals, brains and sweetbreads are tender. Tongue, heart, tripe, beef kidneys are less tender and need longer slow cooking in moisture. An exception is beef heart, which is tender if sliced thinly and stir-fried or sauteed quickly. Pork liver also is at its best when braised. Variety meats are usually cooked well-done, with the exception of liver, which is more moist when cooked only to the medium stage. Variety meats from pork are always cooked well-done.

Sweetbreads are thymus glands of beef, calves and lambs. They are considered great delicacies and are usually quite expensive. To prepare sweetbreads, simmer fifteen minutes in salted water to which one tablespoon of lemon juice or wine vinegar has been added. Drain, plunge in cold water and remove membranes. They may then be pan-fried in a little butter, or broiled after brushing with melted butter. Served with mushrooms they are delicious.

Fish

To retain highest quality, cook all fish the same day you buy it. If you want to put "frozen" fish in the freezer, the quality is best if you buy a still-frozen piece rather than refreezing thawed fish. There is no health hazard in refreezing thawed fish, provided it has not been thawed long and its temperature has not risen above normal refrigerator temperatures.

Fish: A Gift From the Sea

Fish is good for you and tastes good too, when properly prepared. It has about the same amount and quality of protein as a serving of meat or poultry. All proteins from animal sources (fish, eggs, milk, as well as meat) are of high biological value, having all the essential amino acids present in the correct proportions for efficient use by the body.

Fish is lower in both calories and fat than most cuts of beef and pork. Even the so-called "fat fish" such as salmon, butterfish, herring and mackerel average from 5 to 16 percent fat, while a choice grade steak may be 25 percent fat. Fish is suitable for fat-controlled diets because of the low total fat content and because the fat is relatively unsaturated.

Fish contributes B vitamins to the diet and the fat fish contribute some vitamins A, D and E. Fish also contains iodine, iron and copper. Canned fish eaten with the bones, such as salmon, sardines and mackerel, contributes good amounts of calcium and phosphorus.

Not enough of us rely on fish for its nutritive value, or on the variety available. Ask a cook how he or she prepares fish and chances are the answer will be, "flour it and fry it." If you fall into this category, consider these cooking methods:

Broiling: Brush fish with melted butter or oil. Baste lean fish several times during broiling. Preheat broiler. Broil four inches from heat for about twelve to fifteen minutes or until fish flakes and breaks apart easily with a fork. Unless fish is very thick, you will not need to turn it. Use pancake turner to remove fish from broiler pan.

Baking: Bake fish on oiled baking dish or oiled brown paper, either stuffed or unstuffed. Do not fill fish more than two-thirds full of stuffing. Bake in 400°F oven until fish flakes. Brush fat fish with oil, sprinkle with salt and lemon juice. Baste lean fish several times as it bakes with extra oil or butter or with a sauce. This method is also suitable for slices of fillets.

Steaming or poaching: Steam or simmer, do not boil. Add lemon juice or vinegar to water to firm and whiten flesh. Part dry white wine or tomato juice may be used as liquid. Onion, garlic and herbs may be added, or fish may be poached in milk, being sure to keep the milk below the boiling point. Thicken remaining milk and use as cream sauce over the fish. For fat fish, tie in cheese cloth so that the fish may be easily removed from kettle. Place on rack over hot water and cover tightly. Steam. Serve with sauce. This method eliminates excess oil.

Frying: Fry as is or roll fish in seasoned flour or cornmeal or wheat germ, or dip in batter before placing in pan. Fry in butter, oil, bacon or other fat, over moderate heat. Turn only once. Fairly fat fish such as salmon are most suitable for broiling or baking.

General rule is cook fish quickly and for as short a time as possible. The protein of fish sets quickly at a temperature much below the boiling point. Cooking too long or at a temperature higher than necessary ruins the texture and flavor of fish.

Storing fish: Keep fresh fish refrigerated until time to use. Fish loses flavor with any length of storage, therefore, use as soon as possible after purchase, perferably on day you buy it. Keep in the freezing tray or meat compartment of the refrigerator if it is not to be used the day it is bought. Remove store wrapping and re-wrap tightly in waxed or parchment paper. Use it within two days of purchase. If you want to freeze fish after buying it, it would be advisable to buy frozen, not fresh fish for this purpose. Keep frozen fish frozen until time to use. Do not refreeze after thawing, since the quality will deteriorate rapidly. Cooking may be started before the fish is completely thawed. The most desirable way to thaw fish is in the refrigerator and not at room temperature since a considerable amount of dripping usually results.

SQUID IS DELICIOUS

Nutrients in squid and abalone are similar. Nutrient values per one hundred grams (about three and one-half ounces).

	Calories	Protein (grams)	Fat (grams)	Carbohydrate (grams)
Squid	84	16	1	1.5
Sirloin	313	17	27	0
Abalone	98	19	.5	3

About Foods and Buying 165

Cleaning takes skill — so practice. Most cleaning directions are quite complicated. However, there are very simple directions. To prepare, cut the head above the eyes. Slit body and remove cartilage and viscera, along with head. Rinse well and drain on absorbent paper.

In addition, the thin outer skin on the remaining flat section can be slipped off easily under running water to leave the edible legs and a lovely piece of light meat very much like abalone. The trick to keep this piece from curling when fried is to make a small slit on the two cut edges. Then pound lightly a few times with a flat object.

The simplest frying method is to dip cleaned squid ("legs" and flat pieces) in flour that has been seasoned with salt and pepper. Fry quickly to a golden brown. Drain on absorbent paper. Serve immediately.

If you want to be a little fancier, shake cleaned squid in a bag with flour and a bit of salt. Now dip in beaten egg, then cracker or cornflake crumbs and fry in oil about thirty seconds to the side. Delicious! Two pounds will make six moderate servings.

Let's Talk Turkey

New, shorter cooking times for turkey — cook stuffed turkeys to an internal temperature of 180-185°F in 325°F oven. These times are approximately fifteen minutes per pound.

Ready-to-Cook weight	Time in hours*
6 to 8 lbs.	2 to 2½ hours
8 to 12 lbs.	2½ to 3 hours
12 to 16 lbs.	3 to 4 hours
16 to 20 lbs.	4 to 5 hours
20 to 24 lbs.	5 to 6 hours

*These times are approximate and are for birds covered only with cloth. Using foil, paper or other coverings can also affect cooking time. The most accurate "doneness" test is to use a meat thermometer placed in the thickest part of the breast. Be sure the bulb does not touch a bone. Turkey is done when it registers 180-185 degrees F. For stuffed bird, point of thermometer should be in center of stuffing and register 165 degrees F. (For thawed frozen turkeys, 180 degrees is best and they will be less dry if cooked for the minimum time.) The pop-up "doneness" indicators imbedded in turkeys are not reliable. Double-check using a meat thermometer or the "joint test." This "doneness" test is when leg moves easily in joint. Allow bird to rest about one-half hour before carving.

Cook your turkey completely through at one time. Do not partially cook poultry one day and complete the cooking the following day. The poultry may not be heated enough to kill spoilage bacteria, but may instead have reached just the right temperature (between 40- and 140°F) to allow growth of harmful bacteria. It is not a wise procedure to use low oven temperature such as 160-185°F and cook the turkey for many hours, for the same reasons. hours, for the same reasons.

Size of bird to choose. Allow three-fourths to one pound per serving under twelve pounds; allow one-half pound to three-fourths pound for birds over twelve pounds.

How to thaw a turkey. Thaw in original wrapping, on a tray in refrigerator for two to three days. You may also thaw in original wrapping in cold running water, or in cold water that is changed often.

Preparing and stuffing the turkey. Today's processing methods give consumers turkeys that require very little further cleaning. However, stray pinfeathers should be removed and the inside cavity should be well washed to insure that all bits of lung and kidney are also removed.

Care of fresh turkeys. These may be refrigerated at home one or two days before roasting, making sure that the original wrappings are slit to allow for air circulation. Be sure to loosely wrap the giblets and store separately.

After the meal. As promptly as possible after dinner, remove the stuffing from the bird and refrigerate the turkey meat, the stuffing and the gravy, each in its own container. Do not allow any of these foods to stand at room temperature, but refrigerate promptly.

Cooking an unstuffed turkey. For quicker, easier cooking, roast the turkey unstuffed, decreasing the time by three minutes per pound. Bake the stuffing in a casserole during the last hour the turkey is in the oven. Baste occasionally with drippings.

WHOLE CHICKENS AND TURKEY PARTS ARE THE BEST BUYS

You may have wondered which gives you more cooked meat for your money — whole poultry or parts? At current prices, the headline summarizes it all. I drew these conclusions after cutting and weighing, and looking at prices and other price studies of chicken and turkey.

Whole chickens are the best buy. Even whole, cut-up chickens are a good buy. You pay extra if you want chicken parts, in fact, 40 to 60 percent extra. If you do want just the fancy pieces — breasts, thighs, and drumsticks for a party meal — you can probably get them from a whole chicken and get the wings, backs and giblets "free," for another meal. But if you are making Chicken Kiev, you'll want breasts, no matter what the cost.

Turkey parts — hindquarters, drumsticks and wings — are the best buy, compared to whole turkeys. Boneless turkey roasts cost plenty for convenience — about 35 percent more than whole turkey.

Yield of meat increases from backs to wings to whole bird to drumsticks to thighs to breast. You probably knew this. But did you know that you get only a shade more meat on drumsticks than you get on the whole bird?

Poorest buys of all would be frozen "Gravy with Turkey," which may have only 15 percent turkey meat, and "Turkey with Gravy," which may have only 35 percent turkey meat.

10

Milk, Dairy Products and Eggs

MILK

Liquid whole milk contains 87 percent water, not less than 3¼ percent milk fat (butterfat), and at least 8¼ percent nonfat milk solids.

Nutritional Value

Milk is a good source of protein, calcium, riboflavin and some other minerals and vitamins. An eight-ounce cup of whole milk yields the following percentages of the U.S. Recommended Daily Allowance for six nutrients:

Protein	20%	Vitamin D	25%
Vitamin A	4%	Calcium	25%
Riboflavin (Vitamin B$_2$)	30%	Phosphorus	25%

Calories:

1 cup whole milk	160
1 cup low-fat milk	140
1 cup nonfat milk	100

Low-fat milk contains 2 percent fat; nonfat or skim milk contains less than one-half percent fat. Except for calories, their nutritional value is roughly the same as whole milk.

Most milk sold in the United States is pasteurized. This means heating the raw milk to destroy harmful bacteria. A small amount of raw (unpasteurized) milk is sold in some communities. It is labeled as such. It is more expensive, and more perishable.

For the majority of the population, milk is a valuable food to be included in the daily diet. For those who cannot tolerate milk or who have allergic reactions to milk, we suggest you consult your physician. Young children should have two to three cups daily. Children aged nine through teens need three to four cups daily. Adults need two or more. Pregnant women need three or more. Lactating mothers need four or more. Cheese can be eaten as part of the day's milk intake.

Storage

Get milk home quickly and refrigerate for best quality and storage life. The date on the carton is the date after which the store should not sell the milk. However, if properly cared for, milk will keep up to a week after the pull date.

NONFAT DRY MILK

Even with recent increases in prices, nonfat dry milk is widely acclaimed for its economy and nutritive value: A quart of nonfat milk made from the dry powder costs from three-fifths to three-fourths as much as a quart of fresh, whole milk, depending on the size package used. A family using three quarts of milk per day could save as much as $185 a year by switching from whole to nonfat dry milk.

Nonfat dry milk has all the protein, minerals, and the most important of the water-soluble vitamins of fresh whole milk, but only half the calories. In most brands the fat-soluble vitamins A and D have been added.

Can food habits be changed? Advertising, especially television, does it all the time! Food habits can be changed — but not always quickly. We don't eat the way we did twenty-five years ago. In part, we've been cajoled by tantalizing advertising. Keep that in mind.

Be positive and expect to appreciate nonfat milk. Nonfat milk has certain qualities that should be appreciated. Don't present it as a substitute for whole milk, because it is different. Many people prefer nonfat milk. They like its special "mouth feel," and the very cold sensation it gives on swallowing. They even find the taste of whole milk unpleasantly creamy.

When you make the big change — if you decide to change to

About Foods and Buying 171

nonfat milk after years of drinking whole milk — consider either the "Sudden" or "Gradual" methods.

If you choose to use the Sudden change, take the family into your confidence, explaining your reasons for changing to nonfat milk, and acknowledging to them that nonfat is different from whole milk. It is important for everyone in the family to understand that the project will take time and patience. Enthusiasm for the project is an essential ingredient for success.

The Gradual change may be more acceptable. This can be accomplished by mixing a small amount of nonfat milk with whole, gradually increasing the proportion of nonfat as much and as often as your family will accept. Start with one-fourth or less of nonfat, and three-fourths of whole. Use this proportion for two or three weeks before increasing the amount of nonfat milk. Even though a complete change from whole to nonfat milk could take several months, it's worth it! If your family balks at some point and refuses to go any further, give in gracefully. Continue with the proportion acceptable to them and congratulate yourself on succeeding to this extent.

Avoid These Dangers

Careless preparation of the nonfat milk can get you off to a very bad start. Follow directions on the package. Be sure to mix up the milk several hours in advance of the time it is to be used, to give the milk time to thoroughly chill. Warm milk doesn't taste the same, whether it's skim or whole. Many a person has been completely disillusioned by drinking warm, freshly mixed nonfat milk.

The program can be disrupted if your family drinks nonfat milk at home and whole milk at school, or if you lapse into serving whole milk at home when you're too busy to mix up the nonfat. This latter situation is avoidable. After all, nonfat and low-fat fluid milks are both sold at the market! Keep your program going with them. If children are drinking whole milk at school, maybe low-fat milk is your best bet at home. Mix equal amounts of whole and nonfat to make low-fat milk.

Keep nonfat dry milk powder stored properly in a cool, dry place. Unopened packages may be kept for several months. If temperatures reach 90°F or more for long periods, flavor changes may occur. *After mixing with water, refrigerate and use within a few days as you would any other fluid milk.

*If the powder becomes lumpy, it has deteriorated in both flavor and quality. Prevent this change by excluding air; close container tightly.

BUTTERMILK

I thought you should know more about buttermilk, so I asked some experts, friends and relations, and here's what they said:

Fattening? No. Jack (manager of Valley Gold Dairy): Ours is low-calorie (about ninety per glass) and low fat (about 1 percent fat compared to 2 percent for low-fat milk). The thickness doesn't mean it's rich. It's due to adding culture to milk and letting it grow.

Helen: That yummy Bulgarian buttermilk is made from whole milk and has the calories of whole milk.

Salt added? Yes. My Dad: Alas, no buttermilk on my low-sodium diet, unless it's homemade.

How do you use it? Nancy: Make blue cheese dressing with buttermilk — add crumbled blue cheese, few drops olive oil, small clove garlic, something green like fresh basil or parsley. Blend. Other good, cheap, low-calorie salad dressings: one-third mayonnaise and two-thirds buttermilk or equal parts commercial dressing and buttermilk.

A VERY CONTROVERSIAL SUBJECT: MILK

by Helen Black

The next time you sit tongue-tied at a social gathering, why not throw out a remark on some controversial subject? You could mention religion, politics, or milk. All of these subjects are bound to galvanize the group into heated argument. The results, of course, may not be enlightening. It is unclear why milk is so controversial, but plenty of what you hear about it is wrong. Here are some wrong ideas I've heard recently. They range from downright dangerous to merely mild misconceptions.

"Extra nonfat dry milk in a baby's bottle is good" . . . a highly dangerous, wrong idea. Excess protein can have serious, even fatal consequences for young infants. Nonfat dry milk is over 35 percent protein. Neither it nor any other high-protein substance should be added to already adequate baby formulas except under explicit instructions from your doctor.

"Raw milk is better for you" . . . also a dangerous, wrong idea. The problem with raw milk is that it often contains bacteria, straight from the cow. The milk heat treatment of pasteurization removes this risk but reduces the levels of two vitamins. One of the vitamins, thiamine, is reduced only slightly; the other, vitamin C, is abundantly available in other foods.

"The reason fresh milk keeps is that preservatives are put in it." No! This is untrue. But milk does keep better now than it did ten years ago. The reason is that milk is handled more carefully now. For example, in California in 1973 a law was passed requiring a temperature-recording device to continuously monitor farm milk. If the record shows excessive storage temperature, the trucker will not pick up the milk.

"Yogurt is more nutritious than milk." This is not exactly true. Bacteria consume some of the B vitamins as they convert milk to yogurt. However, commercial yogurt is usually made with more added milk solids than fluid milk, hence has correspondingly increased nutrient content.

"Non-instant dry milk has lower heat processing and is more nutritious." Wrong again. This is a very persistent non-truth. The process used to make instant nonfat dry milk does not involve heat at all. In fact, most of the non-instant nonfat dry milk sold is subjected to higher heat treatments, in order to improve performance in bread making in commercial bakeries. Instant nonfat dry milk has been quite thoroughly studied in animal feeding experiments and the nutritional losses from the processing are insignificant.

"Buttermilk contains no fat." Not so. Buttermilk can be made from nonfat milk, but usually it isn't. Valley Gold Buttermilk is 1.5 percent fat. Tuttles Buttermilk is made from whole milk, and is about 3.8 percent fat.

CHEESE

Cheese has been a most useful and versatile food for thousands of years. It is made in many countries around the world. Its use in the United States has, until recent years, been limited to casseroles, sandwiches, or snacks. However, in many countries, it is used with breakfast rolls, at tea time, or is served as a dessert.

Technically, natural cheese is classified by the method of producing the curd, the animal source of the milk and its fat content, and the mold or bacteria used in the ripening process. (During ripening, the flavor, appearance, and texture characteristics of the aged cheese are developed.) However, for convenience the various cheeses may be classified as hard, semi-hard, and soft, depending on their moisture content. The term "natural" used with cheese merely distinguishes it from blended or modified cheeses. It does not mean that the cheese contains no added color, salt, or other additives.

HARD		
Bacteria Ripened 12 - 16 mo.	Bacteria Ripened 3 - 12 mo.	Bacteria Ripened 2 - 3 mo.
Cheshire Parmesan Romano	Cheddar Edam Gjetost Gruyere Provolone Sap Sago Swiss	Nokkelost Kumminost
SEMI-HARD*		
Bacteria Ripened 1 - 8 mo.		Mold Ripened 2 - 12 mo.
Bel Paese Brick Fontina Gouda Jack Muenster Port du Salut Tilsit		Blue Gorgonzola Roquefort Stilton
SOFT		
Bacteria Ripened 1 - 2 mo.	Mold Ripened 2 - 5 mo.	Unripened
Limburger Liederkranz	Brie Camembert	Baker's Cottage Mozzarella Neufchatel Ricotta Teleme

*Some of these cheeses may be fully cured and used for grating.

Besides the natural cheeses, there are other cheeses that have been modified. Pasteurized process cheese is made by blending and heating one or more kinds of pulverized natural cheese with an emulsifying agent; acids such as lactic, acetic, phosphoric; salt and flavorings. The heat used in the processing "fixes" the flavor so that no further aging takes place. The flavor will remain unchanged for several months. The composition is essentially the same as the cheese from which it was made.

Process cheese food is made in the same way as process cheese except that certain dairy products (cream, milk, milk solids, cheese whey, whey albumin) are added. It has more water but less protein and less fat then processed cheese. Examples of process cheese food are limited. However, process cheese spread widely abounds on the grocery shelves. Cheese spreads differ from cheese foods in that the moisture content is higher (maximum 60 percent) and the fat content lower (minimum 20 percent). As a result, the protein content is only about two-thirds as much as in processed cheese.

Cold pack cheese or cheese food merely means that the ground cheese and other ingredients are mixed *without* heat.

Nutritive values. Cheese is an excellent source of animal protein. Equivalent amounts of natural or process cheese can be substituted for boneless meat in the diet. However, the process cheese spreads contain a lesser amount of protein than process cheeses. The protein content of cheese in general varies with the moisture content. It ranges from 8 percent for cream cheese (soft, unripened) to 36 percent for the very hard grating cheeses such as Parmesan.

Cheese contributes varying amounts of calcium, riboflavin, and vitamin A to the diet, which could be important to the non-milk drinker in terms of better nutrition. The fat content of the cheeses is quite high. For those on a fat-restricted diet, dry cottage cheese or baker's cheese is the only cheese with no fat. Creamed cottage cheese has 4 percent fat, and various natural and process cheeses will range from 20 to 35 percent.

Cooking Qualities. Natural cheeses have more distinctive flavors than process cheeses, but some tend to be stringy when melted. For distinctive flavor and better melting qualities, choose a soft, aged, natural cheese. Process cheeses and process cheese spreads melt smoothly and easily in cooking.

Storage. The keeping qualities of cheeses are related to their moisture content. Soft cheeses are perishable and must be refrigerated. The very hard grating cheeses need no refrigeration. While the mold typical of Roquefort cheese is thought to be harmless, it is not known for sure whether cheese that molds in your refrigerator is safe. Prevent cheese from molding by wrapping tightly to exclude air after opening; use up opened packages promptly. If you do trim mold off, cut deeply around moldy spot.

The best protein buy in cheese is cottage cheese, but its calcium content is quite low. Therefore, for the non-milk drinker in particular, the loaf-type cheese spread is a better buy.

Cheese	Grams Protein per pound	Approximate number servings per pound, each serving providing 20 grams of protein	Cost per 20 grams protein (1/3 of adult daily protein allowance)*
Cheddar — natural	113	5	43c - 62c
— process	105	5	59c
Processed cheese spread	73	3.6	55c
Cottage cheese	62	3	26c
Cream cheese	36	2	89c

Of course, there are factors aside from cost that enter into cheese choices, the most important being the flavor and texture and the intended use. Cheese spread would be acceptable to many in a casserole, but it would be hard to imagine eating it with fresh grapes or a crisp apple for dessert!

Process cheese in large loaves is usually cheaper than its natural counterpart. But if it is unique flavor and texture that one wishes, the natural cheeses, whether domestic or foreign, are a great delight!

*Based on August 1979 prices.

CURDLED MILK FOR LUNCH?

Sound unappetizing? Well, lots of us seem to like it. At the Co-op we sell about six thousand five hundred quarts of cottage cheese each week.

Cottage cheese production starts with pasteurized skim milk. A culture of lactic acid developing bacteria and heat curdle or coagulate the milk protein into a soft curd. (Rennet, a coagulating agent obtained from the stomach lining of young mammals, is used only for large curd.) The curd is cut, the whey drained off and the cheese washed. One percent salt and a mixture of cream and milk are added to the creamed varieties.

About Foods and Buying 177

Creamed is available in small or large curd, plain or flavored with chives or pineapple. All are about 4 percent fat and one hundred twenty calories per one-half cup. (Pineapple flavored contains one hundred forty calories per one-half cup.) Low fat contains 2 percent fat and one hundred four calories per one-half cup. Uncreamed or dry curd has no added salt or creaming mixture. Fat content is about ½ percent with ninety-five calories per one-half cup.

Ricotta cheese differs from cottage cheese because it's made with whole milk or a mixture of whole milk and skim milk. Fat content is about 8½ percent with one hundred sixty calories per one-half cup. It's more expensive than cottage cheese and differs slightly in flavor. Ricotta cheese does not keep well once it's opened, so use within two to three days.

Cottage cheese is a good source of protein. One-half cup supplies about seventeen grams or one-third the Recommended Daily Allowance. That's about the same amount of protein as found in three ounces of cooked meat, fish or poultry, two cups of milk or three eggs. Although made from milk, cottage cheese is not a complete substitute for milk because much of the calcium, and some of the other nutrients, remain in the whey that is drained off.

Store cottage cheese tightly covered in the refrigerator. If properly refrigerated, unopened it will keep a week or more beyond the pull date stamped on the bottom of the carton. It spoils more rapidly every time it is opened. Creamed cottage cheese keeps longer than low-fat. Dry curd should be used within two or three days of purchase.

Cottage Cheese Ideas

Combine with spices and seasonings — caraway or poppy seeds, rosemary, tarragon; with fruit — any kind, but especially good with berries, peaches, melons and stewed, dried fruit; with vegetables — mix with diced vegetables in a salad, with chives or green onions on baked potato. For a quick, delicious lunch try cottage cheese with tomato, sliced onions and sour cream. For dips — mix with bleu cheese, horseradish, anchovies, chopped onion, clams, fresh, canned or smoked. Combine with meats — in a casserole such as lasagna made of tomato-meat sauce, cooked noodles, dry curd cottage cheese, mozzarella and Parmesan cheeses. For dessert such as blintzes or cheese cake use one of the dry curd cheeses.

Or, just regular or low-fat cottage cheese sweetened with sugar, flavored with vanilla and cinnamon, and topped with cranberry relish or other fruit is easy and delicious. Also try cottage cheese topped with flavored yogurt.

% FAT IN CHEESE

Cottage cheese, creamed 4%
Ricotta, part skim or whole......................... .8 - 16%
Mozzarella, part skim 17%
Camembert, Swiss process, mozzarella .... 20 - 16%
Provolone, Swiss, American, Edam, blue.............. 27 - 29%
Muenster, Colby cheddar......................... 30 - 33%
Cream 36%

adapted from the Journal of American Dietetic Association.

CULTURED MILK PRODUCTS ARE NOT ALL THE SAME

What is a cultured milk product? It is a whole, low-fat or non-fat fluid milk that may have nonfat dry milk solids added to give it more body and nutrition. It is pasteurized to destroy unwanted bacteria, which might produce flavor during fermentation. It is then innoculated with the appropriate organisms (lactobacillus bulgaricus and streptococcus thermophilus in the case of yogurts) and incubated at about $100°F$ until it is the consistency of junket or custard. It is then refrigerated until used. All ingredients are not yet listed on the labels of all brands, but we are hoping that this will come about soon.

There are different nutritive values among cultured milks. As the percentage of butterfat increases, the total calories go up and the nutrients from the nonfat milk components go down. Comparing sour cream with buttermilk, for instance, sour cream with 20 percent fat has four times as many calories as buttermilk with 1 percent but 25 percent less protein, about 20 percent less calcium but nearly twenty times more vitamin A. Comparing plain lowfat yogurt with lowfat yogurt containing fruit, we find almost double the calories in the fruit yogurt and a reduction of the vitamin A by about one third. The water-soluble vitamins and minerals are reduced, but by a lesser amount (about one-fifth) because nonfat dry milk solids are added to both products. If you think of

About Foods and Buying 179

the fruit yogurts as desserts (they do have added sugar in addition to the sugar in the fruit), then they are very nutritious when compared to most desserts.

Cultured milk products keep longer than non-fermented ones. Non-fermented dairy foods are the fresh milks — whole, lowfat, nonfat, chocolate, etc. The cultured products keep longer, because the fermentation produces acid that inhibits the growth of spoilage organisms. As the cultured products age (in the refrigerator, naturally) the amount of acid gradually increases, and the whey will tend to separate from the milk curds causing a "weeping" of the product. For this reason, most of these cultured milk products contain either gelatin or a vegetable stabilizer to keep the texture smooth. The stabilizer also helps the delicate product withstand handling and transportation. Most cultured milks will keep quite a while after the date on the carton, which is the last day the product should be sold. After this "pull date" most of these products will keep one to two weeks if handled properly. If they develop mold or an unpleasant taste or smell, they should be thrown out.

WHAT'S YOGURT?

What can be learned from comparing the nutrition information on the labels of various yogurts? And how do these products compare with fluid milk and cream as well as frozen dairy desserts? Below is a table giving the grams of fat and the calories in some of these products:

One Cup	Calories	Grams of Fat
Continental Plain Lowfat Yogurt	130	5
Continental Plain Yogurt	270	15
Valley Gold Strawberry Yogurt	240	4
Lucerne Red Raspberry Frozen Yogurt Dessert	240	3
Ice Milk	200	5
Ice Cream	255	14

Why so many calories in Continental Plain Yogurt? If this product were just richer in fat, the calories should be two hundred twenty. Apparently, however, they have also added nonfat dry milk solids, and this would account for the extra fifty calories. The ingredient statement says: "skim milk, cream, Lactobacillus bulgaricus, agar, natural flavor." Doesn't say anything about added milk solids.

Most of us think of yogurt as a low-fat product. Continental Plain Yogurt has three times the fat of other yogurts, and ice milk is lower both in fat and calories than the Continental product. Personally, I don't think this product should be called "yogurt," since it is a manipulated product with more than double the calories in the Continental Lowfat Yogurt. Perhaps it should be called "Extra Rich Yogurt" to call attention to its distinctly different type of composition.

Blue-Veined Cheeses

The name roquefort may only be used for cheese made from ewe's milk in a certain area of France. Similar cheese may be called "Roquefort-type." Gorgonzola is a blue-veined cheese from Italy made from either cow's or goat's milk. Some domestic blue cheeses are colored to give the cheese a creamy color. Most domestic blue is made from cow's milk. The blue veining is the mold with which the cheese was innoculated.

I SCREAM, YOU SCREAM, WE ALL SCREAM FOR ICE CREAM

by Catherine Sinnott

What were Italians doing in the year 1550? Among other things, they were making ice cream, using ice brought down from the mountains. The ice cream business has changed greatly since then.

On checking with the supplier of Valley Gold ice cream, we learned some interesting information about our regular ice cream (sold in the rectangular box) and premium ice cream (sold in a round container).

Valley Gold ice cream is made fron a basic mix (one for regular, one for premium). Included in the mix are cream, butterfat, condensed skim milk, sugar, corn sugar, and stabilizer (from seaweed). Condensed sweet buttermilk and whey powder also are used.

About Foods and Buying 181

Regular ice cream has 10 percent butterfat and premium has 12 percent butterfat. Fruit, nuts, chocolate chips, etc., and flavors are added to the mix to make different varieties. The only color added to these Valley Gold ice creams is annatto, a natural food coloring from the seed of the annatto tree. No color is added in chocolate, strawberry or vanilla (except extra-rich).

Before packaging, the ice cream mix is whipped with air to double its volume. This gives the smooth, creamy texture and "mouth feel" we associate with fine ice cream. Valley Gold's premium ice cream, in the round box, has somewhat less air whipped in.

Ice cream has not been covered by the labeling laws required for many foods. It will be after July 1979 for ice cream shipped interstate.* However, Valley Gold ice cream has had its ingredients on regular ice cream for many years (premium more recently), in line with Co-op member demand. If you have questions about ingredients, you can answer most of them by just reading the box.

*Although extension may be granted to permit supplies of old labels to be used up.

THE VERSATILE EGG

What's oval, white and smooth all over? You're right — an egg! Few of today's convenience foods can beat eggs for packaging, nutrition, low price, versatility and flavor. With eggs as an ingredient, you can be on the way to creating dishes from the world's great cuisines. From France, try a souffle or a quiche; from Italy, zabagalione; from India, curried eggs; from our own shores, don't forget the elegant Baked Alaska. But eggs are worthy of everyday meals as well, from scrambled eggs or omelets, to egg sandwiches, stuffed eggs and custards.

The sooner the egg is removed from the custody of the hen to the refrigerator, the better. Eggs can lose as much quality in a few hours in the hen's nest on a warm day as in a week or two in the refrigerator. Freshness cannot be maintained forever, of course, so plan to use eggs within one to two weeks of purchase. When buying, check the pull date on the end of the carton; the pull date is the date after which the eggs should not be sold. After that date, eggs properly stored should keep at least another week.

Grade AA eggs, purchased at a store where there is rapid turnover and where eggs are refrigerated, should be "upstanding."

That is, when broken into a frying pan, the white does not run all over. Rather it stands up thickly around the yolk, which is small and rounded. With age, or improper storage, the thick white becomes watery and the yolk enlarges and flattens. Such eggs are nutritious but not as good looking.

Eggs are notoriously contaminated with Salmonella bacteria, one of the nastier bacteria that can cause a miserable bout of nausea, diarrhea, stomach cramps and fever beginning about eight hours after eating contaminated foods. This is no problem if the eggs are cooked (to a temperature of $140°F$ at least). If you wish to use raw eggs in eggnog or beer or meringue, use only clean eggs with intact, not cracked, shells.

EGGS ARE NOT SCARY

It is not necessary to be scared of eggs, but some people are. What is terrifying about eggs? Well, the cooking scares some of us. Cholesterol content scares others.

The tough, rubbery egg has been overcooked. It's the protein in eggs that gets tough with too high heat, or too long cooking, or both. An egg boiled three minutes is tougher than one simmered six minutes. That perfect fried egg without nasty frizzled edges, which is not too brown on the bottom, has been cooked gently over moderate heat, just long enough.

A greenish look sometimes afflicts the yolks of hard-boiled eggs. To avoid it, simmer eggs twenty to thirty minutes, then plunge into cold water. The green color is only due to chemical combination of iron from the yolk with sulfur in the white, the result of too high heat or too long cooking. It looks bad, but it's harmless.

Eggs are high in cholesterol, but wait: the question of how dietary cholesterol affects health is still controversial. Not all authorities think normal people should cut out eggs. Since eggs have the highest quality protein of any common food, plus minerals and vitamins too, don't eliminate them unless your doctor advises it. Remember, even low cholesterol diets can include three eggs per week.

(January 30, 1978)

EGGS

Measuring guide — how many to fill a cup?

Egg Size	1 Cup Whites	1 Cup Yolks
Small	10	18
Medium	8	16
Large	7	14
Extra Large	6	12

The Egg . . . and What the Hen Ate

This question of what the hen ate before she laid those eggs is a tough one, and we had to call up the experts at the University of California and talk to our suppliers to get the answers.

Are pale egg yolks low in vitamin A? No. It's true that the brighter yellow vegetables or fruits and the very dark green vegetables are usually higher in provitamin A or carotene. But vitamin A itself is almost colorless. Bright-colored egg yolks are caused by the hen's diet of such feeds as corn or alfalfa, which have other pigments in them.

Arsenic in trace amounts is sometimes used in the feed of layers. Arsenic is an essential nutrient for chickens, and feeds may be low in this element. The arsenic is added in the organic form, not the highly toxic inorganic form. Many years ago, arsenic was used as a growth stimulant added to the feed of fryers, but this is no longer done.

Antibiotics are given layers only when they get sick; antibiotics are not given routinely in their feed. Again, years ago antibiotics were given as growth stimulants; however, the cost of the medication could not be justified for laying hens and the industry dropped the practice.

Are fertile eggs from happier hens? Our experts were unable to answer this question. But they did say that the remnants of sperm and the few cells that could grow into an embryo are so small that it is not possible to detect any chemical differences between fertile and infertile eggs. No difference in lecithin, or cholesterol, or in nutritional value was noted.

Will fertile eggs start to grow? This could happen, if you took them out of the refrigerator and kept them cozy. In some countries, an egg with a well-developed embryo is considered a delicacy! In others, such eggs are not eaten because it is considered to be the taking of life.

Are some eggs low in cholesterol? Alas, no. And the chicken's diet is very unlikely to make any difference in the cholesterol content of the egg.

11

Vegetables

IF YOUR BODY WAS YOUR CAR

How many people do you know who spend more time and money keeping up their cars than they do keeping up their bodies? Just for a minute, think of your body as a car. Cadillac, Rolls-Royce, Volkswagen, or whatever model you like. If you take good care of it and keep it repaired, it will give you good service and performance.

What happens to a car when you put the wrong kind or bad gas into it? Right. It will give you problems. If you continue to do this your problems may become more serious. Your body works the same way. A continuously poor diet leads to ill health. A poor diet may have a lot of junk foods in it and a lack of nourishing foods your body needs in order to keep running well.

Do you need a tune-up? Do you consume many of your meals in fast-food restaurants? Do you eat sweets for snacks? Do you omit vegetables from your meals? Various studies have shown people are eating too few fruits and vegetables. People are eating in restaurants more than ever, which may result in diets high in fat, sugar and salt. Fruits and vegetables, often omitted in restaurant menus, are essential in our diet. They supply us with many vitamins, minerals and the fiber we need to perform necessary body functions.

At picnics, barbecues and parties include raw vegetables instead of chips and/or crackers to nibble on or dip into your dips. Try raw turnips, carrots, celery, jicama, zucchini, bell pepper, cucumber and tomatoes. This will cut down on your fat and salt intake. For sweet munchies replace pies, cakes, cookies and candy with fresh fruit.

I'd Rather Eat Vegetables Than Fruit!

One could say this, if vitamin and mineral content were the only consideration. Many vegetables contain several vitamins and minerals in significant amounts in a one-cup serving. Only a few fruits can make that claim.

While eight vegetables contain seven or more nutrients in a single serving, only avocado of the fruits does as well in a fairly reasonable size serving of one cup of one-half inch cubes. Such a serving is two hundred sixty calories, almost twice the calories of one cup of corn.

Dried apricots, peaches and prunes – uncooked – contain from five to seven nutrients in significant amounts in large servings, such as thirty-five apricot halves or twenty-four whole prunes.

One cup of orange juice, one hundred twenty calories, supplies four nutrients at levels at 10 percent or more of the Recommended Daily Allowance. Like other citrus fruits, it is rich in one nutrient, vitamin C. Fresh orange juice is also quite rich in folacin, a difficult nutrient to include in recommended amounts, especially during pregnancy, and frozen orange juice from concentrate contains good amounts, too. However, vegetables can supply these nutrients in better amounts, plus other nutrients as well, all at much lower caloric levels.

What's a Vegetable?

On these pages the word "vegetable" is used in its common, comfortable menu sense of the term. In this sense, vegetables are the leaves, stems, flowers, roots or tubers and non-sweet fruits of plants. They are extremely important for the minerals and vitamins they contain. In addition, they provide fiber and in a few cases significant amounts of calories.

Leaf vegetables: Because leaves do such vital work for the plant, transforming the energy of the sun into sugar, leaves are among the most nutritious vegetables. This process, photosynthesis, requires vitamins and minerals for the chemical process to occur. Even the protein of green leaves, though small in amount, is high in quality compared to that in other parts of the plant.

Stem vegetables: Asparagus and celery are stem or petioles of plants. The stem transports nutrients between leaves and roots and contains the fiber (lignin), which supports the plant. Nutrient content varies. Asparagus is one of the more nutritious stem vegetables, celery is one of the least.

Root vegetables: Roots, tubers and bulbs store energy for the plant in the form of sugar and starch. Some are high in calories compared to other vegetables; some contain large amounts of carotene or provitamin A.

Flower vegetables: Common vegetables which are truly flowers or buds, include broccoli, cauliflower, artichokes and Brussels sprouts. They vary in the richness of their nutrient content; broccoli is the richest, while artichokes are the poorest.

Immature seed vegetables: Immature seeds commonly eaten as vegetables are green peas, limas and corn. In contrast, mature dry seeds, such as cereals and legumes, are not included as vegetables as we are using the term.

Fruit vegetables: Cucumbers, squash, eggplant, okra and tomatoes are fruits, but in contrast to fruits such as melons, berries and tree fruits are not sweet. Hence, we think of them and serve them as vegetables. With a few exceptions (okra, winter squash, peppers and tomatoes) their nutritive value is low.

VEGETABLES

"Ugh! I hate carrots."

"No vegetable for me, thank you."

Are these the usual comments you hear at the dinner table? If so, maybe a little rethinking on the subject would help change a few minds. It's worth a try.

Why? Because vegetables are low in calories, high in important nutrients (minerals and vitamins) and when eaten raw or cooked properly, they taste good.

Lots of Americans don't like vegetables. Why? Lots of reasons. Maybe because Daddy won't eat them. Maybe because brother and sister say they're "rabbit food." Maybe because Mommy, Uncle Joe or whoever's the cook says they're too much trouble to cook and rarely fixes them. Maybe because they're often overcooked and mushy.

Maybe because most fast-food places don't serve vegetables, and so lots of Americans are out of the habit of eating them. (French fried potatoes are high in fat and salt and don't really count as a vegetable served this way.)

Maybe because when you were little your parents said, "Eat those carrots. They're good for you," so often that you're still rebelling.

It is not as easy to love vegetables as fruits. Fruits, with their natural sugar content, are easily accepted, even by babies. It has been suggested that infants, needing more time to learn to love vegetables, might well be introduced to vegetables before fruits. But everybody, young or old, may benefit from learning to eat new vegetables. Here are some ways to make new vegetables acceptable:

- Introduce the new vegetables when hunger is on your side.
- People are more willing to taste when they are hungry.
- Try growing your own. The taste of home-grown vegetables, the suspense that builds as you watch them grow, will coax anyone to eat them.
- Let children help in preparation — shell the peas, peel the cooked beets, tear the lettuce for salad.
- Mix some of the new vegetable, such as jicama or chard, in a stir-fry with familiar vegetables.
- Make it attractive! Mix green, white, red or yellow vegetables to tempt the eye.
- Try herb or spice seasonings.
- Don't get discouraged too soon! It always takes time, plus a few pleasant experiences, to accept a new food.

Fresh Vegetable Storage Tips

Overbuying and long storage should be avoided as much as possible. Most fresh vegetables should be stored in crisper and/or closed plastic bags in the refrigerator at 40°F. Store mature potatoes in a cool, dark place but not in the refrigerator. New potatoes may be refrigerated.

Before storing vegetables in the refrigerator, remove any bruised or decayed parts, remove tops from root vegetables and wash off any dirt. Drain well before storing.

Ripe fruits should not be mixed with vegetables in crisper. They give off ethylene gas, which causes green vegetables to yellow, russet spots on lettuce, toughening of asparagus and a bitter taste in carrots. Members of the cabbage family (cabbage, broccoli, Brussels sprouts, cauliflower, kale, kohlrabi, etc.) will give strong odors to other foods, so don't keep them more than a day or two in the refrigerator unless they are in closed plastic bags.

About Foods and Buying 189

Although it's a bit of a nuisance, each vegetable can be stored in its own plastic bag fastened with a twist in the crisper or on the lowest shelf of the refrigerator. These plastic bags can be washed, dried and reused as long as they have no holes in them.

Tomatoes and melons should be stored at room temperature until ripe. Onions and garlic should be stored in open-mesh containers at room temperature. (Information from the Department of Vegetable Crops, University of California, Davis.)

Super Vegetables

Some vegetables are sources of several vitamins and minerals in a single serving. The vegetables listed here have four, five, six, seven, or eight vitamins or minerals in amounts of 10 percent or more of the Recommended Daily Allowances. The vitamins and minerals evaluated are vitamins A and C, vitamins B_1, B_2 and B_6, folacin and niacin, and the minerals, calcium, iron and magnesium. Unless otherwise noted, the serving size is one cup, cooked.

THE BEST	SECOND BEST	
8 Nutrients	7 Nutrients	**Turnip Greens**
Collard greens	**Blackeye peas**	Rich in A and C
Rich in A and C	Immature*	**Parsley**
Sweet corn**	**Kale**	Raw, rich in A and C
Fresh	**Green peas**	**Spinach****
	Immature*	Rich in A

STILL EXCELLENT		
6 Nutrients		**Mustard greens**
		Rich in A
		Okra
Asparagus		**Green peas**
Lima beans		Frozen or Canned
Immature*		**Mixed vegetables**
Broccoli		Frozen
Rich in A and C		**Red peppers, hot**
		Rich in A and C

(continued next page)

*Immature means young peas, limas, etc. rather than the mature dry vegetables, such as split peas.

**Nutrient differences between fresh versus cooked, canned or frozen vegetables are due to 1) processing losses or 2) increase in weight of one cup portion on cooking. For example, one cup of cooked spinach weighs about three times as much as one cup of raw spinach.

(continued)

VERY GOOD	
5 Nutrients	**Soybeans**
Brussels sprouts	Immature*
Rich in C	**Sweet corn****
Dandelion greens	Frozen
Rich in A	**Swiss chard**
New Zealand spinach	Rich in A
Rich in A	**Tomato juice**
Spinach, raw**	Canned
Rich in A	**Watercress, raw**
Peas and carrots	Rich in A

GOOD	
4 Nutrients	**Sweet corn****
Green onions	Canned
Tops only, raw	**Sweet potato**
Rutabagas	**Tomato, raw**
	Rich in C

*Immature means young peas, limas, etc. rather than the mature dry vegetables, such as split peas.

**Nutrient differences between fresh versus cooked, canned or frozen vegetables are due to 1) processing losses or 2) increase in weight of one cup portion on cooking. For example, one cup of cooked spinach weighs about three times as much as one cup of raw spinach.

Evaluations by Mary Ruth Nelson based on figures from USDA Agriculture Handbook number 456, 1975; USDA Home Economics Research Report number 36, 1969; Journal American Dietetics Association, 2/77, 6/77, 4/75; and Pennington Dietary Nutrient Guide, 1976.

Fresh Vegetables . . . How to Choose, How to Cook

Choose vegetables by their fresh, crisp look. Avoid limp, old-looking leaves, stalks and flowers. Avoid those with brown or bruised spots.

Buy local produce when available.

Buy in season. At the peak of picking time, vegetables are least expensive and taste best. For example, when fresh corn appears in April or May, it is expensive and not as flavorful as at the height of the season in June, July or August.

About Foods and Buying

How much to buy: just enough to last a few days. The older the vegetable, the greater the loss of nutrients and the tougher to eat. Serve the more perishable ones like corn and asparagus early in the week. Keep the root types like carrots, turnips and potatoes for later.

How to cook: the enemies of vegetables are time, water, light, heat, air, bruising and waste. To save nutrients, fight these enemies.

Use the whole vegetable when possible, not cut up. Trim sparingly. Remove only the tough or discolored portions. Use the outer leaves of lettuce and cabbage. Cabbage leaves are good in soups or stuffed with rice and meat mixtures.

Eat vegetables raw sometimes. Most of us think about raw carrots and celery. How about raw turnips, zucchini, broccoli and jicama? These are good dunked in taco sauce or seasoned cottage cheese.

When you do cook them, cook quickly and use the least possible amount of water (or broth). One-fourth cup water is enough for two to three servings. Greens need only the water that clings to the leaves. Root vegetables and corn need just enough to barely cover them.

Instead of boiling, how about steaming? A proper steamer is fine, but you can improvise. Put the vegetables in a sieve or colander over a pot of boiling water. Cover as tightly as possible while they cook. Check regularly to be sure the water doesn't boil away. Time for steaming varies with the size of the pieces. Check every few minutes until the vegetable is barely tender for best flavor. It won't take long.

For variety, how about stir frying? Cut vegetables in small pieces and cook quickly in a tiny bit of oil, water and soy sauce — an excellent method for asparagus, broccoli and green beans, among others. Experiment with those your family prefers. If any liquid is left after cooking, save it for soups, sauces and stews.

For canned vegetables, use low heat and a covered pan. Save leftover liquid for other uses.

Defrost them partially in your refrigerator before cooking to save energy because of the shorter cooking time required. Season with a dab of butter or margarine and a sprinkle of seasoned salt or such herbs as oregano, thyme, chervil or rosemary.

Other possibilities are parmesan cheese or a squeeze of fresh lemon or lime juice.

Nutrient Losses in Vegetables

The nutritive value of cooked, frozen or canned vegetables is very good even though some destruction as a result of processing does occur.

Nutrient losses in vegetables begin when the foods are harvested. There are physical losses when the outer leaves are stripped away from foods such as broccoli, lettuce or cauliflower. There are chemical losses due to respiration and the activities of the enzymes present in the foods. Vitamin C is the most easily lost nutrient since it is soluble in water and susceptible to chemical destruction. Some vegetables retain it better than others, but all will suffer less loss if they are chilled rapidly after harvest and kept cold until time to process or cook them. Dark green, leafy vegetables — broccoli especially — need to be refrigerated as soon as possible. These are generally shipped packed in crushed ice. Vegetables that retain their vitamin C well are cabbage, peppers, lima and snap beans, and tomatoes. Tubers keep their vitamin C quite well even when not refrigerated.

Canned foods will show some nutrient losses but newer processes and equipment have improved the quality of canned foods. Canned vegetables stored at $65°F$ or higher will lose 15 percent to 25 percent of their thiamin in a year. Don't plan to keep canned foods more than a year because the new crops for processing begin to appear in early summer. This is true for most frozen vegetables also.

THE RAW VEGETABLE EXPERIENCE

I submit that any raw vegetable can be a great chewing experience. Keep a sack of raw vegetables in the refrigerator to satisfy this much-neglected human need. For superior sound and sensation the following are suggested:

Cauliflower: Broken into flowerlets, it can be eaten as is or with kips. It bursts into a thousand small buds between your grinders. Curl your tongue around and scoop them up.

Celery: What a forthright chewing delight! Its noisiness is part of the pleasure. Do not try to conceal it.

Turnips: The raw turnip is somewhat muted in its percussion, possibly due to its smooth, almost velvety texture.

About Foods and Buying 193

Carrots: This experience is part of the Puritan ethic. A raw carrot demands diligence and determination from the jaws. It leaves, however, the pleasant exhaustion of a job well done.

Jicama: The only way to eat jicama — raw — in our opinion. Satisfyingly crisp and somewhat juicy, but not enough to run out the corners of your mouth.

Broccoli: Especially lovable is the stem, peeled and cut into chunks; it's a beautiful green, succulent treat.

BUYING VEGETABLES

Like everything else you can spend lots or relatively little on vegetables. Whatever your budget, it will help to eyeball what you buy and get a rough idea of what you're paying. You get about three small servings (three and one-half ounces or one-half cup each) from:

- 11 - 16 oz. fresh (without a lot of waste)
- 10 oz. frozen package
- 16 oz. can (roughly 1/3 liquid)

For fresh vegetables with moderate waste you get about three small servings per pound. If the vegetable costs 30 cents a pound, that's 10 cents a serving. With almost no waste you get four and one-half servings a pound. The vegetable could cost 44 cents a pound and still cost 10 cents a serving. For 10-cent servings the 16 oz. can or the 10 oz. frozen box would need to cost 30 cents or less, a rare occurrence. (12-cent servings aren't uncommon.)

Don't insist on that out-of-season zucchini. At 79 cents a pound it costs four to eight times what it might be at the height of the season. Some fresh vegetable prices vary wildly, so watch from week to week.

All those fresh vegetables look great, but if you buy too much you may end up with wilted lettuce, bad broccoli and moldy squash. Some vegetables are high priced most of the year: asparagus, artichokes, Chinese pea pods, cauliflower, mushrooms. Consider them special treats.

"By-the-each" vegetables prices need a closer look. Tiny heads of butter lettuce weighing one-fourth pound cost six times as much as a large romaine weighing one and one-half pounds. Potatoes in bags may cost one-third to one-fourth as much as loose potatoes. Maybe you can share a bag with a friend if ten pounds is too much.

Buy Co-op label (or other private labels). Co-op Quality Pack (red label) usually costs several cents less than a national brand and quality is comparable. Economy Pack (green label) costs even less.

Boil-in-bag frozen vegetables with butter or cream sauce often cost 50 to 100 percent more than their plainer cousins. Also the bags take more fuel and cooking time.

12

Canned, Frozen or Fabricated

CANNED, HANDY AND VITAMINS TOO!

Reckless eaters, snacking here, snacking there, too busy to cook vegetables, might consider the charmingly easy can. Are canned vegetables nutritious? Of course. Reports that all vitamins are killed off by canning are exaggerated! Vitamins survive in large numbers!

One cup of canned tomatoes or juice has 60 percent of the day's recommended vitamin C. Canned sweet potatoes and turnip greens have that much vitamin C, too.

Only one-fourth cup of canned carrots or only one-third cup of canned spinach provides all the recommended vitamin A per day.

Canned peas have 30 percent of the day's thiamin; limas have 25 percent of the iron. Quick salad: toss drained vegetables with French dressing, chopped celery, onion, hard-cooked eggs, bacon bits or you name it. Moisten with mayonnaise, serve.

The peach, whether fresh or canned, is hardly a vitamin-rich wonder. Yet what it has is retained well in canning: 20 percent of your vitamin A and 15 percent of your vitamin C in one cup. Try it for dessert sometime.

EASY COOKING WITH TOMATO JUICE, PUREE, SAUCE & PASTE

Tomatoes have been squeezed, squashed and pummeled into a variety of products that greatly simplify the making of spaghetti sauce. All kinds of people use spaghetti sauce, and not just with ground beef, either. Adventurous cooks find it good with fish instead of meat, or with beans, or nuts, or even tofu. For whatever purpose, it's helpful to know something about the various tomato products that can be used.

The Differences Between Tomato Products

All ingredients in tomato products must now be listed on food labels in California. In addition, the Food and Drug Administration has standards that provide for the following:

- Tomato juice is 5 to 6 percent tomato solids.* It is the liquid extracted from tomatoes, with salt added.
- Canned tomatoes also are 5 to 6 percent tomato solids. They must be mature tomatoes, peeled and cored, to which may be added citric acid, calcium salts (to help keep the tomatoes firm), spices, flavoring and salt.
- Tomato puree usually contains from 10 to 12 percent tomato solids. It must contain not less than 8 percent or more than 24 percent. Puree is the extracted and strained liquid from tomatoes; it may be concentrated and it may have salt added. Co-op label tomato puree is unsalted.
- Tomato sauce usually contains from 10 to 12 percent tomato solids, like tomato puree. However, there is no standard for percent solids in tomato sauce. Salt, spices, vinegar, sweetening, vegetables such as onions or garlic may be added.
- Tomato paste must have not less than 24 percent tomato solids. It is liquid extracted from tomatoes and concentrated. Pastes may contain salt, spices, flavoring and baking soda. Co-op tomato paste does not contain ingredients other than tomatoes.

In a pinch, switch sauce for paste. However, substituting one tomato product for another recipe may radically alter the flavor or consistency of the finished product. When substituting a seasoned product for an unseasoned one, add the seasonings called for in the recipe in reduced amounts. Use these rules:

For one pound of fresh tomatoes, simmered and seasoned (or two cups canned tomatoes) use one cup of tomato sauce; for one cup of tomato puree, use one cup tomato sauce, but reduce salt and seasoning in the recipe; for one-half cup tomato paste, use one cup tomato sauce, but subtract one-half cup liquid from recipe and reduce salt and seasonings; for one cup tomato juice, use one-half cup sauce plus one-half cup other liquid (or one-fourth cup paste and three-fourths cup liquid); adjust salt and seasonings.

Using tomato sauce or paste in a recipe is cheaper than using tomato puree and may cost only half as much as canned tomatoes or seasoned spaghetti sauces.

Use within six months of purchase! People worry if the inside of a can, when opened, is black and discolored, as may happen due to the action of acid foods such as tomatoes. If the can is not swollen, leaking or badly dented, it is safe to use. But discoloration can be minimized if canned tomato products are used in a reasonable time after purchase. Keep in a cool place in your home. Rotate the stock to use the oldest first.

After opening, any unused tomato product should be transferred to a glass jar and stored in the refrigerator. Storage in the opened can may cause an unpleasant tinny flavor to develop as well as discoloration of the can lining.

Tomato sauce, puree or paste will contribute important amounts of nutrients to a recipe. They are good sources of vitamin A (carotene) and moderate sources of iron. Vitamin C is present in large amounts but some will be lost in long cooking after opening. Some less familiar nutrients are present. For example, in some spaghetti sauce recipes, more vitamin B_6 (pyridoxine) is provided by the tomato products than by the meat.

*Tomato solids' refers to the solid matter left after all water is evaporated from the product. Fresh tomatoes before processing contain about 5 to 6 percent solids.

CAMPBELL'S SOUP . . . WHAT'S IN IT?

Now I know. For several years, legal problems delayed the nutrition labeling of products containing meat. Now these problems are solved and Campbell's has wasted no time getting this information on some, but not all, of their soup labels. And it makes for interesting reading!

"Nutritious" is a bad word and often associated with soups. It is a bad word because nobody has defined it! It may mean one thing to you and another to me. But nutritionists have not been idle; they are trying to define it. One recent definition would call "nutritious" only food that contains at least four nutrients in amounts that are at least 10 percent of the day's recommended intake (USRDA), in a serving large enough to provide 10 percent of a person's caloric requirement for the day.

With such a scheme, I can tell you that most Campbell's Condensed Soups are not "nutritious"! A surprising exception is Chicken Noodle Soup, which barely makes it.

But Campbell's chunky (do not dilute) soups mostly are "nutritious." Below are those that meet the criteria; that is, they provide at least four nutrients in amounts equal to 10 percent of the USRDA in a half can, or 9½ ounces. Calories in these servings vary from 160 to 260, depending on the soup: Chunky beef, chunky chicken, chunky chicken vegetable, chunky chili beef, chunky clam chowder, chunky sirloin burger.

Canned soup for dinner? Obviously, the Condensed Soups do not have enough nutrients for their calories to make a lunch, let alone dinner. A cheese sandwich or a tuna salad is needed to make up the protein. Chunky soups are better. Some, but not all, contain from eleven to nineteen grams protein in half a can (9½ oz.), or 20 to 30 percent of the USRDA. To compare, most canned dinners such as beef ravioli in meat sauce provide about 6 to 15 percent of the USRDA for protein in the same calorie portion. With bread and salad, a Chunky Soup could be an easy-to-make and adequate dinner.

I also learned that one cup of Campbell's Mushroom Soup (undiluted is only 270 calories, compared to about 400 for one cup of medium white sauce, for which the soup might be substituted in a casserole. Campbell's Golden Mushroom and Cream of Celery Soup are still lower, or about 180 calories per cup.

How Much Meat?

The U.S. Department of Agriculture requires the following minimum amount of meat (based on fresh weight of the meat) in canned or frozen products:

Beef stew	25%
Chili con carne	40%
Chili con carne with beans	25%
Corned beef hash	35%*
Frozen meat pies	25%

*Cooked basis

FROZEN DINNERS: ONE OF LIFE'S LITTLE MYSTERIES

Armchair detectives, please help! How much meat is in frozen dinners? The U.S. Department of Agriculture has given us some clues, but not the answer. The manufacturer has the answer, but he's not telling — yet!

First clue: Frozen dinners must be 25% meat (or meat-food-product). Keep in mind that meat-food-product is not the same as meat. It can be meat with gravy, or sauce, or other ingredients. The USDA has adopted this minimum standard of 25 percent for meat (or meat-food-product) in frozen dinners. While a smaller portion is illegal, it is quite all right to have a larger portion. You don't know if it's larger, of course. This all means that in a frozen beef dinner (sliced beef with gravy, mashed potatoes and corn, total weight 11 oz.) the meat and gravy together must weigh 2¾ oz.

Second clue: The plot thickens, or throw out the appetizer, bread and dessert. Now it isn't always as simple as the beef dinner, of course. Because the standard says not to count any appetizer, bread or dessert in the dinner when you figure the 25 percent meat (or meat-food-product). Now here's a frozen ham dinner (ham, with sauce, sweet potatoes, peas and carrots, corn muffin, total weight 10¼ oz.) Just figure 25 percent of 10¼ minus the weight of the corn muffin, whatever that is.

Third clue: How much meat in a meat-food-product? Well, now, this depends. There's a lot of different combinations, you know! And USDA has put out a separate standard for each, like: In a beef dinner, the beef-with-gravy must be 50 percent beef. This must be 25 percent of the total dinner, or 2¾ oz. So now we know there must be at least 1 3/8 oz. meat in this dinner! Eureka! If the meat portion is sweet and sour pork or beef, it must contain 25 percent meat. So just figure 25 percent of 25 percent of total weight to get actual weight of meat. Don't forget to throw out any bread, appetizer or dessert, first. If the meat portion is Spanish rice with beef or ham, it must contain 20 percent meat. Figure 20 percent of 25 percent, throwing out bread, dessert and appetizer.

Most shoppers don't have these wonderful clues. Even if we did, most of us couldn't figure out this puzzle. Isn't it a pity and a shame that nutrition labeling is not on most of these products? The consumer would know at least if the whole dinner contained an adequate amount of protein.

THIS IS BREAKFAST?

Nine years of research and an investment of more than a million dollars produced this? Modern science's contribution to breakfast (according to a full-page ad in local newspapers): "Sugar, shortening, milk protein, flour (bleached), peanut butter, water, soy protein, brown sugar syrup, dried egg, glycerine, salt, oat flour, mono and diglycerides, leavening, calcium carbonate, artificial flavor, dicalcium phosphate, soy lecithin . . ." and on and on through many vitamins and minerals down to "BHA, BHT, citric acid and propylene glycol added to preserve freshness."

That's General Mills' Breakfast Squares. Remember that ingredients are listed in descending order of predominance, by weight.

Who is kidding whom? This product is so bad that Co-op managers agreed not to carry it as a regular item. With full-page ads and high-pressure TV commercials (and a high-profit margin to boot), we hope we won't be forced to stock it. (A Co-op center manager has the option to order it just for his store.)

Here are a few of my reasons for saying that "Breakfast Squares" is a bad product:

- It's mostly sugar and fat, the two foods most people already eat too much of. Who needs another dose? Who wants their kids to get addicted to sweet rolls for breakfast?

- The Squares undoubtedly contain the vitamins, minerals and protein listed on the box, but they probably don't contain other trace elements present in ordinary, more natural foods.

- The bacon-egg-and-toast breakfast that General Mills chooses to compare its new product with isn't all that good. The egg is okay but the two slices of bacon are high in fat and the two pieces of toast contain more carbohydrates than most of us need. A decent breakfast would include fruit, preferably citrus. It also would be good to have milk — even half a glass.

- The Squares aren't cheap. For a family of four the cost would be 79 cents. For that amount everyone can have orange juice, one egg, toast, milk, and coffee too.

Flavor? Try them. Go ahead. All I can say is that everyone I know who tasted them had a mighty peculiar downturn of the mouth.

The development of this kind of "food" bothers me greatly. What happened to the pleasure of eating real food? Where are we

About Foods and Buying   201

all running so fast? I get the feeling that this kind of product isn't just a response to a demand but feeds and encourages our always-on-the-run, ulcer-producing lifestyle.

But you want a fast breakfast? How about a blender job with a glass of milk, two or three tablespoons of frozen juice and a raw egg (wash the shell before cracking)? Or a peanut butter sandwich, milk and an orange? Or last night's salad and a meat loaf? Or tomato juice and a quesadillo – a tortilla with cheese heated in a frying pan or broiler?

BOO BERRY: GENERAL MILLS HAS DONE IT AGAIN!

Remember Breakfast Squares from General Mills' line of fabricated foods? In a cookie format, all the nutrients you need for breakfast are offered to consumers. The cookie doesn't taste very good, and the Co-op home economists believe a breakfast of real foods has better nutrition as well as better taste. The Co-op doesn't stock GM's Breakfast Squares.

The Buying Committee (two buyers, a store manager and a home economist) screens most of the grocery items that ultimately end up on our shelves. You might think the stuff chosen is not always of the best but you should see what's rejected!

A recent reject was General Mills' new breakfast cereal called Boo Berry. This product joins Count Chocula and Frankenberry as the third scary, spooky cereal advertised so as to appeal to children by promising them a 'glo-in-the-dark' sticker inside the boxes of Boo Berry. This little play on words is perhaps also intended to make the buyer think the product contains blueberries, although labeling laws require that the fact that the blueberry flavor is artificial be declared on the front of the package. Quite a bit more about the product is also artificial. Sugar is the first ingredient. In fact, there is so much sugar used that the 12 percent protein in the oat flour (second ingredient) has been diluted to 5.4 percent in the finished product. The same fate has overtaken the B vitamins and iron of the oats, so the sweet mess has been fortified with eight vitamins and iron. To make sure that the product has the most devastating effect possible on kids' teeth, little bits of blue-colored marshmallows have also been added.

Oatmeal served with a small amount of sugar and plenty of milk makes a good breakfast cereal. It is economical, nourishing and low enough in sugar not to pose too much hazard to tooth enamel.

CARNATION BREAKFAST BAR: SECOND REVOLUTION?

Here we go again with another engineered food: Carnation Granola Breakfast Bars in "six delicious flavors!" This amazing product has thirty-eight ingredients. Most of these are isolated or extracted or otherwise tortured out of ordinary food stuffs, then recombined, glorified with vitamins and minerals, packaged, advertised and sold.

Some researchers say that we are in the midst of a "Second Revolution", the first revolution having been the mass movement of people from country to city in the last century. The first revolution, they say, precipitated the processing of fresh food in order to preserve it in transport from the country where it is raised, to the city where it is eaten. And the Second Revolution, they say, is the elimination of family meals and the substitution of snacks, fortified with vitamins and minerals, as the normal method of eating.

All this causes a kind of nervous quiver among us Co-op home economists, which I like to think of as The Hesitation Waltz. We hesitate, because we wonder if this Second Revolution is really good, necessary or inevitable. For example, do we truly have the nutritional know-how to go this route? Then, what about the economic effect? Is it any cheaper for our society to do this extreme processing and reassembling of nutrients, than it would be just to eat foods in simpler forms?

One of the troubling questions about products such as Carnation Breakfast Bars has to do with the addition of vitamins and minerals. Some new problems have been brought to light by recent nutrition research:

● The Rebound Effect: a dependency, or a developed deficiency, which may occur after large intakes of vitamins C or B_6 are then decreased to average levels.

● Unbalanced Nutrient Intake: Large amounts of certain nutrients may create increased need for others. For example, high-protein diets have been shown to increase the loss of body calcium, and increase amounts of polyunsaturated fats to increase the need for vitamin E. Trace elements are a particular problem because the range between the level of need and that of toxicity is very narrow.

Carnation Breakfast Bars will be sold at $1.09 per package of six bars. That's about 18 cents per bar. Two slices of bread and two teaspoons of butter, about the same in calories as one Breakfast Bar, only cost 7 cents. How about that? The Co-op will be selling this product soon. Buy it if you choose. For the nutritional and economic reasons stated, we don't recommend switching from true meals to snacks such as this. Let the Second Revolution wait until we get a few more answers to our questions.

THE TWINKIES SYNDROME

Are you hooked on this "no taste" product? You're not alone. ITT's Continental Bakery turns out Twinkies at the rate of fifty thousand per hour, three million a week, for gross retail sales last year of $50 million. Two little oblong sausages of sponge cake filled with some kind of white goop consisting of sugar and grease and selling for 25 cents.

Sugar is the most abundant ingredient in Twinkies, followed by flour, corn sweetener, water, shortening, eggs, leavening, whey, modified food starch, salt, skim milk, artificial color and flavor, sorbic acid (a preservative). Children eat 80 percent of the Twinkies sold. These famous grease cups are sold in grocery stores, in liquor outlets and from vending machines. They are popular in lunch boxes, for snacks and as dessert.

People concerned about good food habits and about the taste of well-prepared foods are not great admirers of heavily sugared, mass-produced confections. Children accustomed to eating this type of cake may actually come to prefer it to a homemade product with better-quality ingredients. These same children will not learn to snack on cheeses, raw vegetables and fruits. They can be observed discarding, uneaten, an apple or orange found in their lunch bags or served in the school lunch. And they may grow up with a limited interest in buying, preparing and serving good food in their homes.

Mothers should think carefully before using food as a pacifier. It can become a habit to provide the child with a doughnut, a cupcake or a cookie every time the child accompanies the mother to the food store. So let's be sophisticated. Cut out the junk foods and spend those quarters that used to go into ITT's coffers on better-tasting, more nutritious foods. You can start today.

13

Tips for Creative Cooking

TAKE A TIP FROM A GOURMET COOK

I'm talking about Julia Child, of course, and I want to encourage you to try creative cookery if you haven't already gotten into it. It's easy once you have some practical experience with recipe cookery.

One way to begin is to discover that you're out of cheddar, whole milk and butter — three ingredients needed for twice-baked potatoes. When this happened to me, I rummaged through the refrigerator and found sour cream and mozzarella. These will do just fine. I mixed up some nonfat dry milk using only half the usual amount of water, stirred in the sour cream, added salt and pepper, and warmed the mixture over low heat. I grated the mozzarella, mashed the potatoes, creamed them with the milk-sour cream mix, added the cheese, restuffed the potato shells and topped them with paprika. Marvelous!

Sometimes I take two or three recipes for the same dish and select the ingredients from each that I like or can afford. For example, one recipe for a chicken, shellfish and rice casserole will cost too much if I use frozen shrimp and fresh clams, but I notice that rock cod is on special at a good price, so I make a substitution. Another recipe I looked at used canned tomatoes. I realize this ingredient will add flavor, color and moisture to the casserole, so I substitute two cups of tomatoes for half the chicken broth. Maybe this dish could do with a touch of cheese. How about some grated Swiss sprinkled on top just before serving? The whole thing came out quite well; the flavors didn't fight and the guests gobbled it up.

One day I noted a half head of red cabbage in the crisper. Cole slaw! Don't even need a recipe for this one. Shred the cabbage and moisten it with sour cream and plain yogurt, season with dill weed, celery seed, green onion chopped fine, sugar, salt, pepper and a little lemon juice to taste.

In my herb pot, only three herbs have managed to survive erratic watering, cold weather and stiff breezes — rosemary, a type of sage, and a thyme. Now the main problem I have is to remember that these are growing out on the deck and to make use of them. I like rosemary with fish, with leafy green vegetables and with cheese or egg dishes — but a little goes a long way. The sage can also go with eggs and cheese and fish chowders besides the traditional use in pork and poultry dishes. The thyme complements tomatoes, fish, stews, and most other vegetables. I often use it in a sour cream dip for raw vegetables.

Things never taste exactly the same twice! Variety is achieved by juggling ingredients. It's easier to use up leftovers. You can "stretch" small amounts of meat or fish into a luncheon soup using bouillion cubes or boiling bones for broth and adding a variety of fresh vegetables. And don't forget a complementary herb or spice. It's challenging. It's fun! Try it.

LEAVENING AGENTS

A leavening agent is a gas incorporated or formed in a batter or dough to make it rise. There are three leavening gases: air, water vapor and carbon dioxide. Air can be beaten into the batter or beaten eggs can be folded in. Water, when heated in the dough, forms steam, that causes the mixture to expand. Popovers and cream puffs are largely leavened by steam and air.

But the majority of products are leavened with carbon dioxide gas. Yeast — microscopic single-celled plants — produce carbon dioxide when they multiply in the dough. Recipes made with buttermilk, well-soured milk or molasses need one-half teaspoon baking soda for each cup of acid-containing liquid. The acid combines with the baking soda when heated to produce carbon dioxide.

About Foods and Buying 207

Baking powders contain both acid and baking soda. Commercial baking powders also contain a small amount of cornstarch to keep them from caking. Caking causes a loss of leavening power. To test if your baking powder is still effective, mix one teaspoon with one-third cup hot water. The water should bubble enthusiastically.

Baking powders available in local supermarkets are double-acting, which means that some gas is produced when the liquid is mixed with the dry ingredients but a larger amount of carbon dioxide is formed when the mixture is heated. Therefore, batters and doughs mixed with double-acting powders can sit at room temperature for a while before baking and still make well-leavened products. Check the proportion of baking powder to flour in your recipe before you measure the baking powder. For each cup of flour, use one to one and one-half teaspoons of a double-acting powder.

Double-acting baking powders contain calcium acid phosphate and sodium aluminum sulfate as the two acid ingredients. Some people look upon aluminum as a poison, but actually it poses no health threat in the amount present in baking powder. If you would like to make your own baking powder, here is a recipe from *Joy of Cooking.* For each cup of flour in the recipe, mix one teaspoon of cream of tartar, one teaspoon of baking soda and one-half teaspoon salt. Make it fresh each time you bake, because it doesn't keep very well.

TO COOK! PERCHANCE TO SAVE SOME MONEY!

A cook's inexperience, nowadays, is sheer extravagance. For example, the mere knowledge of how liquids can be thickened is the key to soups, sauces or souffles. The cook, conniving against penny-waste here or nickel-down there uses up the vegetable cooking water, the scraps of left-over meat, or the egg yolk lurking in the depths of the refrigerator. More, such a skill provides a curious stiffening of the spine in the supermarket! A pox on high beef prices! And alternative eating may even taste better.

These three are essential to the thickened soup, the sauce, or the souffle. The trick is in the combining:

- Melt the fat — it's easy. Most any kind of fat will do — bacon grease, butter, margarine, oil. Use the chart below for proportions.

- Adding the flour — it's easy too. The flour is stirred into the melted fat. It seems too easy! Stir and cook the fat and flour together for several minutes over low heat, until well blended.
- Adding the liquid is the trick. The liquid must be added slowly, with steady stirring, until a smooth, thick mixture results. Use any kind of liquid. Milk, or broth, or a combination of both is commonly used. Broth or left-over vegetable cooking water can be used to reconstitute canned milk, concentrated milk or dry milk.

Use the trick for clam chowder. Drain one can chopped clams or baby clams; reserve liquid. Using proportions for soup, prepare white sauce with the drained liquid plus enough milk to make one cup. If desired, saute one or two tablespoons each of chopped onions and celery in the melted fat before adding flour. Combine white sauce and clams, correct the seasoning, heat thoroughly. Serves two.

Or curry the leftovers. Use proportions for sauce or gravy. When fat is melted, add one-half to one teaspoon curry powder. If desired, saute one-half cup chopped onions and celery in the fat. Add flour, stirring and cooking. Add liquid, using broth. When hot and smooth stir in one and one-half to two cups cooked, boneless meat or fish. Season with lemon juice, salt and pepper to taste. Serve over rice, for two.

Basic Proportions For White Sauce

	soup (or thin sauce)	sauce or gravy	souffle
Fat	1 tablespoon	2 tablespoons	3 tablespoons
Flour*	1 tablespoon	2 tablespoons	3 - 4 tablespoons
Liquid	1 cup	1 cup	1 cup

*1 tablespoon of cornstarch, potato or arrowroot starch is equal to 2 tablespoons of flour.

WHAT'S WITH HONEY?

Shoppers frequently ask about honey — is it cooked, unblended, or organic? Is it better nutritionally than other sweeteners? What does sage or orange blossom mean on a label? How do you substitute honey for sugar in a recipe?

Honey production is a fascinating subject, but let's leave the explanation of how the bees make honey to others better qualified. Commercial honey is a byproduct the beekeeper or apiarist sells. His bees are essential for the pollination of fifty or more important crops in California, which is why this is a large honey-producing state. The fees for this pollination service are an important part of the beekeeper's income. The bees are moved to wherever they are needed for pollination, or wherever there is a honey crop.

What does organic honey on a label mean? If you define "organic" as meaning no chemical pesticides used and no chemical fertilizers applied, this doesn't fit honey very well. The beekeeper has no control over where the bees go to gather honey except in the rather general sense of choosing the area in which the hives are placed.

Honey production is seasonal but, with the protracted growing season in California, the bees are working most of the year. Sage (which is a wild plant of the mint family growing along the coast in central California) and orange blossom are spring crops. Alfalfa, clover, and wild flowers are summer crops. Honey from eucalyptus and safflower has an unpleasant taste and, if too much is present in the honey, cannot be marketed.

Honey that is sold as "blended" honey means that no one floral flavor predominates. Of course, the beekeeper can't tell the bees which flowers to visit so, unless it's certain that the product contains at least 60 percent honey with the flavor designated on the label, it can't be sold as anything but a blend. But, by the same token, honey labeled orange blossom or clover will undoubtedly contain traces of other flavors. Although the law says the label flavor must predominate, there is no laboratory test for particular flavors.

The beekeeper removes the honey from the comb by slicing the caps off an entire section with a knife. The comb in its supporting wooden frame is then spun (centrifuged) to extract the liquid honey. The empty comb can then be replaced in the hive for reuse by the bees.

The extracted honey is allowed to stand in large settling tanks for two or three weeks. Foam, bits of wax, and some of the lighter-weight debris rise to the top and are skimmed off. The honey is then put into large, bulk containers and stored until shipped to the packer.

A small amount of honey is sold in the wooden frames — just as the bees stored it. This is comb honey. If it's been taken from the frame, but left in one piece, it's called out-comb honey. Chunk honey is pieces of honey in the comb (sold in the jar) with liquid honey filling up the spaces. This may be especially enjoyable for city slickers who would like the fun of chewing on the comb.

When the packer receives the honey, some of it may have crystallized. In order to label it U.S. Fancy, (U.S. Grade A is another designation that means the same), it must be strained through, at the very least, an eighty-mesh screen. The packer is required to be sure that it contains not more than 18.6 percent water.

An eighty-mesh screen is fairly coarse. To get honey that is sparkling clear, it must be clarified by filtration through material fine enough to remove all the tiniest specks of pollen and dust. To liquify the honey if it has crystallized and to aid in filtering it, it is heated to about 140°F for a few hours. Or the packer may "flash heat" it to a higher temperature for a shorter time. Since both color and flavor are damaged by either a high temperature for a short time or a lower one for longer periods, packers use as little heat as possible. Whether these processes produce a "cooked" honey or not, you can decide. It definitely cannot be clarified without some heating, but 140°F is a long way from boiling (212°F). Perhaps the only uncooked honey is that in the comb.

Honey should be stored in a dry place at room temperature, since it is more likely to crystallize if it is cold. However, it may crystallize anyhow, because it is a super-saturated solution. Shaking, jarring, or temperature fluctuations may cause crystal formation. Freezing does not impair color or flavor but may hasten granulation. To liquify honey, place the jar in a pan of warm water until the crystals melt.

You wish to replace sugar in a recipe with honey? If more than half the sugar in a cake recipe is replaced with honey, the volume of the baked cake will be less and the cake will brown too much. Half a cup or less of sugar may be replaced with honey without adjusting the liquid in the recipe. If a cup or more of honey is used, often the liquid in the recipe should be decreased by one-fourth cup for each cup of honey used. To minimize burning, lower the oven temperature by 25°F and bake a little longer. Many baked products except light layer cakes are quite acceptable with less sugar. You may experiment by substituting for the sugar one-half as much honey.

Nutritive value of honey? Honey is mostly sugars. They are simple sugars (monosaccharides) rather than double sugars (disaccharides) such as are found in cane or beet sugar. Double sugars must go through an extra step in digestion — they must be split into simple sugars before they can be absorbed into the blood.

About Foods and Buying 211

However, your digestive juices contain enzymes that do this very readily, so claims that honey is "easy to digest" are technically true but practically unimportant. Honey provides twenty-one calories per teaspoon, regular sugar has sixteen. Honey furnishes little except calories. The traces of vitamins and minerals in it are too small to be significant considering the amount that is used in an average person's diet. The best reason for using honey is that you prefer the flavor. Who wants to sprinkle sugar on biscuits when you can use honey?

Other Quick Ideas For "Gourmet" Dishes

Preseasoned rices may be made easily by placing one cup rice, two cups cold water, one teaspoon butter and one teaspoon, or more, of any spice or herb you fancy such as curry powder, powdered cardamon, oregano, or thyme, into a heavy saucepan with a close-fitting lid. Bring to a boil, lower heat and simmer for twelve to fifteen minutes. The rice may also be cooked in a double boiler for twenty to twenty-five minutes.

An easy-to-make fried rice or noodle dish may be prepared by sauteing leftover rice or noodles in oil with a minced onion, green pepper, leftover chicken, beef, pork or seafood until the rice or noodles are lightly browned. Add a beaten egg, salt and pepper and saute another five minutes. This may be served topped with chopped nuts, minced parsley and chives or sesame seeds.

FAST FOOD AT HOME

Can you spare thirty minutes (not counting shopping time) to fix a tasty meal? One that the family will enjoy, be inexpensive and have the bonus of more nutrients and fewer calories than many foods the fast-food outlets offer?

Americans are eating more and more meals outside the home, for a variety of reasons. Many of these meals may not provide a vegetable or salad and most are high in fat and calories.

Alternatives? Yes! For example: Very Fast Chicken Dinner, and others.

Very Fast Chicken Dinner

Put chicken parts on greased baking sheet. Sprinkle with herbs. Start broiling. Scrub potatoes, slice one inch thick lengthwise and put with chicken. Turn both after fifteen minutes. If potatoes get too brown remove for a few minutes. Meantime, wash and slice vegetables onto platter; add dressing. Other family members are setting table, putting out bread and beverage, such as milk or juice. Cut up fruit for dessert. Chicken cooks in thirty minutes total. Makes four servings.

Quick, Almost-Pizza Dinner

Figure two to three English muffin halves per person. Top each with sliced mozzarella or jack cheese, spoonful tomato sauce and sprinkle of oregano, basil, garlic powder and grated parmesan. Bake at 400°F for ten to fifteen minutes or broil several inches below heat until hot and bubbly. Drain one can each green, kidney and garbanzo beans. Add oil and vinegar dressing and toss well. Top sliced fresh fruit with spoonful cottage cheese and/or yogurt.

Part Four
Keeping Food Safely

14

Food Spoilage

DON'T SPOIL YOUR SUMMER FUN

Let me remind you of a few safety ideas so you won't get sick from the food you take to the barbecue or picnic.

Keep hot foods hot — cold foods cold. Ice chests or insulated bags with ice, dry ice or reusable cold packs are good for keeping food cold. Chill food before packing. Hot foods are hot when they are above 140°F. Harmful bacteria may grow in foods that are lukewarm. It is a good practice not to let food sit around at room temperature, especially in warm weather. Chances for foodborne illness are greater if you do.

You may not get sick right away. Symptoms can take as long as seventy-two hours to develop. Foodborne illness can be a lot like a virus. You may experience any one or all of the following symptoms: vomiting; diarrhea; stomach cramps.

Wash hands with soap and water before preparing, serving and eating foods. Bacteria from nose, cuts or not washing after using the bathroom can cause harmful bacteria to multiply in food. Wash the knife after you use it for cutting raw chicken. Don't use the unclean knife to cut up the watermelon. It may pass bacteria from one food to another.

Be extra careful with: seafood, dishes made with eggs, poultry, soups, cooked meats, foods containing milk, and cream pies. Keep cold until ready to use. Put leftovers in refrigerator or on ice right away.

WASH YOUR HANDS, DEARIES

Working around food? Just been to the restroom? Wash your hands, dearie. Why? Because not doing so could contribute to making someone sick.

We're not trying to make you into fidgety worriers, scared of every single germ. Germs (bacteria) are everywhere. We take in millions every day — some "good" some "bad." But with careful hand washing and good food handling practices we can cut way down the number of "bad" bacteria we gulp down and thus cut the odds on getting sick.

Bacteria are everywhere, but those that might make you sick, especially staphylococcus, are concentrated around people's noses, and salmonella are concentrated in the intestinal tracts of animals, including humans. Many people are regular carriers of these bacteria without knowing it.

Most illness we get from food we get because bacteria reach the food and then multiply to huge numbers. Bacteria divide and two become four, forty become eighty and if conditions are right, millions become billions.

Why dirty hands while preparing food are a no no. Example: Your hands are full of bacteria; you eat cold turkey without washing (not recommended naturally); you ingest a mere hundred thousand bacteria, which your body might fight off. But if you handle the cooked turkey with unwashed hands, let it sit in a warm room while bacteria multiply, and then you feast before bed, everyone might get sick — not right away but hours later. (That's why we say refrigerate leftovers promptly.)

What else goes wrong? It might be cross contamination. You cut up a chicken. It's full of salmonella. Later you cook the chicken thoroughly so it's okay. You have the wit not to slice the meatloaf for sandwiches on the same board. But you don't wash your hands. The salmonella are carried by your hands to that warm meatloaf. They multiply; your husband saves the sandwich for the end of swing shift — and trouble.

Pity the maligned mayonnaise. You've heard about food poisoning after the political picnic. Everyone blamed the mayonnaise in the potato salad. But mayonnaise by itself is acid and not a good place for bacteria to grow. It's more likely due to all those bacteria from the unwashed hands, hands that cut and mixed the warm potatoes. The bacteria probably incubated to millions and billions for hours on a hot day while everyone played baseball.

Use that soap. Washing your hands thoroughly with soap, even with that yukky piece in the public washroom, will get your hands cleaner than just a quick rinse.

Preparing lots of food at a lunch counter or school kitchen? It's good to have a pot with chlorine sanitizer to keep your hands in from time to time. Use one tablespoon chlorine bleach for each quart water. Use this for sponges and cutting boards too.

PLEASE DON'T EAT MOLDY FOODS

Years ago we said, "Don't worry about moldy food — it's harmless." No more. Research in the last fifteen years has shown that there are dozens of different toxins produced by molds. Sometimes the mold itself may be hazardous to your health. True, there are many useful molds, but since there's no easy way to distinguish these from those that might hurt us, we say don't eat any moldy foods.

What does it do to you? Different molds produce different toxins, and these do different things in the body. Aflatoxin is the best known toxin and is a potent cancer causer. Most peanuts are inspected for aflatoxin. Aflatoxin may also be produced by mold in grains, beans, nut meats, spices, bread. Do not eat these foods if they are moldy. Don't even sniff mold; it can enter your body through the respiratory tract. Mold growing on acid food such as pickles may alter the acidity and allow food spoilage, so throw this food out, too.

Throw it out or cut it off? There's some difference of opinion here among experts, but most conclude it's best to throw out moldy food. Mold spores can imbed themselves below the surface. But if you do cut, on cheese for example, cut deep, don't just wipe the surface.

What about naturally moldy cheese such as roquefort? The mold that's there to produce cheese is apparently okay.

What to do? Don't buy moldy food. At home wash and dry your refrigerator and bread box frequently. Keep foods as cool and dry as possible. And don't keep them too long. Cooking will not destroy the toxins produced by mold.

15

Food Storage

THE GROCERIES ARE BOUGHT
WHERE DO YOU STORE THEM?

Wait a moment! There are two things to consider before you get the groceries home.

In the store buy the non-refrigerated foods first, such as crackers, paper products, canned foods. Get the meat, dairy and frozen items last because thirty to forty minutes in your shopping cart can contribute to a loss of quality.

Head home quickly — Don't do errands while the food is in a warm car. Bacteria and molds love those cozy temperatures and start multiplying at a rapid rate. If you must make a stop or two, bring a picnic chest with you and put the perishables in it so cold foods can keep their cool.

Home at last — unpack quickly — The cold items go into the refrigerator or freezer right away. Meat for the freezer is wrapped tightly in freezer paper and dated so you'll have a record of how old it is. Store vegetables in plastic bags in crisper. Do not wash until ready to use.

Cans, boxes and bags of food under the sink? No way! — Do you put some of them under the sink? Some people do, but it's not recommended. This is a favorite spot for insects and rodents, and it's only a step further into your food supply. There are pipes under the sink which may leak, and moisture is a no-no for safe storage. It can cause rust on cans and molds on grains, cereals and similar foods.

Next to the stove? — Cupboards close to the stove or other heat sources aren't best for food, either. The heat dries up mixes, bread and flour and encourages insect infestation. Use those cupboards for dishes. Use the coolest areas for food.

Household cleaners and food are a dangerous combination — Wherever you store cleansers, ammonia and other cleaning compounds, food shouldn't go near them. It's just too easy for a child or babysitter to pick up a bottle of furniture polish and add it to the salad dressing!

Rotate your canned foods frequently — Mark the date of purchase on the can label to remind you to use it before its first birthday. If you're suspicious of a food's safety because a can is badly rusted or swollen or shows any sign of leakage, do not taste it. This could be dangerous to your health. Tasting doesn't always tell you food is safe, anyway. Throw it out.

No Refrigeration?

Living without a refrigerator is hard but not impossible. You need to plan carefully, understand what must not be kept at room temperature (so that you won't poison yourself), shop more often and maybe spend a little more, because you can't store leftovers.

You will probably need to shop every day for fresh food, or shop every other day and on alternate nights have dinner from the cupboard — maybe tuna and noodles with cut up fresh celery (a little limp from yesterday) and fresh tomato salad.

Your shelf should include some of your favorite canned items that will make the basis of a quick dinner, and can be finished at one meal — tuna, sardines, beans, corned beef hash, tamales or what have you.

There are many foods that normally are kept in the refrigerator but may be kept a day or two at room temperature. These include:

- Eggs (in shell or hard cooked)
- Hard cheeses such as cheddar and cheese food, but not soft cheeses such as cottage cheese, cream cheese, ricotta
- Raw vegetables: carrots, turnips, even lettuce or celery (put in plastic bag and closed with a rubber band)
- Margarine and butter
- Half a grapefruit
- Pickles

For Safety's Sake If You Have No Refrigeration

Do not keep any cooked food or leftovers without refrigeration. Certain kinds of spoilage problems are not taken care of by boiling before eating, so just don't keep fresh or cooked meat, cooked vegetables, milk or cooked dishes from one day to the next.

Do not store canned food after it is opened. It is not safe to use half the canned hash for supper and the rest for lunch the next day. Potentially dangerous bacteria may grow. If you want milk in your coffee, use powdered cream or nonfat dry milk, not canned milk.

Fresh milk and cottage cheese should be used all in one meal. Dry milk can be mixed a glass at a time. A little instant coffee or vanilla improves the flavor for some people or you can try Milkman, which is more expensive than dry milk but costs less than fresh milk.

STORING DAIRY PRODUCTS

Concentrated milk. To increase the keeping quality of fresh concentrated milk, it may be quickly frozen and held frozen until ready to use. Like other frozen foods, it must be used soon after defrosting. When defrosted, there may be a texture change to a somewhat grainy consistency. Keep frozen or refrigerated at all times.

Cottage cheese and other uncured cheeses. Cottage cheese is perishable. It needs always to be kept covered in the refrigerator. It should keep five days after the "pull" date on the carton, if handled carefully. It spoils more rapidly every time it is opened and even more quickly if left unrefrigerated. When using these uncured cheeses (cottage cheese, ricotta, baker's or farmer's) be sure to use a clean spoon or knife when removing portions from the remainder. Do not eat cottage cheese directly from the carton; the spoon that has been in your mouth contaminates any product remaining in the carton. Creamed cottage cheese keeps longer than low-fat. Baker's, farmer's and ricotta keep after opening for even shorter periods and so are best used within two days of purchase.

Yogurt. Yogurt should be stored in the refrigerator at all times. Most of the storage information for cottage cheese (see above) applies to yogurt. However, because the fermentation process produces acid that inhibits the growth of bacteria other than the innoculating organism, yogurt will keep for a week or more in the refrigerator. However, with longer storage, the whey will tend to separate from the milk curds, causing a "weeping" of the product. Should an unpleasant taste or smell develop during storage, discard the product. There are wild bacteria that may grow even at refrigerator temperatures. The innoculating organisms used to make the yogurt also grow slowly in the refrigerator, causing the product to get increasingly acid. This is perfectly all right.

Non-fat milk. This product may be purchased as a fresh milk or as a dry powder. Fresh, non-fat milk should always be refrigerated. The date on the carton is the "pull" date, the date after which the store should not sell the milk. However, if properly cared for, this product will keep up to a week beyond the pull date.

Non-fat dry milk. For best quality, keep the package tightly closed. Store in a cool, dark, dry place. The quality of the dry milk will be best if kept only two to three months after opening the package. If the powder becomes lumpy, it has deteriorated in both flavor and quality. You may want to transfer the powder as the original container becomes empty, to a smaller one with a tight-fitting lid, since air in the package hastens deterioration of most food products. If the temperature reaches $90°F$ or more for long periods, flavor changes may occur.

Careless preparation of the non-fat dry milk can cause additional problems. Follow the directions on the package. Use clean utensils and cold water. Mix milk several hours before using and refrigerate to improve flavor. Reliquified dry milk is perishable. Store and use as you would fresh milk. If the same container is used over and over to store non-fat milk, scald occasionally to prevent bacteria buildup.

Whole milk, extra-rich milk, low-fat milk. All these fresh milks are perishable. Get them home quickly and refrigerate for best quality and longer storage life. These cartons also have a pull date, but if properly stored they should keep at least a week after the pull date.

Shelf life of dairy products can be a guide to their keeping life at home. Shelf life is the time between the processing date and the pull date on the carton. Under good conditions and unopened, these products should keep at least a week after the date on the carton. Those with longer shelf lives should keep even longer.

Product	Shelf life
All fluid milks	10 days
Cottage cheeses	13 days

Sour cream, sour half and half   21 days
Yogurts   30 - 35 days

Eggs. The carton tells you the size and grade. Grade AA eggs, if refrigerated both in the store and at home, will keep for two to three weeks after the pull date on the carton and still retain their AA quality. The pull date on most brands of eggs is twenty-one days after packing.

You will occasionally find a blood spot in the egg when you crack it, or you may notice that the white has a brownish tinge. Both of these conditions are due to the rupturing of blood vessels in the oviduct of the hen as the egg passes down this tube to the outside world. The brown tinge in the albumin results from a ruptured vessel near the beginning of the egg's trip down the oviduct. The bright red blood spot occurred near the end of the journey. There is no need to discard such eggs.

Because of the hen's anatomy, as the egg is laid the egg shell may be contaminated with fecal material containing salmonella, since hens can be carriers of this bacteria. This poses no problem if the egg is broken and then either cooked or refrigerated again immediately. However, a tiny piece of shell in an unrefrigerated eggnog that stood at room temperature for an appreciable length of time could pose a health hazard if consumed. Either eat raw eggs immediately after shelling or refrigerate them again. Cracked eggs should not be used raw.

Eggs provide a nearly perfect medium for the growth of bacteria. Dishes such as custards, quiches, souffles, and other foods containing large amounts of egg in a moist product should be refrigerated if there are any leftovers after the meal. Mayonnaise, while containing eggs, also contains either vinegar or lemon juice, the acid of which inhibits bacterial growth. Therefore, it may safely be stored in a cool place if refrigeration is not available.

STORAGE OF MEAT, FISH, AND POULTRY IN THE REFRIGERATOR AND FREEZER: HOW TO DO IT AND HOW LONG TO STORE

The range in time reflects recommendations for *maximum storage time* from several authorities. Keep prepackaged fresh meats in original wrappers, but loosen to allow good air circulation. Rewrap (using wax paper) fresh meats wrapped in plain market paper; keep wrappings loose.

STORAGE TIME CHART

Type of Meat, Poultry or Fish	Refrigerator 38° to 40°F	Freezer 0°F or lower
Roasts		
Beef, veal and lamb	4 - 6 days	6 - 9 months
Pork	4 - 6 days	3 - 6 months
Steaks and chops		
Beef	3 - 5 days	6 - 8 months
Pork, veal and lamb	3 days	3 - 4 months
Ground meat		
Beef, veal and lamb	1 - 2 days	3 - 4 months
Pork	1 - 2 days	1 - 3 months
Variety meats	1 - 2 days	3 - 4 months
Luncheon meats	1 week	not recommended
Sausage		
Fresh pork	1 week	2 months
Smoked	3 - 7 days	not recommended
Dry and semi-dry, unsliced	2 - 3 weeks	not recommended
Frankfurters	4 - 5 days	not recommended
Bacon	5 - 7 days	not recommended
Smoked ham		
Whole or half	1 week	2 months
Slices	3 - 4 days	not recommended
Corned beef	1 week	2 weeks
Leftover cooked meat	2 - 4 days	2 - 3 months
Poultry		
Raw	2 days	6 months
Cooked	2 - 4 days	2 - 3 months
Fish		
Raw	1 day	2 - 4 months
Cooked	2 - 3 days	1 month
Frozen cooked combination foods		
Meat pies		3 months
Swiss steak		3 months
Stews		3 - 4 months
Meat dinners		3 - 4 months

FREEZING IS NOT ECONOMICAL COMPARED TO CANNING

You need a low cost supply of food: So you have a home garden, or you're going to the country to pick ripe peaches or apricots, or there are some really good buys in the market. Cost alone is not enough. Bruised, underripe or overripe foods have a lot of waste. Now, how should you process these foods?

Keeping Food Safely

Studies by Cornell University Extension nutritionists recently found that food frozen at home costs 19 cents per pound more than when fresh food is simply purchased and eaten. This figure assumes that the freezer is full and electric rates are relatively low. When the freezer is half empty and operating inefficiently, using high-cost electric current, home freezing can add as much as 53 cents per pound to the cost of food. This cost figure includes the cost of the freezer spread over its life expectancy and cost of electricity to run it. Keep the freezer full, rotate the stock and use it regularly. Packaging that is rigid with flat tops and bottoms is the most efficient shape, because more can be packed into a given space. Any rigid container that is capable of being sealed to keep oxygen out and moisture in can be used, whether made of glass, metal, plastic or cardboard. To prevent breakage of glass, leave sufficient headspace to take care of the expansion of the food during freezing. Do not tighten screw tops until food is frozen.

What about canning? Canning is much more economical than freezing, but only if your family likes canned fruits and vegetables. Also, choose the right foods to can. Why can carrots if fresh ones are available year-round at reasonable prices? Don't can or freeze more food than you will use within a year. If canning supplies or freezer space is limited, choose foods with high nutritive values.

TIPS ON FREEZING

In August, fresh fruits and vegetables are at or nearing their peaks of ripeness and best prices. Also, backyard produce is nearly ready for harvesting. Perhaps you have questions?

What kinds freeze well? All fresh fruits and most vegetables except those with high water content such as cukes, lettuces, and tomatoes. Tomatoes may be peeled, brought to a rolling boil and then packed in jars or plastic containers and frozen. The flavor is excellent, very similar to fresh.

What to do to produce before freezing? Cantaloupe and most berries can be frozen "as is," No fruits need blanching. However, fruits packed in syrup or sugar keep their colors, shapes and flavors better. Ascorbic acid is usually added to light-colored fruits to retain the color. But they can be steamed quickly to prevent browning and then coated with sugar. The flavor will not be harmed. All vegetables must be blanched before freezing to kill bacteria and stop enzyme action, which can cause spoilage.

How long can frozen produce be stored for best quality? Up to one year at 0°F. Check the temperature of your freezer. Date packages with day of processing.

What kinds of packaging to use? Almost any airtight container (glass or plastic) that doesn't give off odors and won't break at freezer temperatures. Plastic wrap, plastic bags and heavy aluminum foil are all right but can be punctured during handling. Recycled plastic cartons (such as cottage cheese containers and milk cartons) are great but you should use freezer bags for liners and seal the cartons with freezer tape (which also makes an excellent label if you write on it with ink).

Does freezing affect nutritive values? Freezing foods quickly, immediately after harvest, reduces nutrient loss. Some loss of water-soluble nutrients results from blanching of vegetables.

PLAN AND PREPARE... DON'T PANIC

Holiday time is busy-time for most homemakers. One partial solution to this problem for those who have freezer space is to use your free hours in the weeks before holidays to prepare and freeze several main dishes plus some baked goods. These can then be used on those days when the seemingly endless round of washing and cleaning leaves little time for meal preparation. Certain basic rules can serve as guides to what will or will not freeze successfully.

Foods that freeze well include: combination dishes such as lasagna, spaghetti, meat balls, meat loaf, chicken casseroles, stewed or pot roasted beef, most seafood recipes (in all of these remove excess fat from cooked dish before freezing); baked goods such as bread, rolls, cakes and pies, sandwiches of many varieties (see exceptions below); soups of all types excluding potatoes.

Avoid freezing the following:

1. Fried foods (except French fried potatoes and onion rings), which lose their crispness.

2. Milk sauces, custards, cream fillings, since they may curdle, become watery or lumpy.

3. Potatoes, which do not have a good texture after freezing.

4. Lettuce, other fresh greens, and tomatoes lose their crispness.

5. Cooked egg whites and meringues, since they toughen and get rubbery.

Keeping Food Safely

Packaging frozen foods: 1) Pack in amounts to be used in one meal. 2) Exclude as much air as possible before wrapping. 3) Use moisture-resistant containers, bags, or paper. Materials may include glass, metal, plastic, or waxed cartons. All covers should fit tightly, but leave one-half inch headspace for expansion. 4) Casseroles lined with heavy foil may be used. After freezing contents, wrap the foil-covered food in freezer wrapping and the empty casserole can then be used for other cooking.

Freezing and storing: Freeze food rapidly. Place the packages in coldest part of freezer. Allow for cold air circulation. The food temperature must be lowered to below $40°F$ within four hours to reduce growth of bacteria. Freezer temperature should be kept at $0°F$; for every $5°$ increase in temperature, the storage time for the food is decreased by half. That is, food that keeps for six months at $0°F$ will start to deteriorate in quality after three months at $5°F$.

Thawing and cooking: Precooked foods may be defrosted in the refrigerator or at room temperature (This is least desirable since bacteria may grow as the outer layer of food defrosts.) or by heating. Leave wrapping material on when possible. Uncooked casseroles may be put directly into the oven from the freezer. Add about twenty minutes to the baking time. Unbaked doughs and batters are always defrosted before baking.

Refreezing: When foods have partially thawed and are refrozen, they will lose some of their quality. Use these refrozen foods as soon as possible. Consider wholly thawed foods perishable and keep them under refrigeration until needed.

The conditions under which the food has thawed will determine if it should be refrozen. You may safely refreeze partially thawed food if it has been thawing for only a brief time (for instance, if it was stored overnight in the refrigerator during a temporary power failure in the freezer), and it still feels cold and contains ice crystals.

On the other hand, if foods have slowly thawed over a period of several days, to a temperature above $40°F$, they are not likely to be fit for refreezing. Meats, poultry, most vegetables and some prepared foods may become unsafe to eat. Most fruits and fruit products soon develop an undesirable flavor. Discard any unpleasant-looking or smelly food since it may contain microorganisms that make it unsafe.

Recommended Reading

The following books, also available from Anderson World, can augment your exercise and fitness program. They are available from major bookstores or can be ordered directly from the publisher: 1400 Stierlin Road, Mountain View, CA 94043.

RUNNER'S WORLD NO TIME TO COOK COOKBOOK by Diana Frank. This 340-page cookbook is what every busy, active person needs in the kitchen. There are hundreds of simple, yet tasty recipes for your enjoyment, from Dried Fruit Soup to Hamburger Quiche. Frank incorporates many of the new specialty foods such as tofu and bulgur and has her own ideas on using a basic tomato sauce to add zest to a meal. Spiral bound $11.95.

RUNNER'S WORLD NATURAL FOODS COOKBOOK by Pamela Hannan. An easy-to-follow guide to recipes without sugar, with special attention to the vitamins that can be received from properly prepared food. Extensive recipes in a variety of categories complete the 284-page book. Spiral bound $11.95.

RUNNER'S WORLD WEIGHT CONTROL BOOK by Dr. Michael Nash. A logical, realistic approach to losing weight and keeping it off — forever — that ignores the fad diets and gets to the real problem: one's own self-image. A complete course in getting away from the multi-course meal. Spiral bound $11.95; paperback $9.95.

RUNNER'S WORLD INDOOR EXERCISE BOOK by Richard Benyo and Rhonda Provost. A simple-to-understand guide to fitness and the body, and how it responds to beginning exercise programs. Programs are keyed to the beginner and helping you get started indoors in the privacy of your livingroom. Spiral bound $11.95; paperback $9.95.

RUNNER'S WORLD YOGA BOOK by Jean Couch with Nell Weaver. A complete guide to using the principles of yoga for stretching, strengthening and toning the body. A good book to graduate to after making the initial commitment to embark on a fitness and health program. This 228-page book has more than 400 photos and line drawings. Spiral bound $11.95; paperback $9.95.

DANCE AEROBICS by Maxine Polley. The rage that has swept the nation. Getting in shape and staying there through an ambitious program of enjoyable, fast-moving dance that builds aerobic fitness while toning the muscles and doing away with unwanted weight. Paperback $5.95.